Oracle Global Data Services for Mission-critical Systems

Maximizing Performance and Reliability in Complex Enterprise Environments

Y V Ravi Kumar
Mariami Kupatadze
Sambaiah Sammeta

Apress®

Oracle Global Data Services for Mission-critical Systems: Maximizing Performance and Reliability in Complex Enterprise Environments

Y V Ravi Kumar
IRVING, TX, USA

Mariami Kupatadze
Bethesda, MD, USA

Sambaiah Sammeta
Flower Mound, TX, USA

ISBN-13 (pbk): 978-1-4842-9552-6
https://doi.org/10.1007/978-1-4842-9553-3

ISBN-13 (electronic): 978-1-4842-9553-3

Managing Director, Apress Media LLC: Welmoed Spahr
Acquisitions Editor: Celestin Suresh John
Development Editor: Laura Berendson
Editorial Project Manager: Mark Powers

Cover designed by eStudioCalamar

Cover image by Bolivia Inteligente on Unsplash (www.unsplash.com)

Distributed to the book trade worldwide by Springer Science+Business Media New York, 1 New York Plaza, Suite 4600, New York, NY 10004-1562, USA. Phone 1-800-SPRINGER, fax (201) 348-4505, e-mail orders-ny@springer-sbm.com, or visit www.springeronline.com. Apress Media, LLC is a California LLC and the sole member (owner) is Springer Science + Business Media Finance Inc (SSBM Finance Inc). SSBM Finance Inc is a **Delaware** corporation.

For information on translations, please e-mail booktranslations@springernature.com; for reprint, paperback, or audio rights, please e-mail bookpermissions@springernature.com.

Apress titles may be purchased in bulk for academic, corporate, or promotional use. eBook versions and licenses are also available for most titles. For more information, reference our Print and eBook Bulk Sales web page at http://www.apress.com/bulk-sales.

Any source code or other supplementary material referenced by the author in this book is available to readers on GitHub (http://github.com/apress). For more detailed information, please visit http://www.apress.com/source-code.

Paper in this product is recyclable

Table of Contents

About the Authors

Y V Ravi Kumar is an Oracle ACE Director (ACED) and Oracle Certified Master (OCM) with 25+ years of experience in banking, financial services, and insurance (BFSI). He has worked as a vice president (DBA), senior database architect, Oracle engineered systems architect, and technology advisor. He is an Oracle Certified Professional (OCP) for Oracle 8i/9i/10 g/11 g/12c/19c and an Oracle Certified Expert (OCE) in Oracle GoldenGate, RAC, Performance Tuning, Oracle Cloud Infrastructure, Terraform, and Oracle Engineered Systems (Oracle Exadata, Oracle Database Appliance, ZFS, and ZDLRA), as well as Oracle Security and Maximum Availability Architecture (MAA) certified. He is also certified as a Multi-Cloud Certified Architect, Oracle Cloud Infrastructure Architect Professional, AWS Certified Solutions Architect Professional, and Google Cloud Architect Professional.

He has published more than 100+ Oracle technology articles, including ones for Oracle Technology Network (OTN), OraWorld Magazine, UKOUG, OTech Magazine, and Redgate. He has spoken twice at Oracle Open World (OOW). He has designed, architected, and implemented the core banking system (CBS) database for the central banks of two countries: India and Mahé, Seychelles. Oracle Corporation has published his profile in its Oracle ACE Program as well as on its OCM list and in its Spotlight on Success stories. He is the author of two other Apress books, *Oracle Database Upgrade and Migration Methods* and *Oracle High Availability, Disaster Recovery, and Cloud Services.*

Mariami Kupatadze holds the distinction of being the first Oracle Certified Master (OCM) in her country, Georgia, and is a former member of the ACE program, having previously held ACE status. Mari has published multiple articles in prominent industry publications, such as the OraWorld e-magazine and Oracle Technology Network (OTN), and has been a featured speaker at prestigious events, such as the APAC Oracle Users Groups Community (APACOUC) and the Luxembourg Oracle Users Group (LUXOUG). In 2019, she authored a chapter on Oracle Sharding for the Apress book *Oracle High Availability, Disaster Recovery, and Cloud Services*. A prolific blogger since 2010, Mari has published more than 400 posts on her blog, which has been recognized as one of the Top 60 Oracle blogs.

Sambaiah Sammeta is an Oracle Certified Professional (OCP) with 15 years of experience working as an Oracle Database administrator consultant. He has provided DBA support for various clients in the banking, retail, healthcare services, automobile, and financial services sectors. He has the following certifications: Oracle Cloud Architect Professional (2020 and 2019), Oracle Autonomous Database Cloud, and Oracle Database Cloud Certified Specialist (2020). He planned and performed all the 11g to 19c and 12c to 19c database upgrades for several major banking and healthcare clients.

About the Technical Reviewer

 **Biju Thomas** is an Oracle ACE Director and heads the Global Oracle Practice at Data Intensity. He is a senior technical leader with hands-on Oracle skills as well as expertise in enterprise-wide team leadership, Oracle applications and e-business suite architecture solutions, and cloud migrations. His focus is efficiently and cost-effectively running Oracle workloads in the public cloud. He is also an author, speaker, and mentor.

Biju started administering Oracle databases in 1993. He is a frequent presenter at Oracle conferences and has authored several books about Oracle products. Biju lives in Dallas and enjoys outdoor activities, especially gardening when it is not cold. Biju's social media URLs and blog are at `www.bijoos.com`.

Acknowledgments

I am grateful to God who gave me strength, courage, perseverance, and patience in this sincere and honest attempt of knowledge sharing. This fourth book of mine as a coauthor would not have been possible without the following people:

- Shri Late Yenugula Venkatapathi and Smt. Yenugula Krishnakumari, my parents, for instilling in me good thoughts and values. They encouraged me to work hard and always be a step ahead in learning new things.

- Shri B. Suresh Kamath (founder of LaserSoft and Patterns Cognitive), my mentor, my guru, my strength, and my guide, who has inspired me for the last 25 years. He is an immensely talented and technically sound individual. He taught me how to be well-read with no compromises. He led by example in being content yet hungry for knowledge. He motivated me to go that extra mile in experimenting with newer technologies/environments and in being regularly out of my comfort zone.

- Anitha Ravi Kumar, my wife, for being immensely tolerant with me. "Behind every successful man there is a woman," as they say. I believe she is the embodiment of this well-known belief. Special thanks to my daughter, Sai Hansika, and my son, Sai Theeraz, for giving me time to write a fourth book.

- Mr. Biju Thomas, for agreeing to be the technical reviewer for this book.

- My friends and colleagues, for backing me up and sharing with me their knowledge, laughter, joy, wisdom, and strengths. I received continuous encouragement from each one, and most of them were instrumental in shaping me into what I am.

ACKNOWLEDGMENTS

- The reader, for picking up this book. I have attempted to be as simple and straightforward as possible when sharing this knowledge, and I truly believe that it will help you, the reader, to steadily deep dive into various interesting concepts and procedures.

I would also like to express my gratitude to the Oracle professionals Vijay Cherukuri, Nivas Nadimpalli, Satyendra Kumar, Binay Rath, Mohit Singh (my RAC guru), Mariami Kupatadze, Jennifer Nicholson (OTN), Bal Mukund Sharma, Shailesh Dwivedi (vice president of product management at Oracle), Pankaj Chandiramani (product management for the Oracle Distributed Database), Deeksha Sehgal (product manager at Oracle), Nassyam Basha, Krishnakumar, and all my LaserSoft colleagues.

Special thanks to Celestin Suresh John, Shobana Srinivasan, Joseph Quatela, Laura Berendson, and Mark Powers at Apress for giving me an opportunity to write my fourth book for Apress.

—Y V Ravi Kumar

After the release of my first book on Oracle's AutoUpgrade, I did not expect that I would contribute to writing another book, but here we are. When Y V Ravi Kumar first mentioned writing a book about Oracle GDS, I got excited, so we started working on it. I was also pleased when Mariami Kupatadze joined us as coauthor.

First, I would like to thank the Apress team for giving us the opportunity to write this book and for being patient throughout this journey. I would like to thank both my coauthors, Mariami Kupatadze and Y V Ravi Kumar, for their excellent support throughout the writing process.

I want to express a very special thanks to my wife, Sujitha Chalamalasetty, and to my daughter, Sarayu Sammeta, for being very patient and supportive during all the hours that I spent writing this book. I want to thank my parents from whom I learned to be nice to others. I want to thank my brother, Shiva Shankar, and my sister, Sheshawati, who helped me make the right decisions in a few tough times. I also want to share this happiness with my good friend, Srinivas Kolipaka. We both know what this achievement means for both of us.

Finally, I thank all the readers for selecting this book; we included the most typical scenarios that we see in production environments and have explained them in a simple and straightforward way. I hope that this book will help you in configuring Oracle GDS and Oracle Sharding in your environment.

—Sambaiah Sammetta

I would like to express my deepest gratitude and acknowledge the invaluable contributions of all those who have played a part in the creation of this book. Without their unwavering support, expertise, and dedication, this project would not have come to fruition.

In loving memory of my dear husband, Giorgi Beridze, I dedicate this book to celebrate the extraordinary man he was and the everlasting impact he had on my life. His presence continues to be felt in the greatest gift he left behind, our precious little kids, Salome Beridze and Ana Beridze. They are the radiant sunshine that illuminates my world, bringing immeasurable joy to my heart.

Salome and Ana, throughout the process of writing this book, you have been my constant source of inspiration. Your innocent curiosity, boundless energy, and unwavering love have ignited my determination to create something meaningful and impactful.

—Mariami Kupatadze

Introduction

Oracle Global Data Services (GDS) is an automated workload management feature introduced in Oracle Database 12c that provides workload routing, load balancing and inter-database service failover, replication lag-based routing, role-based global services, and centralized workload management for a set of replicated databases that are globally distributed or located within the same data center.

Over the course of the book, we cover the following salient capabilities of Oracle GDS using test cases:

- Global service failover

- Role-based global services

- Replication lag-based routing

- TAF-enabled global service in a GDS environment

- Local-based routing

- High availability of global service manager (GSMs)

- A crash of the GDS catalog database

This book also covers the following test cases:

- Configuring and installing GSMs

- Configuring and administering GDS

- GDS test cases with Active Data Guard

- GDS test cases with Oracle GoldenGate

- GDS test cases in RAC with Active Data Guard

This book also covers Oracle Sharding, a scalability and availability feature for custom-designed OLTP applications that enables distribution and replication of data across a pool of discrete Oracle databases that share no hardware or software. The pool of databases is presented to the application as a single logical database. Applications elastically scale (data, transactions, and users) to any level, on any platform, simply by adding additional databases (shards) to the pool. Scaling up to 1,000 shards is supported in the first release. This book deals with how to configure Oracle Sharding for mission-critical environments using the Oracle Active Data Guard (ADG) and RAFT replication feature from the Oracle 23c release.

Written by experts who have a lot of experience with Oracle technologies, this book is for people who work with databases or applications. It provides practical advice, tips, and examples to help you understand and use GDS effectively.

Whether you are new to GDS or already have some knowledge, this book will give you the tools and knowledge to make the most of this powerful technology and keep your mission-critical systems running smoothly.

Foreword

No matter what kind of data collection interface an application has, the possibilities for data monetization and the responsibilities of governance will define the downstream lifecycle of the data. How this can be done effectively, to create lasting value, differs across industries and organizations.

In my 25+ years at Oracle, our customers and partners have unfailingly agreed on a common theme: regulatory requirements aside, losing data would result in a serious loss of business equity. Consequently, data replication strategies for data preservation are important for bespoke and packaged applications alike.

The arrival of hybrid and multicloud scenarios has created new security challenges, as well as data governance practices such as FAIR for research asset monetization and preservation.

This book provides a view of how a slew of technologies can be combined to advance the current data practices at each organization, alleviating some of the common architectural restrictions of the past.

This book, written by Y V Ravi Kumar, Mariami Kupatadze, and Sambaiah Sammeta, will clarify the working principles of Oracle Global Data Services and the underlying building blocks of the technology. Readers can borrow ideas from the many test cases involving Active Data Guard, GoldenGate, and more. The authors also offer insights on Oracle Sharding and Raft Replication that can be applied across industries.

I would like to take the opportunity to congratulate the authors on writing this book at a time when many of technologies showcased within are being implemented in next-generation cloud deployments. This book will have tremendous value for architects and data lifecycle strategists alike.

Binay Rath
Senior Director, APAC Alliances and Channels, Oracle Health Sciences Global
Business Unit
Oracle Corporation

CHAPTER 1

Introduction to Oracle Global Data Services

One of the key challenges in database environments is ensuring seamless failover and transparent client connections. When a server that clients are connected to fails, both the clients and the application servers typically encounter errors, and new connections are not automatically redirected to an online database. This can result in disruptions and downtime for the application.

Prior to Oracle Database 12c's maximum availability architecture (MAA), third-party load balancers were necessary to optimally distribute workloads **across synchronized copies** in the same or different datacenters. This created significant integration costs and difficulties in handling support because multiple vendors had to be contacted to resolve issues.

With Oracle Database 12c and the introduction of Global Data Services (GDS), these challenges have been resolved. GDS is a database load balancer for **replicated databases** that offers automation and simplicity by providing workload routing, load balancing, service failover, and centralized service management for a set of replicated databases.

GDS delivers automated workload management, which includes built-in transparent failover capabilities. This eliminates the need for separate load balancers or custom connection managers, and client connections are seamlessly redirected to an online database in the event of a server failure. GDS simplifies the management of client connections and ensures continuous availability and uninterrupted operation of the application.

This chapter provides an overview of the key components of GDS, including their functionality and utilization. By becoming familiar with the GDSCTL command-line interface and exploring various examples, you will gain confidence in working with GDS.

© Y V Ravi Kumar, Mariami Kupatadze, Sambaiah Sammeta 2023
Y V Ravi Kumar et al., *Oracle Global Data Services for Mission-critical Systems*,
https://doi.org/10.1007/978-1-4842-9553-3_1

We also cover the difference between systems not using GDS, and we explore how to use GDS according to best practices. The chapter gives an overview of the GDS role in all possible architectures such as maximum availability, distributed transactions, and multitenant architecture.

You will also see the high-level steps of GDS deployment, including its restrictions, licenses, and compatibility.

At the end of the chapter, you will find a troubleshooting section that shows the necessary logs and commands that can be used during root-cause analysis (RCA).

GDS Components

GDS consists of several key components that work together to provide efficient workload management and high availability for replicated databases.

Global service managers (GSMs) act as listeners in different regions and are known as *global listeners*. They can understand the current workload of the system in real time. Their main tasks are to balance the load of services, handle failures, and manage the system in a centralized manner. GSMs collect performance information from the databases in the GDS setup and also measure the time it takes for data to travel between regions. Based on this information, GSMs create a guidance system for load balancing while the system is running and share it with the client connection pools. If a database fails, it is the responsibility of the GSMs to inform the clients about the issue.

A GSM must be associated with one GDS setup, and it is important to have at least one GSM in each region. To enhance system performance and availability, it is recommended to have three GSMs.

The **GDS catalog** is a database that stores important information about the GDS configuration. It includes details about hosts, regions, GSMs, global services, databases, and more. The size of the GDS catalog database is typically small and usually doesn't exceed 100GB.

Each catalog is linked to a single GDS configuration. To enhance system availability, it is highly recommended to utilize technologies such as Oracle Real Application Cluster (RAC), Oracle Data Guard, and Oracle Clusterware. These technologies help improve the availability of the system.

A **GDS region** consists of a collection of databases and clients that are connected to each other on a nearby network. The databases within the same region have faster network connections and lower latency compared to databases in different regions. Typically, a region corresponds to a local area network (LAN) or a metropolitan area network (MAN).

To ensure uninterrupted access to the GDS configuration, it is advisable to designate a buddy region for each GDS region. This buddy region should have GSMs that can take over and continue providing the necessary services if the GSM in the primary region goes offline or becomes unavailable.

A **GDS pool** is a group of replicated databases that fall under a specific administrative domain. Dividing the GDS configuration databases into multiple pools offers enhanced security and simplifies administration by allowing each pool to be managed by a different administrator.

There are certain limitations when placing databases into the same pool.

- A database can belong to only one GDS pool.

- While databases within a pool don't necessarily need to have the same set of global services, if some of them do provide the same global service, then those databases must be part of the same pool.

The **global service** is a database service that is provided by multiple replicated databases. In earlier versions of Oracle databases, only local services were available. However, starting from Oracle Database 12c and later versions, global services can be provided.

The GSM acts as a mediator between the databases and the clients. When a client wants to connect to a global service, they connect to the regional GSM without specifying a specific database or instance. The GSM then forwards the client's request to the most suitable instance based on real-time statistics.

The status of global services is stored not only in the GDS catalog but also in each member database's system dictionary tables or the Oracle Clusterware Registry (OCR).

When a new member database joins the configuration or an existing database restarts, the GSM compares the metadata information between the GDS catalog and the database. If any inconsistencies are found, the GSM is responsible for synchronizing the member database's metadata with the catalog.

If a database instance fails, all GSMs are notified about the failure, and they stop directing client requests to the failed instance until it is recovered. If the failed instance was the only running instance for the configuration, the GSM can automatically start the service on another database in the GDS pool (if configured), or the administrator can manually perform the same action.

To manage and control Global Data Services, the Global Data Services Control command-line utility (GDSCTL) should be used.

GDS clients use the **Oracle Notification Service (ONS)** to receive real-time load balancing advice and high-availability (HA) events from GDS. The ONS server is located with the GSM.

GDS Features

Many third-party solutions are not fully integrated with Oracle software, which makes it difficult for them to benefit from the features that GDS has, such as **runtime load balancing**.

In the replica set, some databases may have a slower response because of the high load, while others may have room to serve new connections. GDS uses load statistics from all databases in the pool to route the connection to the best database. This is one of the key features that distinguishes it from other vendors.

GSM gathers performance data for each service from all the configured database instances. Also, GSM measures the latency of inter-region networks by exchanging messages with GSMs located in other regions. Utilizing these metrics, GSM is able to dynamically adjust and balance the workload in real time based on the specified option.

Here is the syntax to add the service:

```
[-rlbgoal {SERVICE_TIME|THROUGHPUT}]
```

- SERVICE_TIME is the default setting that ensures connection balance by considering response time. It maintains a well-balanced distribution of connections.

- THROUGHPUT is used for connection balancing based on throughput, taking into account the actual data transmitted or processed, rather than relying on the response time.

Here is a real-world example:

```
GDSCTL> add service -service hr_srvc -gdspool hr –preferred_all  –rlbgoal
SERVICE_TIME
```

Interdatabase service failover is another important feature of GDS that helps it efficiently handle failures. In the event of a failure where services are shifted to another available database, GDS promptly sends Fast Application Notification (FAN) events. These events enable clients to quickly reconnect to the newly available database without having to wait for a timeout period. This ensures faster and seamless resumption of services for the clients.

In real-world scenarios, the default timeout for reconnection without utilizing FAN can be as long as 60 seconds. This duration can be quite significant for production systems, potentially causing delays and disruptions in service availability.

Replication lag-based workload routing allows clients to configure lag tolerance for a specific application. GDS can route connections to the standby server that has a lag below the acceptable threshold. If lag increases so that it exceeds the limit, then the service is relocated to another standby database satisfying the condition.

In the worst case, when no such database is available, then the service is shut down, but whenever the lag is within the acceptable limit, GDS starts the service automatically.

Here is the syntax to add a service:

```
[-lag {lag_value | ANY}]
```

- lag_value: This is defined in seconds.

- ANY: This is the default option in which there is no specific upper limit for lag. It implies that any amount of lag is acceptable within the system.

Here are some real-world examples:

```
GDSCTL> add service -service hr_srvc -gdspool hr -preferred_all -role
physical_standby -lag ANY
```

```
GDSCTL> add service -service hr_srvc -gdspool hr -preferred_all -role
physical_standby -lag 180
```

For applications that cannot tolerate lag, you can set -lag 0. This means requests for this global service are forwarded only to the primary database or to the standby database if it is synchronized with the primary.

If the lag is exceeded for the service, then it is brought down only after all current requests are completed.

Role-based global services offer the capability to detect role changes within Data Guard Broker. In the event that the role of a service aligns with the new role of the database, these services are automatically relocated to the new primary database.

Here is how to add a service:

```
[-role {PRIMARY | PHYSICAL_STANDBY [-failover_primary] | LOGICAL_STANDBY |
SNAPSHOT_STANDBY}]
```

- PHYSICAL_STANDBY -failover_primary: This clause means that the service will be running on the standby database. If the standby database fails, then the service will be relocated to the primary database.

Here is a real-world example:

GDSCTL> add service -gdspool hr -service hr_srvc -preferred_all **-role physical_standby -failover_primary**

This parameter is better explained with the -lag option. If we set the -lag attribute to 10 seconds and no data has arrived for more than 10 seconds, for example, when the apply process is stopped, then GDS automatically relocates the global service to the primary database because the -failover_primary option was used.

Centralized workload management for replicas - one way to simplify workload management for replicas is by centralizing it. Using the GDSCTL command-line utility or the Oracle Enterprise Manager Cloud Control (OEMCC) graphical user interface, you can administer the global resources of regionally or globally replicated databases.

If you need information about the options provided by a specific tool, you can access the help feature.

[gsmosuser@gsmnode bin]$ **echo $PWD**
/u01/app/oracle/product/19.0.0/gsmhome_1/bin

Directly pass the help option to the tool:

[gsmosuser@gsmnode bin]$ **./gdsctl -help**

Or you can use the help option in the interface:

GDSCTL> **help**

Connect-time load balancing ensures that network traffic is evenly distributed across multiple servers. This distribution prevents any single server from becoming overloaded and maximizes the efficient use of resources. In simple terms, it helps balance the workload and prevents servers from being overwhelmed, leading to better resource management.

Here is how to add or modify a service:

```
[-clbgoal {SHORT | LONG}]
```

- SHORT: This is the default option. It is well-suited for load balancing during runtime. Here is an example of its use:

```
GDSCTL> add service -service hr_srvc -gdspool hrpool -preferred_all -clbgoal
SHORT
```

- LONG: This is an option suitable for applications that involve long-lived connections, such as batch jobs. It prioritizes connection persistence, aiming to minimize disruptions caused by connection reassignments. Here is an example of its use:

```
GDSCTL> add service -service hr_srvc -gdspool hrpool -preferred_all -clbgoal
LONG
```

Region-based workload routing allows businesses to direct user requests to the nearest available database location based on the user's geographical region.

By routing requests to the closest database, the latency is reduced, resulting in faster response times and improved user experience.

For example, if a user in Europe tries to access data, the request can be automatically routed to a database located in Europe, rather than going through a database in a different region, such as Asia or the Americas.

Here is how to add or modify a service:

```
[-locality {ANYWHERE | LOCAL_ONLY [-region_failover]}]
```

- ANYWHERE: This is the default option. The connections from the clients are routed to any region for load balancing or failover. The choice of the database is based on its performance and network latency between regions where the client and database reside. If databases in different regions have the same load, then the policy gives preference to the local region. Here is an example of its use:

GDSCTL> add service -service hr_srvc -gdspool hr –preferred_all **-locality
ANYWHERE**

- LOCAL_ONLY: GDS will never route connections to databases in other regions. Inter-region failover is disabled. The client connection is routed to the best database in the client's region. The database in the local region is chosen based on its performance. If there is no database in the local region offering the global service, then the client connection request fails; it is never redirected to another region even if the remote region has available instances. Here is an example of its use:

GDSCTL> add service -service hr_srvc -gdspool hr –preferred_all **-locality
LOCAL_ONLY**

- LOCAL_ONLY -region_failover: The connections are routed to another region if all databases in the local region have failed. Here is an example of its use:

GDSCTL> add service -service hr_srvc -gdspool hr –preferred_all –locality
LOCAL_ONLY -region_failover

Active Data Guard and Oracle GoldenGate are replication technologies extensively utilized in Oracle databases. These technologies enable the replication of data across various sites, which can consist of either RAC or single-instance databases. GDS plays a crucial role in facilitating seamless service failovers and load balancing between these diverse sites.

Figures 1-1 and 1-2 are simple illustrations of maximum availability architecture without and with GDS.

In the absence of GDS, client connections lack transparency during failover events. If the server to which clients are connected experiences a failure, both the clients and the application servers will encounter errors, and subsequent connections will not be automatically redirected to an available database, as illustrated in Figure 1-1.

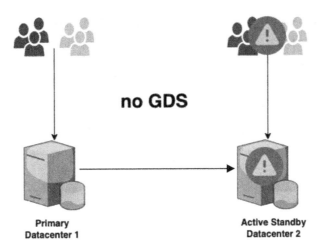

Figure 1-1. *No failover without GDS*

GDS offers automated workload management, effectively addressing failover scenarios, as illustrated in Figure 1-2. It removes the need for specialized custom connection managers and load balancers dedicated to handling database workloads.

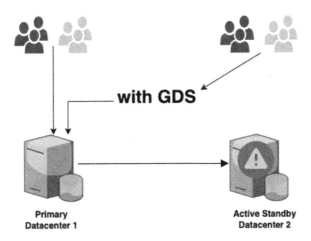

Figure 1-2. *Global service failover with GDS*

The GDS configuration needs to be stored in a separate database called the **Global Data Services catalog**. The catalog is associated with only one GDS configuration. The minimum version of the database is Oracle Database 12c.

Similar to any of the Oracle databases, the GDS repository also needs to be configured using high-availability technologies such as Oracle RAC, Oracle Data Guard, and/or Oracle Clusterware.

In Figure 1-3, you can see the GDS catalog database is in an Active Data Guard configuration, and the sales database uses GoldenGate. A GDS configuration contains multiple GSMs per region. Placing and partitioning databases into GDS pools simplifies service management and provides higher security by allowing each pool to be administered by a different administrator.

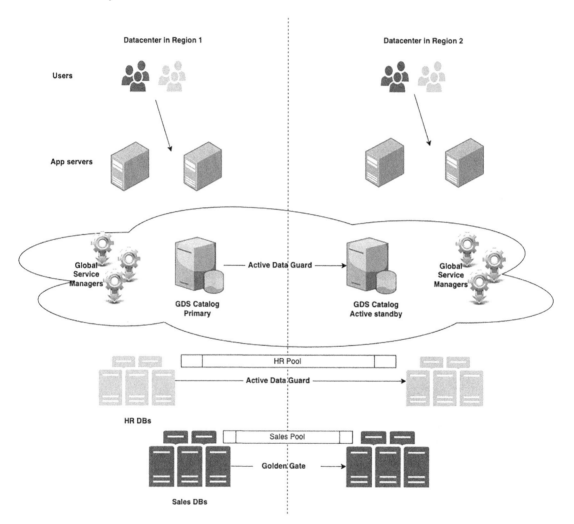

Figure 1-3. *GDS components and architecture*

Configuration Best Practices of GDS in Maximum Availability Architecture

Each region should have a total of three GSMs, with each GSM residing on dedicated hardware. This setup ensures redundancy, as even if one GSM experiences an outage, the other two will continue to provide the required services.

The GDS catalog, which is essential for GDS operations, must be protected using Data Guard. The primary and standby databases that host the GDS catalog should be deployed on separate hardware.

To further enhance the reliability and manageability of the GDS catalog database, it is recommended to consolidate it with Oracle Enterprise Manager Cloud Control.

Additionally, regular backups using Recovery Manager (RMAN) should be performed to safeguard the GDS catalog database against any potential data loss.

Global Services and Distributed Transactions

Using global services in XA transactions on a multi-instance Oracle RAC environment can potentially result in performance degradation. To mitigate this issue, it is advised to enable the -dtp parameter and set it to TRUE for any service utilized by XA transactions. Setting this parameter guarantees that all XA transactions will be performed through the service having tightly coupled branches running on a single instance.

Global Services in Multitenant Architecture

The container database (CDB) can be part of the GDS configuration. The service can be created at the CDB$ROOT or pluggable database (PDB) level. If the PDB property is not set, then the global service is created at the CDB root level.

Global Service Failover Details

When a global service or database fails, the GSM considers **preferred** databases as failover targets before **available** databases.

If the failover was intentional, using GDSCTL, then the service does not failover to another database. Settings will remember the current database as a failover target, and if another replicated database fails, then the previously mentioned service can start again on the remembered database.

The GDS framework supports role-based global services. If the GDS pool contains databases that are part of the Oracle Data Guard broker configuration, the GDS framework can automatically start the global service when the database role matches the role specified for this service. Valid roles are PRIMARY, PHYSICAL_STANDBY, LOGICAL_STANDBY, and SNAPSHOT_STANDBY.

The global service cannot failover between regions if the locality parameter is set to LOCAL_ONLY and the inter-region failover is not enabled.

It is recommended to have fast connection failover enabled for the Oracle clients, which provides rapid failover of the connections in the case of service outages. Instead of waiting for the response from the failed database, which can be as many as 60 seconds, depending on the failure, clients receive FAN events and react immediately.

If something blocks the GSM from connecting to the Global Data Services catalog, then the GSM will not be able to automatically failover a service.

GDS Restrictions, License, and Compatibility

GDS operates as a shared infrastructure, allowing a single GDS configuration to handle the following:

- Management of up to 300 database instances

- Support for 1,000 global services

- Provision of 20 GDS pools

- Organization of 10 GDS regions

- Availability of five GSMs per region

- Facilitation of 1,000 mid-tier connection pools

The databases included in the GDS configuration need to fulfill the following requirements:

- Licensing for either Oracle Active Data Guard or Oracle GoldenGate is mandatory.

- The Oracle Database version must be Enterprise Edition (EE) 12.1 or higher.

- The deployment can be either a single Instance or a RAC configuration.

- The database can be Oracle multitenant or not.

- The deployment is compatible with Oracle Exadata and Oracle Database Appliance (ODA).

The following are the high-level steps involved in installation and configuration:

1) Install GSM software on GSM servers, with a minimum of one GSM per region. According to best practices, it is recommended to have three GSMs per region.

2) Set up GDS Administrator accounts and privileges.

3) Create a GDS catalog.

4) Add GSM, regions, pools, databases, and global services.

5) Start services.

6) Set up client connectivity.

7) Adjust the settings in your application servers.

Comprehensive installation and configuration procedures will be covered in subsequent chapters, providing detailed guidance on the necessary steps.

Troubleshooting

The majority of troubleshooting time is spent on searching for information within logs. This section provides an overview of the various tools and logs that should be examined during the troubleshooting phase.

- GSM alert log location: `/u01/app/oracle/diag/gsm/<GSM-node>/gsm?/trace/alert*.log`

- GSM agent log: `$ORACLE_HOME/data/agent.log`

- GSM Listener Trace: GDSCTL> **status**

GSM tracing is enabled in the Global Data Services catalog database and all GDS pool databases using `GWM_TRACE` levels.

The following statement provides immediate tracing, but the trace is disabled after a database restart:

```
SQL> alter system set events 'immediate trace name GWM_TRACE level 7';
```

The following statement enables tracing that continues in perpetuity, but only after restarting the database:

```
SQL> ALTER SYSTEM SET EVENT='10798 trace name context forever, level 7' SCOPE=spfile;
```

To enhance safety, it is advisable to enable both traces.

To trace everything, you will need to set this on the GDS catalog and all GDS pool databases. The traces are written to the RDBMS session trace file for either the GDSCTL session (on the GDS catalog) or the sessions created by the GSMs (on the GDS pool databases).

Note   Typically, shared servers handle connections to the GDS catalog and GDS pool databases, resulting in the tracing information being stored in a shared server trace file e.g

`named _s00*.trc`

The status command can be used to obtain the running status of the GDS components, as shown here:

GDSCTL> **status gsm**

```
Alias                        gsmwest
Version                      19.0.0.0.0
Start Date                   28-NOV-2022 05:23:01
Trace Level                  off
Listener Log File            /u01/app/oracle/diag/gsm/gsmnode/gsmwest/
                             alert/log.xml
Listener Trace File          /u01/app/oracle/diag/gsm/gsmnode/gsmwest/trace/
                             ora_5059_140388162772032.trc
Endpoint summary             (ADDRESS=(HOST=gsmnode.mycompany.mydomain)
                             (PORT=1571)(PROTOCOL=tcp))
GSMOCI Version               3.0.180702
Mastership                   N
Connected to GDS catalog     N
Process Id                   5070
Number of reconnections      0
Pending tasks.      Total    0
Tasks in process. Total   0
Alert: catalog database is not registered on GSM listener.
Regional Mastership          TRUE
Total messages published   6
Time Zone                    +00:00
Orphaned Buddy Regions:
    None
GDS region                   west
```

GDSCTL> **status service**

```
Service "salesrv.sales.oradbcloud" has 2 instance(s). Affinity: ANYWHERE
    Instance "sales%1", name: "orcl1", db: "orcl", region: "west",
    status: ready.
    Instance "sales%2", name: "orcl2", db: "orcl", region: "west",
    status: ready.
```

GDSCTL> **status database**

Database: "orcl" Registered: Y State: Ok ONS: Y. Role: PRIMARY Instances: 2
Region: west
   Service: "salesrv" Globally started: Y Started: Y
            Scan: N Enabled: Y Preferred: Y
   Registered instances:
     sales%1
     sales%2

The gdsctl config command can be used to obtain the static configuration
information of various GDS components.

GDSCTL> **config**

Regions
----
east
regionora
west

GSMs
----
gsmwest

GDS pools
----
dbpoolora
sales

Databases
----
orcl

Services
----
salesrv

GDSCTL pending requests

```
Command                     Object                        Status
-------                     ------                        ------

Global properties
-----------------------
Name: oradbcloud
Master GSM: gsmwest
DDL sequence #: 0
```

GDSCTL> **config gsm**

```
Name       Region   ENDPOINT
----       ------   --------
gsmwest    west     (ADDRESS=(HOST=gsmnode.mycompany.mydomain)(PORT=1571)
                    (PROTOCOL=tcp))
```

GDSCTL> **config region**

```
Name                    Buddy
----                    -----
east
regionora
west
```

GDSCTL> **config gdspool**

```
Name            Broker                  Sharded
----            ------                  -------
dbpoolora       No                      No
sales           No                      No
```

GDSCTL> **config database**

```
Name      Pool     Status   State   Region   Availability
----      ----     ------   -----   ------   ------------
orcl      sales    Ok       none    west     ONLINE
```

```
GDSCTL> config service
```

```
Name      Network name              Pool   Started Preferred all
----      ------------              ----   ------- -------------
salesrv   salesrv.sales.oradbcloud  sales  Yes      Yes
```

You can enable tracing using the set trace_level command from the GDSCTL command-line interface.

```
GDSCTL> set trace_level -gsm gsm_name SUPPORT
trace_level is set to SUPPORT
```

The SUPPORT option provides a trace with troubleshooting information for Oracle Support Services. The other options are ADMIN and USER.

To disable tracing, use this:

```
GDSCTL> set trace_level -gsm gsm_name OFF
trace_level is set to OFF
```

The exact location of a given global service manager's log and trace files can be obtained using the status gsm command.

```
GDSCTL> status gsm
```

Summary

Global Data Services is an automated workload management feature that was introduced in Oracle Database 12c. It provides connect-time and runtime load balancing, replication lag-based workload routing, interdatabase service failover, role-based global services, centralized workload management for replicas, and region-based workload routing.

Since Oracle Database 12c, customers are allowed to use all these features without contacting third-party vendors.

GDS provides better performance, availability, automation, and simplicity.

The next chapter explores the Oracle Sharding technology alongside Global Data Services. It helps you understand the benefits of sharding, the significance of high availability, and the various methods that can be used in this architecture.

CHAPTER 2

Introduction to Oracle Sharding

In this chapter, we'll cover Oracle Sharding technology along with Global Data Services (GDS), and we will describe the benefits of sharding and high availability. We'll also cover methods that can be used in this type of architecture.

We will also introduce the GDSCTL commands used for Oracle Sharding, with all the possible options and arguments.

We've also included an "Oracle Sharding Workshop" section to guide you through the GSM software installation and configuration steps that are necessary for setting up an Oracle Sharding architecture and GSM in your lab environment.

Let's start by defining exactly what the sharding is.

What Is Sharding?

Oracle Sharding is a technology that distributes user data across multiple databases, called **shards**, within the same or different datacenters. In a shared-nothing architecture, the data is horizontally partitioned across a number of physically independent databases.

Sharding is similar to the table partitioning. The difference between them is that the table partitioning technology places partitions into the same database, while in sharding, partitions are located in different databases.

Shards together make up a single logical database, called a **sharded database (SDB)**. The distribution of the data is completely transparent to applications.

Shard-aware Oracle tools are SQL Developer, EM Cloud Control, RMAN, and Data Pump.

© Y V Ravi Kumar, Mariami Kupatadze, Sambaiah Sammeta 2023
Y V Ravi Kumar et al., *Oracle Global Data Services for Mission-critical Systems*,
https://doi.org/10.1007/978-1-4842-9553-3_2

Extensions for sharding are included in the following interfaces: JDBC, OCI, UCP, ODP.NET, and PL/SQL.

Figure 2-1 shows a table that is horizontally partitioned between three different databases/shards.

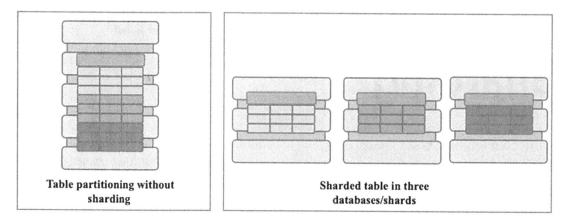

Figure 2-1. *Unsharded and sharded table partitioning*

Benefits of Sharding

Sharding **linearly scales** performance and capacity by adding shards into the existing system.

The architecture provides **fault isolation** by using a shared-nothing method, which means no hardware or software will be shared between shards.

In a sharding architecture, you can **geographically distribute** data by placing shards into the datacenters that are close to its consumers.

Downtime is reduced by using **rolling upgrades**. Patches or configuration changes can be applied on one shard at a time, without affecting other shards.

Oracle Sharding supports on-prem, cloud, and hybrid deployment models.

Sharding High Availability

Each shard can optionally be deployed on an Oracle Real Application Cluster (RAC) to protect against node failure. You can set up the shards in Oracle Data Guard and open the standby database with read-only access.

For active-active replication, you can use Oracle GoldenGate. Please note that Oracle GoldenGate replication support for sharding is deprecated in Oracle Database 21c.

Sharding Methods

Oracle data placement is controlled by the sharding method. The methods used in this technology are covered in this section.

The **system-managed** sharding method implies that the user does not map data to shards. A consistent hash algorithm ensures that the data is randomly and evenly distributed across all shards.

Before creating a sharded table, a set of tablespaces has to be created to store the table partitions.

You create the tablespaces by executing the following SQL statement:

```
CREATE TABLESPACE SET ts1;
```

While creating a sharded table, you specify the sharding method and a tablespace location using the following:

```
CREATE SHARDED TABLE transactions
( tran_id     NUMBER NOT NULL
...
, CONSTRAINT tran_pk PRIMARY KEY(tran_id)
)
PARTITION BY CONSISTENT HASH (tran_id)
PARTITIONS AUTO
TABLESPACE SET ts1
;
```

The **user-defined** method considers that the user maps data to individual shards. This method is necessary when there is a strict requirement to have some type of data on a particular shard.

The benefit of this method is that the user knows what data becomes unavailable during a particular sharding failure. The disadvantage is that the database administrator (DBA) must maintain the balance distribution of the data.

Partitioning can be performed either by list or by range in Oracle Sharding. It is important to note that no tablespace set is used; the method requires the manual creation of tablespaces associated with the shardspace. A **shardspace** is a set of shards that store data corresponding to a range or list of key values.

The DBA must create shardspaces using the GDSCTL command and populate the command with specific shards, as shown here:

```
GDSCTL> ADD SHARDSPACE -SHARDSPACE east
GDSCTL> ADD SHARDSPACE -SHARDSPACE west

GDSCTL> ADD CDB -CONNECT cdb1
GDSCTL> ADD CDB -CONNECT cdb2

GDSCTL> ADD SHARD -CONNECT shard1 -CDB cdb1 -SHARDSPACE east;
GDSCTL> ADD SHARD -CONNECT shard2 -CDB cdb2 -SHARDSPACE west;
```

Tablespaces must be created individually and explicitly associated with a shardspace.

```
SQL> CREATE TABLESPACE ts1 IN SHARDSPACE east;
SQL> CREATE TABLESPACE ts2 IN SHARDSPACE west;
```

The following is the SQL statement for creating a user-defined table:

```
CREATE SHARDED TABLE int_students
( id             NUMBER
, student_number NUMBER
...
, state          VARCHAR(2) NOT NULL
)
PARTITION BY LIST (state)
( PARTITION p_northeast VALUES ('NY', 'VM', 'NJ') TABLESPACE ts1
, PARTITION p_southeast VALUES ('FL', 'GA') TABLESPACE ts1
, PARTITION p_northwest VALUES ('OR', 'WA') TABLESPACE ts2
, PARTITION p_southwest VALUES ('AZ', 'UT', 'NM') TABLESPACE ts2
);
```

Composite sharding is a combination of the system-managed and user-defined sharding methods.

In this method, data is first partitioned by list or by range across shardspaces and then partitioned by a consistent hash algorithm across multiple shards in each shardspace.

Using GDSCTL, the DBA must create shardspaces and populate them with specific shards.

```
GDSCTL> ADD SHARDSPACE -SHARDSPACE shspace1;
GDSCTL> ADD SHARDSPACE -SHARDSPACE shspace2;

GDSCTL> ADD CDB -CONNECT cdb1
GDSCTL> ADD CDB -CONNECT cdb2

GDSCTL> ADD SHARD -CONNECT shard1 -CDB cdb1 -SHARDSPACE shspace1;
GDSCTL> ADD SHARD -CONNECT shard2 -CDB cdb2 -SHARDSPACE shspace2;
```

A separate tablespace set must be created in each shardspace.

```
CREATE TABLESPACE SET ts1 IN SHARDSPACE shspace1;
CREATE TABLESPACE SET ts2 IN SHARDSPACE shspace2;
```

The following is an example of creating a table using this method:

```
CREATE SHARDED TABLE int_students
( id              NUMBER
, student_number  NUMBER
...
, state           VARCHAR(2) NOT NULL
)
PARTITION BY LIST (state)
PARTITION BY CONSISTENT HASH (id)
PARTITIONS AUTO
(PARTITIONSET p_northeast VALUES ('NY', 'VM', 'NJ') TABLESPACE SET ts1
,PARTITIONSET p_southeast VALUES ('FL', 'GA') TABLESPACE SET ts1
,PARTITIONSET p_northwest VALUES ('OR', 'WA') TABLESPACE SET ts2
,PARTITIONSET p_southwest VALUES ('AZ', 'UT', 'NM') TABLESPACE SET ts2
);
```

GDSCTL Commands Used for Oracle Sharding

The following GDSCTL commands are commonly used in an Oracle Sharding configuration:

- `add cdb`: This adds a CDB to the shard catalog.

```
GDSCTL> add cdb -connect connect_identifier
          [-pwd password]
          [-savename]
          [-cpu_threshold cpu]
          [-disk_threshold disk]
          [-rack rack_id]
          [-force]
```

- `add credential`: This adds a credential that can be used by the Remote Scheduler Agent to execute jobs.

```
GDSCTL> add credential -credential credential_name
              -osaccount account_name
              -ospassword password
          [-windows_domain domain_name]
```

- `add file`: This adds the contents of a file to the catalog, which can be used by GDSCTL commands.

```
GDSCTL> add file -file file_name -source local_filename
```

- `add gsm`: This adds a GSM.

```
GDSCTL> add gsm -gsm gsm_name
        -catalog connect_id
      [-pwd password]
      [-wpwd password]
      [-region region_name]
      [-localons ons_port]
      [-remoteons ons_port]
      [-listener listener_port]
```

```
[-endpoint gmsendpoint]
[-remote_endpoint remote_endpoint]
[-trace_level level]
```

- add invitednode (add invitedsubnet): This adds a host address or subnet information to the valid node checking for registration (VNCR) list in the catalog.

```
GDSCTL> add {invitednode | invitedsubnet}
        [-group group_name]
        [-catalog catalog_dbname [-user user_name/password]]
      vncr_id
```

- add region: This adds a region.

```
GDSCTL> add region -region region_list [-buddy region_name]
```

- add service: This adds a global service to a Global Data Services pool.

```
GDSCTL>  add service
        [-gdspool gdspool_name]
        -service service_name
        (-preferred_all | (-preferred dbname_list [-available
        dbname_list]))
        [-locality {ANYWHERE | LOCAL_ONLY [-region_failover]}]
        [-role {PRIMARY | PHYSICAL_STANDBY [-failover_primary] |
           LOGICAL_STANDBY | SNAPSHOT_STANDBY}]
        [-lag {lag_value | ANY}]
        [-notification {TRUE | FALSE}]
        [-rlbgoal {SERVICE_TIME | THROUGHPUT}]
        [-dtp {TRUE | FALSE}]
        [-sql_translation_profile stp_name]
        [-clbgoal {SHORT | LONG}]
        [-tafpolicy {BASIC | NONE | PRECONNECT}]
        [-policy policy]
        [-failovertype {NONE | SESSION | SELECT | TRANSACTION | AUTO}]
```

```
        [-failovermethod {NONE | BASIC}]
        [-failoverretry failover_retries]
        [-failoverdelay failover_delay]
        [-edition edition_name]
        [-commit_outcome {TRUE | FALSE}]
        [-retention retention_seconds]
        [-session_state {DYNAMIC | STATIC | AUTO}]
        [-replay_init_time replay_init_time]
        [-pdbname pdbname]
        [-drain_timeout]
        [-stop_option  {NONE,IMMEDIATE, TRANSACTIONAL}]
        [-failover_restore {NONE|LEVEL1|AUTO}]
        [-table_family family]
```

- add shard: This adds a shard to the shard catalog.

```
GDSCTL> add shard -connect connect_identifier
        [-pwd password]
        [-savename]
        [-region region_name]
        [-force]
        [-cdb cdb_name]
        [-cpu_threshold cpu]
        [-disk_threshold disk]
        [{-shardgroup shardgroup_name | -shardspace shardspace_name}]
        [-deploy_as {PRIMARY | STANDBY | ACTIVE_STANDBY}]
        [-rack rack_id]
        [-replace old_db_name]
        [-gg_service (http|https):ogg_host:sm_port/GGHOME_directory]
```

- add shardgroup: This adds a shardgroup.

```
GDSCTL> add shardgroup -shardgroup shardgroup_name
            [-region region_name]
            [-shardspace shardspace_name]
            [-deploy_as {PRIMARY | STANDBY | ACTIVE_STANDBY}]
            [-repfactor number]
```

- add shardspace: This adds a shardspace to the shard catalog.

```
GDSCTL> add shardspace -shardspace shardspace_name
            [-chunks number]
            [-protectmode dg_protection_mode]
```

- config: This displays the configuration data for all components.

```
GDSCTL> config [-support]
```

- config cdb: This displays the properties of a CDB.

```
GDSCTL> config cdb [-cdb cdb_name]
```

- config chunks: This displays the properties of a chunk.

```
GDSCTL> config chunks [-support]
   ( [-shard shd] | [-shardgroup sh] | [-show_reshard] | [-cross_shard] )
   ( [-chunk chunk_id] | [-key key [-superkey superkey] )
```

- config credential: This displays the remote credentials available for shard jobs.

```
GDSCTL> config credential [-support]
```

- config file: This displays file objects.

```
GDSCTL> config file [-support] [-file file_name]
```

- config gsm: This displays the configuration data for the specified GSM.

```
GDSCTL> config gsm [-gsm gsm_name] [-support]
```

- config region: This displays the configuration data for the specified region.

```
GDSCTL> config region [-region region_name] [-support]
```

- config sdb: This displays the configuration data for the sharded database.

```
GDSCTL> config sdb [-support]
```

- `config service`: This displays the configuration for the services that are located in a database pool.

```
GDSCTL> config service [-gdspool gdspool_name] [-service service_name]
[-support]
```

- `config shard`: This displays the properties of a shard.

```
GDSCTL> config shard -shard shard_name [-support]
```

- `config shardgroup`: This displays the properties of a shardgroup.

```
GDSCTL> config shardgroup [-shardgroup shardgroup_name] [-support]
```

- `config shardspace`: This displays the properties of a shardspace.

```
GDSCTL> config shardspace [-shardspace shardspace_name] [-support]
```

- `config vncr`: This displays the configuration data for valid node checking for registration.

```
GDSCTL> config vncr [-group group_name] [-support]
```

- `configure`: This configures the GDSCTL parameters.

```
GDSCTL> configure [-gsmport port]
           [-timeout seconds]
           [-show]
           [-driver {THIN | OCI}]
           [-resolve {IP | HOSTNAME | QUAL_HOSTNAME}]
           [-log {ALL|OFF|INFO|FINE|FINER|FINEST|SEVERE|WARNING}]
           [-log_file log_file]
           [-gsm gsm_name]
           [-showtime ON|OFF]
           [-verbose ON|OFF]
           [-save_config]
           [-gsmdebug (1|0)]
           [-spool]
           [-width]
```

- connect: This specifies the credentials to administer a GSM environment.

```
GDSCTL> connect [user_name[/password]]@connect_identifier
```

- create shard: This creates a new shard and adds it to a shardspace or shardgroup.

```
GDSCTL> create shard [{-shardgroup shardgroup_name | -shardspace
shardspace_name}]
                [-region region_name]
                [-deploy_as {primary | standby | active_standby}]
                [-rack rack_id]
                [-gg_service (http|https):ogg_host:sm_port/deployment
                  -gg_password gg_user_password]
                -destination destination_name
                {-credential credential_name |
                  -osaccount account_name
                  -ospassword password
                 [-windows_domain domain_name]}
                [-dbparam db_parameter_file |
                  -dbparamfile db_parameter_file]
                [-dbtemplate db_template_file |
                  -dbtemplatefile db_template_file]
                [-netparam net_parameter_file |
                  -netparamfile net_parameter_file]
                [-serviceuserpassword pwd]
                [-sys_password]
                [-system_password]
```

- create shardcatalog: This creates a shard catalog.

```
GDSCTL> create shardcatalog -database connect_identifier
                [-user username[/password]]
                [-region region_name_list]
                [-configname config_name]
```

```
                    [-autovncr {ON | OFF}]
                    [-force]
                    [-sdb sdb_name]
                    [-shardspace shardspace_name_list]
                    [-agent_password password]
                    [-repl DG | OGG}]
                    [-repfactor number]
                    [-sharding {system | composite | user}]
                    [-chunks number]
                    [-protectmode dg_protection_mode]
                    [-agent_port port]
```

- delete catalog: This deletes the catalog.

```
GDSCTL> delete catalog [-connect [user/[password]@]conn_str] [-force]
```

- deploy: This deploys and configures the sharded databases.

```
GDSCTL> deploy [-no_rebalance]
```

- disable service: This disables specified global services.

```
GDSCTL> disable service [-gdspool gdspool_name]
               [-service service_name_list]
               [-database db_name |[-override -connect conn_str
               [-pwd password]]]
```

- enable service: This enables the global service.

```
GDSCTL> enable service [-gdspool gdspool_name]
               [-service service_name_list]
               [-database db_name|[-override -connect conn_str
               [-pwd password]]]
```

- modify catalog: This modifies the properties of the catalog.

```
GDSCTL> modify catalog [-autovncr {ON | OFF}]
               [-oldpwd oldpassword -newpwd newpassword]
               [-pwd password -newkeys]
               [-agent_password password]
```

```
[-agent_port port]
[-region region]
[-recover]
```

- modify cdb: This modifies CDB attributes.

```
GDSCTL> modify cdb -shard cdbname_list
            [-connect connect_identifier]
            [-pwd gsmrootuser_pwd]
            [-scan scan_address [-ons port]]
            [-savename]
```

- modify credential: This modifies a credential that will be used by the Remote Scheduler Agent to execute jobs.

```
GDSCTL> modify credential -credential credential_name
                -osaccount account_name
                -ospassword password
              [-windows_domain domain_name]
```

- modify file: This updates the contents of a file in the catalog.

```
GDSCTL> modify file -file file_name -source local_filename
```

- modify gsm: This modifies the configuration parameters of the GSM.

```
GDSCTL> modify gsm -gsm gsm_name
            [-catalog connect_id [-pwd password]]
            [-region region_name]
            [-localons ons_port]
            [-remoteons ons_port]
            [-endpoint gmsendpoint [-remote_endpoint remote_endpoint]]
            [-listener listener_port]
            [-wpwd wallet_password]
```

- modify region: This modifies the configuration parameters for a region.

```
GDSCTL> modify region -region region_name_list [-buddy region_name]
[-weights weight]
```

- `modify service`: This modifies the service attributes.

```
GDSCTL> modify service [-gdspool gdspool_name] -service service_name
            {-preferred db_name_list | -available db_name_list}
```

- `modify shard`: This modifies the properties of a shard.

```
GDSCTL> modify shard -shard shname_list
            [-region region_name]
            [-connect connect_identifier]
            [-pwd password]
            [-scan scan_address [-ons port]]
            [-savename]
            [-cpu_threshold cpu]
            [-disk_threshold disk]
            [-destination destination_name]
            [-credential credential_name |
             [[-osaccount account_name]
              [-ospassword password]
              [-windows_domain domain_name]]]
```

- `modify shardgroup`: This modifies the shardgroup attributes.

```
GDSCTL> modify shardgroup -shardgroup shardgroup_name
              [-region region_name]
              [-shardspace shardspace_name]
              [-repfactor number]
              [-deploy_as {PRIMARY | STANDBY | ACTIVE_STANDBY}]
```

- `modify shardspace`: This modifies the parameters of the shardspace.

```
GDSCTL> modify shardspace -shardspace shardspace_name
              [-chunks number]
              [-protectmode dg_protection_mode]
```

- `move chunk`: This moves chunks from one shard to another shard.

```
GDSCTL> move chunk -chunk {chunk_id_list | ALL}
           -source shard_name
         [-target shard_name]
```

```
[-timeout]
[-verbose]
```

- `relocate service`: This stops a service on one database and starts it on a different database.

```
GDSCTL> relocate service [-gdspool gdspool_name]
                -service service_name
                -old_db db_name
                -new_db db_name
                [-force]
                [-override [-oldpwd oldpassword] [-newpwd newpassword]]
```

- `remove cdb`: This removes CDBs from the shard catalog but does not destroy them.

```
GDSCTL> remove cdb -cdb {cdb_name_list | ALL} [-force]
```

- `remove credential`: This deletes an existing credential.

```
GDSCTL> remove credential -credential credential_name
```

- `remove file`: This deletes a file object from the catalog.

```
GDSCTL> remove file -file file_name
```

- `remove gsm`: This removes a GSM.

```
GDSCTL> remove gsm [-gsm gsm_name]
```

- `remove invitednode (remove invitedsubnet)`: This removes information about the host from the valid VNCR list.

```
GDSCTL> remove invitednode {[-group group_name]|vncr_id}
```

- `remove region`: This removes the specified regions.

```
GDSCTL> remove region -region region_list
```

- `remove service`: This removes a service from a database pool.

```
GDSCTL> remove service [-gdspool gdspool_name] -service service_name
```

- `remove shard`: This removes shards from the sharded database.

```
GDSCTL> remove shard {-shard {shard_name_list | ALL} |
                -shardspace shardspace_list |
                -shardgroup shardgroup_list}
            [-force]
```

- `remove shardgroup`: This removes a shardgroup.

```
GDSCTL> remove shardgroup -shardgroup shardgroup_name
```

- `remove shardspace`: This removes a shardspace.

```
GDSCTL> remove shardspace -shardspace shardspace_name
```

- `services`: This displays information about the services that are registered with the specified GSM.

```
GDSCTL> [status service | services] [-gsm gsm_name]
                            [-service service_name]
                            [-raw | -verbose | -support]
```

- `set gsm`: This sets the GSM in the current session. The GSM name is resolved from the `gsm.ora` file.

```
GDSCTL> set gsm -gsm gsm_name
```

- `set inbound_connect_level`: This sets the `INBOUND_CONNECT_LEVEL` listener parameter.

```
GDSCTL> set inbound_connect_level [-gsm gsm_name] timeout_value
```

- `set log_level`: This sets the log level for the listener associated with a specific GSM.

```
GDSCTL> set log_level [-gsm gsm_name] log_level
```

- `set outbound_connect_level`: This sets the timeout value for the outbound connections.

```
GDSCTL> set outbound_connect_level [-gsm gsm_name] timeout_value
```

- set trace_level: This sets the trace level for the listener associated with the GSM.

```
GDSCTL> set trace_level [-gsm gsm_name] trace_level
```

- split chunk: This splits each chunk into two chunks with an equal number of records.

```
GDSCTL> split chunk -chunk chunk_id_list [-shardspace shard_space_list]
```

- sql: This executes a SQL statement or stored procedure against a sharded database.

```
GDSCTL> sql "sql_statement"
```

- start gsm: This starts a specific GSM.

```
GDSCTL> start gsm [-gsm gsm_name]
```

- start service: This starts services.

```
GDSCTL> start service [-gdspool gdspool_name]
              -service service_name
           [{-database db_name |
               -override [-pwd password] -connect connect_identifier}]
```

- status gsm: This displays the status of a GSM.

```
GDSCTL> status (gsm)? [-gsm gsm_name] [-raw | -verbose | -support]
```

- status service: This shows the status of a service.

```
GDSCTL> {status service | services} [-gsm gsm_name]
                            [-service service_name]
                            [{-raw|-verbose|-support}]
```

- stop gsm: This stops the GSM.

```
GDSCTL> stop gsm [-gsm gsm_name]
```

- **stop service**: This stops the service.

```
GDSCTL> stop service [-gdspool gdspool_name]
            [-service service_name_list]
            [{-database db_name |
                -override -connect connect_identifier [-pwd password]}]
            [-force]
            [-drain_timeout time]
            [-stop_option {NONE|IMMEDIATE|TRANSACTIONAL}]
```

- **validate catalog**: This checks the GDS catalog, global service manager status, and pool databases, and reports errors.

```
GDSCTL> validate [catalog]
        [-gsm gsm_name]
        [ {-config | -database db_name} ]
        [-catpwd cpwd]
        [-dbpwd dpwd]
```

Oracle Sharding Workshop

In this interactive section, we will present detailed instructions and real-life scenarios showcasing the implementation of Oracle Sharding with GDS. This practical approach will equip you with the necessary tools and commands to apply sharding techniques in your own environments. At the end of this section, you will have the opportunity to validate the methodology, ensuring the completeness of your setup.

You will need five servers to set up a lab environment.

- gsmcat: Shard catalog database (gsmcatdb) and shard director

- prsh01: Primary shard database server

- prsh02: Primary shard database server

- stsh01: Standby read-only shard database server for prsh01

- stsh02: Standby read-only shard database server for prsh02

Configuration Steps

Install the Oracle Database 19c (19.3) database software on all database and catalog servers.

Note   While writing this chapter, the bug that interferes with shard registration on the agent is still not corrected in Oracle Database 19c (19.17). If you have the Oracle Database 19c (19.17) RDBM software on the catalog server and you try to register a shard server with the agent, you may get the following error:

[oracle@prsh01 bin]$ **schagent -registerdatabase gsmcat.mycompany.mydomain 8080**

Agent Registration Password ? *******
Failed to get agent Registration Info from db: DB agent registration version is not supported for this agent

If you downgrade the catalog server software to 19.03, then the registration will be successful.

So, keep Oracle Database 19c (19.3) on all servers until the bug is corrected.

Installing the GSM Software

On gsmcat, we are choosing to co-locate the shard director software on the same host, which requires installing the 19c GSM software on a separate Oracle home. Here are the steps for installing the GSM software:

1. Download the GSM software for your platform from http://www.oracle.com/technetwork/database/enterprise-edition/downloads/index.html.

2. Under the Oracle Database 19c (19.3) - Enterprise Edition section, click See All.

3. Download the GSM software (LINUX.X64_193000_gsm.zip) and place it on the GSM server under the /u01/install directory.

4. Unzip the GSM media and run `runInstaller`.

```
[oracle@gsmcat install]$ cd gsm/
[oracle@gsmcat gsm]$ ./runInstaller
```

When prompted, fill in the following fields:

- Oracle base: /u01/app/oracle

- Sofware location: /u01/app/oracle/product/19.3.0/gsmhome_1

When you see a pop-up window, connect to the server via SSH and run the requested `.sh` scripts via the root user. Then return to the installation and click OK.

```
[root@gsmcat ~]# /u01/app/oracle/product/19.3.0/gsmhome_1/root.sh
```

Creating the Catalog Database

On the `gsmcat` server, create the `gsmcatdb` database using DBCA from the RDBMS home and follow these instructions:

1. The shard catalog database `gsmcatdb` must use a server parameter file (spfile).

2. The database character set and national character set chosen for `gsmcatdb` must contain all the possible characters that will be inserted into the shard catalog or any of the shards.

3. Because the shard catalog database can run multiple shard queries that connect to shards over database links, the database initialization parameters `OPEN_LINKS` and `OPEN_LINKS_PER_INSTANCE` must be greater than or equal to the number of shards that will be part of the sharded database configuration.

```
SQL> alter system set open_links=16 scope=spfile;
SQL> alter system set open_links_per_instance=16 scope=spfile;
SQL> shut immediate
SQL> startup
```

4. We are planning to use CREATE SHARD to add shards to the sharding configuration, so the SHARED_SERVERS and DISPATCHERS database initialization parameters must be set to allow the Remote Scheduler Agent to connect to the catalog over an Oracle XML Database (XDB) connection.

    - SHARED_SERVERS must be greater than 0 (zero) to allow shared server connections to the shard catalog from the Remote Scheduler Agent processes running on the shard hosts.

    - DISPATCHERS must contain a service for XDB, based on the Oracle SID value.

    ```
    SQL> alter system set shared_servers=5;
    SQL> show parameter dispatchers

    NAME          TYPE         VALUE
    ----------    ---------    ----------------------------------------
    Dispatchers   string       (PROTOCOL=TCP)(SERVICE=gsmcatdbXDB)
    ```

    - After setting these parameters, run this:

    ```
    SQL> alter system register;
    ```

5. Set the db_create_file_dest, db_recovery_file_dest, and db_recovery_file_dest_size parameters in the catalog database.

    ```
    SQL> alter system set db_recovery_file_dest_size=10G;
    SQL> alter system set db_recovery_file_dest='/u01/app/oracle/fast_recovery_area';
    SQL> alter system set db_create_file_dest='/u01/app/oracle/oradata';
    ```

6. Verify the parameter values.

    ```
    SQL> show parameter db_recovery_file_dest_size

    NAME                          TYPE          VALUE
    --------------------------    ------------  ------
    db_recovery_file_dest_size    big integer   10G
    ```

```
SQL> show parameter db_recovery_file_dest
```

NAME	TYPE	VALUE
db_recovery_file_dest	string	/u01/app/oracle/fast_ recovery_ area

```
SQL> show parameter db_create_file_dest
```

NAME	TYPE	VALUE
db_create_file_dest	string	/u01/app/oracle/oradata

Setting Up the GDS Administrator Accounts and Privileges

The GSMCATUSER account is created by default during the Oracle Database 19c installation. The DBA of the catalog database must unlock the account and give the account password to the Global Data Services administrator.

Whenever a new GSM is added to the GDS configuration, the GDS administrator must specify the GSMCATUSER account password. The password is encrypted and stored in the wallet for future use by the GSM.

Via SSH, connect to the catalog server gsmcat.mycompany.mydomain. Using sqlplus, connect to the catalog database, gsmcatdb in our case, and do the following:

```
$ export ORACLE_SID=gsmcatdb
$ export ORACLE_HOME=/u01/app/oracle/product/19.3.0/dbhome_1
$ export ORACLE_BASE=/u01/app/oracle
$ export PATH=$ORACLE_HOME/bin:$PATH

[oracle@gsmcat ~]$ sqlplus / as sysdba

SQL> alter user GSMCATUSER account unlock;
SQL> alter user GSMCATUSER identified by Oracle123;
```

The GSD administrator who creates the GDS catalog must have a user account on the catalog database, which will be granted the GSMADMIN_ROLE role.

```
SQL> create user gsm_admin identified by Oracle123;
SQL> grant connect, gsmadmin_role to gsm_admin;
SQL> grant inherit privileges on user SYS to gsmadmin_internal;
```

If you planning to add existing databases, then you need to do the following on each shard database being added to the configuration.

The GSM connects to the pool databases using the GSMUSER account, which also exists by default in Oracle 19c Database, but it is locked. The password for GSMUSER is given to the GDS administrator who adds the database to a GDS pool (GDSCTL> add database). The password is stored in the GDS catalog for future use by all GSMs.

Connect to each shard server (prsh01, prsh02, stsh01, stsh02) and unlock the GSMUSER user and set the password.

```
SQL> alter user GSMUSER account unlock;
SQL> alter user GSMUSER identified by oracle;
```

In our test case, we do not have existing databases, but we are creating them using the CREATE SHARD command. This means GSMUSER and the shard database do not exist yet.

Creating the Shard Catalog

Connect to the catalog database server via SSH and create the catalog database using GDSCTL.

```
[oracle@gsmcat ~]$ export ORACLE_HOME=/u01/app/oracle/product/19.3.0/
gsmhome_1
[oracle@gsmcat ~]$ export ORACLE_BASE=/u01/app/oracle
[oracle@gsmcat ~]$ export PATH=$ORACLE_HOME/bin:$PATH

[oracle@gsmcat ~]$ gdsctl
```

```
GDSCTL> create shardcatalog -database gsmcat.mycompany.mydomain:1521/
gsmcatdb -region region1 -user gsm_admin/Oracle123 -agent_port 8080
-agent_password oracle -chunks 12
```

Here, gsmcat.mycompany.mydomain is a catalog database server hostname, 1521 is a listener port number, and gsmcatdb is a catalog database service name.

We are planning to use the CREATE SHARD method to add shards to the configuration, which requires the following two additional parameters to be defined while creating a shardcatalog. These parameters are required for Remote Scheduler Agent registration.

- -agent_password specifies the password that will be used by the Remote Scheduler Agent to register with the shard catalog.

- -agent_port specifies the port number that the agent uses to create an XDB connection to the shard catalog. The default for this parameter is 8080.

Make sure after creating the catalog database that the listener has registered the HTTP endpoint.

```
[oracle@gsmcat ~]$ lsnrctl status
...
 (DESCRIPTION=(ADDRESS=(PROTOCOL=tcp)(HOST=gsmcat.mycompany.mydomain)
(PORT=8080))(Presentation=HTTP)(Session=RAW))
...
```

Creating the Global Service Manager

Create the GSM using gdsctl add and start gsm and name it mygsm.

```
GDSCTL> add gsm -gsm mygsm -catalog gsmcat.mycompany.mydomain:1521/
gsmcatdb -region region1
"gsmcatuser" password:
GSM successfully added

GDSCTL> start gsm -gsm mygsm

GDSCTL> config gsm -gsm mygsm
Name: mygsm
Endpoint 1: (ADDRESS=(HOST=gsmcat.mycompany.mydomain)(PORT=1522)
(PROTOCOL=tcp))
Local ONS port: 6123
Remote ONS port: 6234
ORACLE_HOME path: /u01/app/oracle/product/19.3.0/gsmhome_1
GSM Host name: gsmcat.mycompany.mydomain
Region: region1
```

Buddy

```
GDSCTL> status gsm -gsm mygsm
```

```
Alias                       MYGSM
Version                     19.0.0.0.0
Start Date                  16-DEC-2022 03:08:58
Trace Level                 off
Listener Log File           /u01/app/oracle/diag/gsm/gsmcat/mygsm/
                            alert/log.xml
Listener Trace File         /u01/app/oracle/diag/gsm/gsmcat/mygsm/trace/
                            ora_4096_140438574529600.trc
Endpoint summary            (ADDRESS=(HOST=gsmcat.mycompany.mydomain)
                            (PORT=1522)(PROTOCOL=tcp))
GSMOCI Version              3.0.180702
Mastership                  Y
Connected to GDS catalog    Y
Process Id                  4098
Number of reconnections     0
Pending tasks.     Total    0
Tasks in  process. Total    0
Regional Mastership         TRUE
Total messages published    0
Time Zone                   +00:00
Orphaned Buddy Regions:
     None
GDS region                  region1
```

Setting Up a TNS Entry on the Catalog

Add a TNS entry of the GDS catalog database under the GSM home's tnsnames.ora file.

/u01/app/oracle/product/19.3.0/gsmhome_1/network/admin/tnsnames.ora

```
GSMCATDB =
  (DESCRIPTION =
    (address = (protocol = tcp)(host = gsmcat)(port = 1521))
```

```
(CONNECT_DATA =
  (SERVICE_NAME = gsmcatdb)
)
)
```

Creating the Operating System Credentials

These credentials are the operating system (OS) username and password on the shard hosts (prsh01, prsh02, stsh01, stsh02), and the credentials are used by the Remote Scheduler Agent to run jobs on the shard hosts.

Reset the Oracle password on all the shard servers if you don't remember it exactly.

passwd oracle

Connect to the catalog server and run gdsctl.

[oracle@gsmcat ~]$ **gdsctl**

GDSCTL> **connect gsm_admin/Oracle123@GSMCATDB**
GDSCTL> **add credential -credential oracred -osaccount oracle**
-ospassword oracle

Note   If gdsctl is not connected to the database before running the previous command, you will get GSM-45034.

GDSCTL> **add credential -credential oracred -osaccount oracle**
-ospassword oracle

GSM-45034: Connection to GDS catalog is not established

Registering and Starting the Scheduler Agents on Shards

Connect each shard server and register it with the agent. The password specified here is the one we used when the catalog database was created.

Remember, this was the command we used:

*(create shardcatalog -database gsmcat.mycompany.mydomain:1521/gsmcatdb
-user gsm_admin/Oracle123 -agent_port **8080** -agent_password **oracle** -chunks
12 -region region1)*

Connect to the primary shard server prsh01 and pass the password using echo to the schagent command.

```
[oracle@prsh01 bin]$ which schagent
/u01/app/oracle/product/19.3.0/dbhome_1/bin/schagent
```

```
[oracle@prsh01 ~]$ echo "oracle"|schagent -registerdatabase gsmcat.
mycompany.mydomain 8080
```

```
[oracle@prsh01 ~]$ schagent -start
Scheduler agent started using port 37049
```

```
[oracle@prsh01 ~]$ schagent -status
Agent running with PID 13641

Agent_version:19.3.0.0.0
Running_time:00:00:07
Total_jobs_run:0
Running_jobs:0
Platform:Linux
ORACLE_HOME:/u01/app/oracle/product/19.3.0/dbhome_1
ORACLE_BASE:/u01/app/oracle
Port:37049
Host:prsh01.mycompany.mydomain
```

Repeat the same steps for other hosts. Connect to prsh02, stsh01, and stsh02 and run the following:

```
$ export ORACLE_HOME=/u01/app/oracle/product/19.3.0/dbhome_1
$ export PATH=$ORACLE_HOME/bin:$PATH
$ export ORACLE_BASE=/u01/app/oracle
```

```
$ which schagent
/u01/app/oracle/product/19.3.0/dbhome_1/bin/schagent
```

```
$ echo "oracle"|schagent -registerdatabase gsmcat.mycompany.mydomain 8080
$ schagent -start
$ schagent -status
```

Creating the Regions and Shard Groups

Add the second region using gdsctl.

Note   The first region named region1 has already been created when we run the create shardcatalog command.

```
[oracle@gsmcat ~]$ gdsctl
```

```
GDSCTL> add region -region region2
The operation completed successfully
```

```
GDSCTL> config region
Name                        Buddy
----                        -----
region1
region2
```

Add the primary and standby shardgroups.

```
GDSCTL> add shardgroup -shardgroup primary_shardgroup -deploy_as primary
-region region1
```

```
GDSCTL> add shardgroup -shardgroup standby_shardgroup -deploy_as active_
standby -region region2
```

Setting Up Valid Node Checking for Registration

Add each shard's host address to the VNCR list in the shard catalog.

```
GDSCTL> add invitednode prsh01
GDSCTL> add invitednode prsh02
GDSCTL> add invitednode stsh01
```

```
GDSCTL> add invitednode stsh02

GDSCTL> config vncr

Name                          Group ID
----                          --------
192.168.1.3
prsh01
prsh02
stsh01
stsh02
```

Creating Directories on Shards

On **every shard server**, log in as an Oracle user and create the necessary directories under /u01/app/oracle.

```
# su - oracle
$ cd /u01/app/oracle
$ mkdir oradata
$ mkdir fast_recovery_area
```

Creating a Shard Template for DBCA

This step is optional. If the default template values are acceptable for your environment, then you can skip this section and use a default (/u01/app/oracle/product/19.3.0/dbhome_1/assistants/dbca/templates/General_Purpose.dbc) template.

Connect to the catalog server and run dbca to generate a new creation template containing all the desired parameters for shard databases.

Please note that we are not creating a database using dbca, but we are generating a template that will be used by the create shard command.

```
$ dbca
```

Select "Manage templates" and assign a meaningful name for the template, CreateShard in our case, as shown in Figure 2-2.

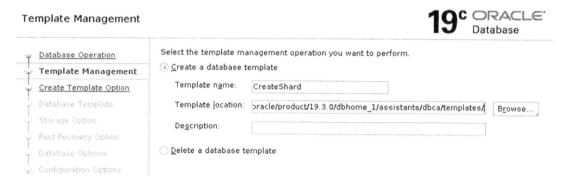

Figure 2-2. *DBCA template management operation*

Choose "Create template from an existing template," select Custom Database, and select the "Use following for the database storage attributes" radio button. Fill in the following field:

- Database file location: /u01/app/oracle/oradata

Select Specify Fast Recovery Area and indicate the desired Fast Recovery Area size (e.g., 10) and the path (e.g., /u01/app/oracle/fast_recovery_area).

Increase the number of processes up to the necessary value (e.g., 800).

Follow the wizard and choose all the necessary settings; for this test we are not modifying any other parameters.

Creating Shards

Create two shards (prsh01, prsh02) in primary_shardgroup in region1 and another two shards (stsh01, stsh02) in the standby_shardgroup in region2.

Note If any of the create shard commands fail, then the shard's DB Unique Name number will still be incremented. This means if you were expecting the DB Unique Name value to be sh1 for your first shard, you might be surprised to find that it is sh21 because your command failed several times before. You don't have to worry about the shard unique name; it must be unique but is not sequential.

```
GDSCTL> create shard -shardgroup primary_shardgroup -destination prsh01
-credential oracred -dbtemplatefile /u01/app/oracle/product/19.3.0/
dbhome_1/assistants/dbca/templates/CreateShard.dbt
The operation completed successfully
DB Unique Name: sh1

GDSCTL> create shard -shardgroup primary_shardgroup -destination prsh02
-credential oracred -dbtemplatefile /u01/app/oracle/product/19.3.0/
dbhome_1/assistants/dbca/templates/CreateShard.dbt
The operation completed successfully
DB Unique Name: sh2

GDSCTL> create shard -shardgroup standby_shardgroup -destination stsh01
-credential oracred -dbtemplatefile /u01/app/oracle/product/19.3.0/
dbhome_1/assistants/dbca/templates/CreateShard.dbt
The operation completed successfully
DB Unique Name: sh3

GDSCTL> create shard -shardgroup standby_shardgroup -destination stsh02
-credential oracred -dbtemplatefile /u01/app/oracle/product/19.3.0/
dbhome_1/assistants/dbca/templates/CreateShard.dbt
The operation completed successfully
DB Unique Name: sh4
```

Reviewing the Configuration

Review the configuration from the gsmcat server, using the gdsctl config commands.

```
GDSCTL> config

Regions
-----------------------
region1
region2

GSMs
-----------------------
mygsm
```

```
Sharded Database
-----------------------
orasdb

Databases
-----------------------
sh1
sh2
sh3
sh4

Shard Groups
-----------------------
primary_shardgroup
standby_shardgroup

Shard spaces
-----------------------
shardspaceora

Services
-----------------------

GDSCTL pending requests
-----------------------
Command                         Object                          Status
-------                         ------                          ------

Global properties
-----------------------
Name: oradbcloud
Master GSM: mygsm
DDL sequence #: 0
```

GDSCTL> **config shardspace**

```
Shard space              Chunks
-----------              ------
shardspaceora            12
```

```
GDSCTL> config shardgroup

Shard Group          Chunks Region            Shard space
-----------          ------ ------            -----------
primary_shardgroup   12     region1           shardspaceora
standby_shardgroup   12     region2           shardspaceora

GDSCTL> config shard

Name  Shard Group          Status  State   Region   Availability
----  -----------          ------  -----   ------   ------------
sh1   primary_shardgroup   U       none    region1  -
sh2   primary_shardgroup   U       none    region1  -
sh3   standby_shardgroup   U       none    region2  -
sh4   standby_shardgroup   U       none    region2  -
```

Configuring the TNS Entries for Shards

After we know what our shard names will be, we can set up the TNS entries.

Connect to gsmcat, prsh01, prsh02, stsh01, and stsh02 and add the entries in the tnsnames.ora file of the database home.

```
SH1 =
  (DESCRIPTION =
    (ADDRESS = (PROTOCOL = TCP)(HOST = prsh01.mycompany.mydomain)(PORT = 1521))
    (CONNECT_DATA =
      (SERVER = DEDICATED)
      (SERVICE_NAME = sh1.mycompany.mydomain)
    )
  )

SH2 =
  (DESCRIPTION =
    (ADDRESS = (PROTOCOL = TCP)(HOST = prsh02.mycompany.mydomain)(PORT = 1521))
    (CONNECT_DATA =
      (SERVER = DEDICATED)
```

```
        (SERVICE_NAME = sh2.mycompany.mydomain)
      )
    )

SH3 =
  (DESCRIPTION =
    (ADDRESS = (PROTOCOL = TCP)(HOST = stsh01.mycompany.mydomain)(PORT = 1521))
    (CONNECT_DATA =
      (SERVER = DEDICATED)
      (SERVICE_NAME = sh3.mycompany.mydomain)
    )
  )

SH4 =
  (DESCRIPTION =
    (ADDRESS = (PROTOCOL = TCP)(HOST = stsh02.mycompany.mydomain)(PORT = 1521))
    (CONNECT_DATA =
      (SERVER = DEDICATED)
      (SERVICE_NAME = sh4.mycompany.mydomain)
    )
  )

SH1.mycompany.mydomain =
  (DESCRIPTION =
    (ADDRESS = (PROTOCOL = TCP)(HOST = prsh01.mycompany.mydomain)(PORT = 1521))
    (CONNECT_DATA =
      (SERVER = DEDICATED)
      (SERVICE_NAME = sh1.mycompany.mydomain)
    )
  )

SH2.mycompany.mydomain =
  (DESCRIPTION =
    (ADDRESS = (PROTOCOL = TCP)(HOST = prsh02.mycompany.mydomain)(PORT = 1521))
    (CONNECT_DATA =
      (SERVER = DEDICATED)
```

```
      (SERVICE_NAME = sh2.mycompany.mydomain)
    )
  )

SH3.mycompany.mydomain =
  (DESCRIPTION =
    (ADDRESS = (PROTOCOL = TCP)(HOST = stsh01.mycompany.mydomain)(PORT = 1521))
    (CONNECT_DATA =
      (SERVER = DEDICATED)
      (SERVICE_NAME = sh3.mycompany.mydomain)
    )
  )

SH4.mycompany.mydomain =
  (DESCRIPTION =
    (ADDRESS = (PROTOCOL = TCP)(HOST = stsh02.mycompany.mydomain)(PORT = 1521))
    (CONNECT_DATA =
      (SERVER = DEDICATED)
      (SERVICE_NAME = sh4.mycompany.mydomain)
    )
  )
```

Running the Deployment

Connect to the catalog server (gsmcat) using the gdsctl command and deploy the configuration. At the end of the deployment, all shards will be created and configured on specific servers.

```
GDSCTL> deploy
deploy: examining configuration...
deploy: deploying primary shard 'sh1' ...
deploy: network listener configuration successful at destination 'prsh01'
deploy: starting DBCA at destination 'prsh01' to create primary shard
'sh1' ...
```

```
deploy: deploying primary shard 'sh2' ...
deploy: network listener configuration successful at destination 'prsh02'
deploy: starting DBCA at destination 'prsh02' to create primary shard 'sh2'
```

<The output has been intentionally shortened>

```
deploy: DBCA standby creation job succeeded at destination 'stsh02' for
shard 'sh4'
deploy: DBCA standby creation job succeeded at destination 'stsh01' for
shard 'sh3'
deploy: requesting Data Guard configuration on shards via GSM
deploy: shards configured successfully
The operation completed successfully
```

Reviewing the Deployment

Connect to the catalog server (gsmcat) using gdsctl and review the deployment and the configuration using the following commands:

GDSCTL> **databases**

```
Database: "sh1" Registered: Y State: Ok ONS: N. Role: PRIMARY Instances: 1
Region: region1
Alert: Data Guard observer is not running.
   Registered instances:
     orasdb%1
Database: "sh2" Registered: Y State: Ok ONS: N. Role: PRIMARY Instances: 1
Region: region1
Alert: Data Guard observer is not running.
   Registered instances:
     orasdb%11
Database: "sh3" Registered: Y State: Ok ONS: N. Role: PH_STNDBY Instances:
1 Region: region2
   Registered instances:
     orasdb%21
```

Database: "sh4" Registered: Y State: Ok ONS: N. Role: PH_STNDBY Instances:
1 Region: region2
    Registered instances:
        orasdb%31

GDSCTL> **config shard**

Name	Shard Group	Status	State	Region	Availability
sh1	primary_shardgroup	Ok	Deployed	region1	ONLINE
sh2	primary_shardgroup	Ok	Deployed	region1	ONLINE
sh3	standby_shardgroup	Ok	Deployed	region2	READ ONLY
sh4	standby_shardgroup	Ok	Deployed	region2	READ ONLY

Configuring Global Services

Add a global service that will run on all the primary databases.

GDSCTL> **add service -service prim_srv -role primary**
The operation completed successfully

GDSCTL> **config service**

Name	Network name	Pool	Started	Preferred all
prim_srv	prim_srv.orasdb.oradbcloud	orasdb	No	Yes

Start and check its status.

GDSCTL> **start service -service prim_srv**

GDSCTL> **status service**
Service "prim_srv.orasdb.oradbcloud" has 2 instance(s). Affinity: ANYWHERE
    Instance "orasdb%1", name: "sh1", db: "sh1", region: "region1",
    status: ready.
    Instance "orasdb%11", name: "sh2", db: "sh2", region: "region1",
    status: ready.

Add a global service that will run on all the standby databases.

GDSCTL> **add service -service stby_srv -role physical_standby**

GDSCTL> **config service**

Name	Network name	Pool	Started	Preferred all
prim_srv	prim_srv.orasdb.oradbcloud	orasdb	Yes	Yes
stby_srv	stby_srv.orasdb.oradbcloud	orasdb	No	Yes

GDSCTL> **start service -service stby_srv**

GDSCTL> **status service**
```
Service "prim_srv.orasdb.oradbcloud" has 2 instance(s). Affinity: ANYWHERE
   Instance "orasdb%1", name: "sh1", db: "sh1", region: "region1",
   status: ready.
   Instance "orasdb%11", name: "sh2", db: "sh2", region: "region1",
   status: ready.
Service "stby_srv.orasdb.oradbcloud" has 2 instance(s). Affinity: ANYWHERE
   Instance "orasdb%21", name: "sh3", db: "sh3", region: "region2",
   status: ready.
   Instance "orasdb%31", name: "sh4", db: "sh4", region: "region2",
   status: ready.
```

Verifying the Data Guard Broker Configuration

For the Data Guard Broker configuration, you need to set a desired password for the GSMUSER user. The user has the SYSDG role and is also in the password file, so we need to copy a modified password file to the standby shards.

Connect to prsh01.

```
[oracle@prsh01 ~]$ export ORACLE_SID=sh1
[oracle@prsh01 ~]$ export ORACLE_HOME=/u01/app/oracle/product/19.3.0/dbhome_1
[oracle@prsh01 ~]$ export ORACLE_BASE=/u01/app/oracle
[oracle@prsh01 ~]$ export PATH=$ORACLE_HOME/bin:$PATH
[oracle@prsh01 ~]$ sqlplus / as sysdba
```

```
SQL> col username for a9
SQL> set linesize 800
SQL> select username, sysdba, SYSOPER,SYSDG from v$pwfile_users;

USERNAME   SYSDB SYSOP SYSDG
---------  ----- ----- -----
SYS        TRUE  TRUE  FALSE
GSMUSER    FALSE FALSE TRUE
```

Connect to the primary shards (sh01 and sh02) and reset the password.

```
SQL> alter user GSMUSER identified by oracle;
```

For simplicity, copy the password file to all the standby shard servers.

Note   SSH passwordless authentication is not enabled by default; you need to enable it; otherwise, use other tools to place the /u01/app/oracle/ product/19.3.0/dbhome_1/dbs/orapwsh1 file on other servers with the correct SID in the password filename.

```
[oracle@prsh01 ~]$ scp /u01/app/oracle/product/19.3.0/dbhome_1/dbs/orapwsh1
stsh01:/u01/app/oracle/product/19.3.0/dbhome_1/dbs/orapwsh3

[oracle@prsh02 ~]$ scp /u01/app/oracle/product/19.3.0/dbhome_1/dbs/orapwsh2
stsh02:/u01/app/oracle/product/19.3.0/dbhome_1/dbs/orapwsh4
```

Connect to prsh01 and run the following:

```
[oracle@prsh01 admin]$ export ORACLE_SID=sh1

[oracle@prsh01 ~]$ dgmgrl /
...
Connected to "sh1"
Connected as SYSDG.
DGMGRL> connect GSMUSER/oracle
Connected to "sh1"
Connected as SYSDG.
```

GMGRL> **show configuration**

Configuration - sh1

  Protection Mode: MaxPerformance
  Members:
  sh1 - Primary database
    Warning: ORA-16819: fast-start failover observer not started

    sh3 - (*) Physical standby database
      Warning: ORA-16819: fast-start failover observer not started

Fast-Start Failover: Enabled in Potential Data Loss Mode

Configuration Status:
WARNING   (status updated 55 seconds ago)

    Connect to prsh02 and run the following:

[oracle@prsh02 ~]$ **dgmgrl GSMUSER/oracle@sh2**

...
Connected to "sh2"
Connected as SYSDG.
DGMGRL> **show configuration**

Configuration - sh2

  Protection Mode: MaxPerformance
  Members:
  sh2 - Primary database
    Warning: ORA-16819: fast-start failover observer not started

    sh4 - (*) Physical standby database
      Warning: ORA-16819: fast-start failover observer not started

Fast-Start Failover: Enabled in Potential Data Loss Mode

Configuration Status:
WARNING   (status updated 47 seconds ago)

    The observer must be configured properly; for testing purposes, we will start it temporarily.

```
[oracle@prsh01 ~]$ nohup dgmgrl -silent GSMUSER/oracle@sh1
  "start observer" &
```

```
[oracle@prsh02 ~]$ nohup dgmgrl -silent GSMUSER/oracle@sh2
  "start observer" &
```

Double-check the configuration.

```
[oracle@prsh01 ~]$ dgmgrl GSMUSER/oracle@sh1
...
Connected to "sh1"
Connected as SYSDG.
```

```
DGMGRL> show configuration
```

```
Configuration - sh1

  Protection Mode: MaxPerformance
  Members:
  sh1 - Primary database
    sh3 - (*) Physical standby database

Fast-Start Failover: Enabled in Potential Data Loss Mode

Configuration Status:
SUCCESS   (status updated 51 seconds ago)
```

Do the same on the second node.

```
[oracle@prsh02 ~]$ dgmgrl GSMUSER/oracle@sh2
...
Connected to "sh2"
```

```
DGMGRL> show configuration
```

```
Configuration - sh2

  Protection Mode: MaxPerformance
  Members:
  sh2 - Primary database
    sh4 - (*) Physical standby database

Fast-Start Failover: Enabled in Potential Data Loss Mode
```

Configuration Status:
SUCCESS   (status updated 58 seconds ago)

Connect to the catalog using gdsctl and update the password for shards.

```
GDSCTL> modify shard -shard sh1 -pwd oracle
GDSCTL> modify shard -shard sh3 -pwd oracle
GDSCTL> modify shard -shard sh2 -pwd oracle
GDSCTL> modify shard -shard sh4 -pwd oracle
```

Creating the Schema for Testing

Export the Oracle environment variables. Enable the shard DDL for the session, create the schema, and grant the necessary privileges to it.

```
[oracle@gsmcat ~]$ export ORACLE_SID=gsmcatdb
[oracle@gsmcat ~]$ export ORACLE_HOME=/u01/app/oracle/product/19.3.0/
dbhome_1
[oracle@gsmcat ~]$ export ORACLE_BASE=/u01/app/oracle
[oracle@gsmcat ~]$ export PATH=$ORACLE_HOME/bin:$PATH
[oracle@gsmcat ~]$ sqlplus / as sysdba

SQL> alter session enable shard ddl;

SQL> create user app_shard identified by app_shard;

SQL> grant connect, resource, alter session, select_catalog_role, gsmadmin_
role, dba to app_shard;

SQL> grant all privileges to app_shard;

SQL> grant execute on dbms_crypto to app_shard;

SQL> grant create table, create procedure, create tablespace, create
materialized view to app_shard;

SQL> grant unlimited tablespace to app_shard;

SQL> create tablespace set TSP_SET_1;
```

Connect to the catalog database using the newly created user and create a sharded table.

```
SQL> CONNECT app_shard/app_shard

SQL> create sharded table Customers
  (
    CustId       varchar2(100) NOT NULL,
    FirstName    varchar2(100),
    LastName     varchar2(100),
    Passwd       raw(60),
    CONSTRAINT pk_customers PRIMARY KEY (CustId)
  ) tablespace SET TSP_SET_1
  partition by CONSISTENT HASH (CustId) partitions AUTO;
```

Connect using gdsctl and see if any of the DDLs failed.

```
GDSCTL> show ddl

id    DDL Text                                      Failed shards
--    --------                                      -------------
1     create user app_shard identified by *...
2     grant connect, resource, alter sessio...
3     grant all privileges to app_shard
4     grant execute on dbms_crypto to app_s...
5     grant create table, create procedure,...
6     grant unlimited tablespace to app_shard
7     create tablespace set TSP_SET_1
8     create sharded table Customers
```

Verify that there were no DDL errors on each shard.

```
GDSCTL> config shard -shard sh1
Name: sh1
Shard Group: primary_shardgroup
Status: Warnings
State: Deployed
Region: region1
```

Connection string: prsh01.mycompany.mydomain:1521/sh1.mycompany.
mydomain:dedicated
SCAN address:
ONS remote port: 0
Disk Threshold, ms: 20
CPU Threshold, %: 75
Version: 19.0.0.0
Failed DDL:
DDL Error: ---
Failed DDL id:
Availability: ONLINE
Rack:

Supported services

Name   Preferred Status
----   --------- ------
prim_srv   Yes   Enabled
stby_srv   Yes   Enabled

GDSCTL> **config shard -shard sh2**
Name: sh2
Shard Group: primary_shardgroup
Status: Ok
State: Deployed
Region: region1
Connection string: prsh02.mycompany.mydomain:1521/sh2.mycompany.
mydomain:dedicated
SCAN address:
ONS remote port: 0
Disk Threshold, ms: 20
CPU Threshold, %: 75
Version: 19.0.0.0
Failed DDL:
DDL Error: ---
Failed DDL id:

Availability: ONLINE
Rack:

Supported services

Name   Preferred Status
----   --------- ------
prim_srv   Yes   Enabled
stby_srv   Yes   Enabled

GDSCTL> **config shard -shard sh3**
Name: sh3
Shard Group: standby_shardgroup
Status: Warnings
State: Deployed
Region: region2
Connection string: stsh01.mycompany.mydomain:1521/sh3.mycompany.
mydomain:dedicated
SCAN address:
ONS remote port: 0
Disk Threshold, ms: 20
CPU Threshold, %: 75
Version: 19.0.0.0
Failed DDL:
DDL Error: ---
Failed DDL id:
Availability: READ ONLY
Rack:

Supported services

Name   Preferred Status
----   --------- ------
prim_srv   Yes   Enabled
stby_srv   Yes   Enabled

GDSCTL> **config shard -shard sh4**

Name: sh4

Shard Group: standby_shardgroup

Status: Ok

State: Deployed

Region: region2

Connection string: stsh02.mycompany.mydomain:1521/sh4.mycompany.
mydomain:dedicated

SCAN address:

ONS remote port: 0

Disk Threshold, ms: 20

CPU Threshold, %: 75

Version: 19.0.0.0

Failed DDL:

DDL Error: ---

Failed DDL id:

Availability: READ ONLY

Rack:

Supported services

Name	Preferred	Status
prim_srv	Yes	Enabled
stby_srv	Yes	Enabled

Verifying the Data Distribution

Connect to the catalog database using SQL*Plus and fill the sharded table with demo data.

```
SQL> connect app_shard/app_shard

SQL> insert into Customers values(1,'Mari','Kupatadze',utl_raw.cast_to_
raw('hello world'));

SQL> insert into Customers values(2,'Salome','Beridze',utl_raw.cast_to_
raw('hello world1'));
```

```
SQL> insert into Customers values(3,'Ana','Beridze',utl_raw.cast_to_
raw('hello world2'));
```

```
SQL> commit;
```

Verify how the chucks were distributed between shards.

```
GDSCTL> config chunks
Chunks
------------------------
Database                  From      To
--------                  ----      --
sh1                       1         6
sh2                       7         12
sh3                       1         6
sh4                       7         12
```

Connect to each shard and check what data is stored in the app_shard.
Customers table.

Connect to the primary databases (sh1, sh2) and run the following:

```
[oracle@prsh01 bin]$ sqlplus app_shard/app_shard
```

```
SQL> set linesize 800
SQL> col LASTNAME for a11
SQL> col FIRSTNAME for a10
SQL> col PASSWD for a35
SQL> col CUSTID for a5
SQL> select * from Customers;
```

```
CUSTI FIRSTNAME  LASTNAME     PASSWD
----- ---------- -----------  -------------------------
1     Mari       Kupatadze    68656C6C6F20776F726C64
2     Salome     Beridze      68656C6C6F20776F726C6431
```

```
[oracle@prsh02 bin]$ sqlplus app_shard/app_shard
```

```
SQL> set linesize 800
SQL> col LASTNAME for a11
SQL> col FIRSTNAME for a10
```

```
SQL> col PASSWD for a35
SQL> col CUSTID for a5
SQL> select * from Customers;

CUSTI FIRSTNAME   LASTNAME    PASSWD
----- ---------- ----------- -----------------------------------
3     Ana        Beridze     68656C6C6F20776F726C6432
```

Let's check that the rows were also synchronized in Data Guard.
Connect to the standby servers (sh3, sh4).

```
[oracle@stsh01 onlinelog]$ sqlplus app_shard/app_shard

SQL> set linesize 800
SQL> col LASTNAME for a11
SQL> col FIRSTNAME for a10
SQL> col PASSWD for a35
SQL> col CUSTID for a5
SQL> select * from Customers;

CUSTI FIRSTNAME   LASTNAME    PASSWD
----- ---------- ----------- -----------------------------------
1     Mari       Kupatadze   68656C6C6F20776F726C64
2     Salome     Beridze     68656C6C6F20776F726C6431

[oracle@stsh02 ~]$ sqlplus app_shard/app_shard

SQL> set linesize 800
SQL> col LASTNAME for a11
SQL> col FIRSTNAME for a10
SQL> col PASSWD for a35
SQL> col CUSTID for a5
SQL> select * from Customers;

CUSTI FIRSTNAME   LASTNAME    PASSWD
----- ---------- ----------- -----------------------------------
3     Ana        Beridze     68656C6C6F20776F726C6432
```

Troubleshooting

In this section, we'll explore some common troubleshooting scenarios.

Problem 1

Say you received the following error while adding shard server to the agent:

```
[oracle@prsh01 bin]$ schagent -registerdatabase gsmcat 8080
Agent Registration Password ? *******

Remote host terminated the handshake
Neither HTTP nor HTTPS servers are correctly set up in gsmcat.mycompany.
mydomain:8080
Database is unavailable at gsmcat.mycompany.mydomain:8080
```

Connect to the catalog database server and check the listener.log file under the RDBMS home.

```
07-DEC-2022 20:59:04 * http * (ADDRESS=(PROTOCOL=tcp)(HOST=192.168.1.1)
(PORT=54688)) * handoff * http * 12519
TNS-12519: TNS:no appropriate service handler found
```

Workaround

Increase the processes parameter in the catalog database and restart.

```
SQL> show parameter processes

NAME          TYPE         VALUE
------------  -----------  -----------
processes     integer      300

SQL> alter system set processes=800 scope=spfile;

SQL> shut immediate;

SQL> startup
```

Problem 2

Registering the shard server with the catalog agent is failing when the catalog RDBM software is 19.17.

```
[oracle@prsh01 bin]$ which schagent
/u01/app/oracle/product/19.3.0/dbhome_1/bin/schagent
```

```
$ schagent -registerdatabase gsmcat.mycompany.mydomain 8080
Agent Registration Password ? *******
```

```
Failed to get agent Registration Info from db: DB agent registration
version is not supported for this agent
```

Workaround

The bug mentioned in several MOS notes is not fixed in 19.17. The only way to fix it for now, until a patch is released, is to downgrade the catalog database from Oracle 19.17 to 19.3.

The current patch on the catalog server is DBRU 19.17.0.0.221018.

```
[oracle@gsmcat ~]$ $ORACLE_HOME/OPatch/opatch lspatches
34411846;OJVM RELEASE UPDATE: 19.17.0.0.221018 (34411846)
34444834;OCW RELEASE UPDATE 19.17.0.0.0 (34444834)
34419443;Database Release Update : 19.17.0.0.221018 (34419443)
```

Here's how to roll back the patch on the catalog database:

```
[oracle@gsmcat ~]$ $ORACLE_HOME/OPatch/opatch rollback -id 34419443
```

```
[oracle@gsmcat ~]$ $ORACLE_HOME/OPatch/opatch lspatches
34411846;OJVM RELEASE UPDATE: 19.17.0.0.221018 (34411846)
34444834;OCW RELEASE UPDATE 19.17.0.0.0 (34444834)
29517242;Database Release Update : 19.3.0.0.190416 (29517242)
```

Run the post-patch script.

```
[oracle@gsmcat ~]$ cd $ORACLE_HOME/OPatch
```

```
[oracle@gsmcat OPatch]$ ./datapatch -verbose
...
```

```
Adding patches to installation queue and performing prereq  checks...done
Installation queue:
 No interim patches need to be rolled back
 Patch 34419443 (Database Release Update : 19.17.0.0.221018  (34419443)):
    Rollback from 19.17.0.0.0 Release_Update 220924224051 to  19.3.0.0.0
    Release_Update 190410122720
 No interim patches need to be applied
...
Validating logfiles...done
```
Patch 34419443 rollback: SUCCESS
```
  logfile: /u01/app/oracle/cfgtoollogs/sqlpatch/34419443/24972075/34419443_
  rollback_GSMCAT_2022Dec15_21_59_04.log (no errors)
```

[oracle@gsmcat ~]$ **/u01/app/oracle/product/19.3.0/dbhome_1/bin/schagent -version**
```
Oracle Scheduler Agent Version 19.3.0.0.0
```

Recompile all the invalid objects.

After rollback is complete, continue registering shards.

$ **schagent -registerdatabase gsmcat.mycompany.mydomain 8080**
```
Agent Registration Password ?
Oracle Scheduler Agent Registration for 19.3.0.0.0 Agent
Agent Registration Successful!
```

Problem 3

Say you get this error:

```
GSM-45034: Connection to GDS catalog is not established
```

Solution

Connect to the catalog database before running commands:

GDSCTL> **connect gsm_admin/Oracle123@GSMCAT**

Problem 4

While creating the shardcatalog, you get the following error:

```
GDSCTL> create shardcatalog -database gsmcat.mycompany.mydomain:1521/gsmcat
-region region1 -user gsm_admin/Oracle123 -agent_port 8080 -agent_password
oracle -chunks 12
GSM-45029: SQL error
No more data to read from socket
```

The catalog database alert log shows the following:

```
$ tailf /u01/app/oracle/diag/rdbms/gsmcat/gsmcat/trace/alert_gsmcat.log
```

```
2022-12-15T21:54:58.610813+00:00
Exception [type: SIGSEGV, Address not mapped to object] [ADDR:0x0]
[PC:0x520EE7B, pisoch()+59] [flags: 0x0, count: 1]
Errors in file /u01/app/oracle/diag/rdbms/gsmcat/gsmcat/trace/gsmcat_
ora_26288.trc  (incident=51731):
ORA-07445: exception encountered: core dump [pisoch()+59] [SIGSEGV]
[ADDR:0x0] [PC:0x520EE7B] [Address not mapped to object] []
Use ADRCI or Support Workbench to package the incident.
See Note 411.1 at My Oracle Support for error and packaging details.
```

Solution

If you rolled back the 19.17 patch from the catalog server, you need to run the post-rollback steps if you have not done so yet.

```
[oracle@gsmcat ~]$ cd $ORACLE_HOME/OPatch
```

```
[oracle@gsmcat OPatch]$ ./datapatch -verbose
```

Problem 5

While starting GSM, the following error happens:

```
GDSCTL> start gsm -gsm mygsm
GSM-45054: GSM error
GSM-40070: GSM is not able to establish connection to GDS catalog
```

Check the GSM log.

$ tailf /u01/app/oracle/diag/gsm/gsmcat/mygsm/trace/alert_gsmcat.log

```
2022-12-15T22:21:36.633294+00:00
GSM-40122: OCI Catalog Error. Code: -1. Message: BEGIN GSMADMIN_INTERNAL.
dbms_gsm_nopriv.GETCATALOGLOCK( gsm_version => :vers, gsm_name => :name
,currentChangeSeq => :changeid,catalog_version => :catvers );END;
GSM-40122: OCI Catalog Error. Code: 932. Message: ORA-00932: inconsistent
datatypes: expected - got BLOB
ORA-06512: at "GSMADMIN_INTERNAL.DBMS_GSM_NOPRIV", line 106
ORA-06512: at line 1
```

Check the catalog database's invalid objects.

SQL> select count(*) from dba_objects where status='INVALID';

```
  COUNT(*)
----------
       355
```

Solution

Recompile the objects.

SQL> @?/rdbms/admin/utlrp.sql

SQL> select count(*) from dba_objects where status='INVALID';

```
COUNT(*)
----------
0
```

Note   We are assuming no critical configuration is saved in the catalog and the database was created for testing purposes. Please don't do the following on production systems:

If you were not able to start the GSM after recompiling objects, then you need to delete the current catalog database and re-create it using dbca. There is a chance that downgrading the database from 19.17 to 19.03 introduced bugs and corrupted the system package, especially GSMADMIN_INTERNAL.DBMS_GSM_NOPRIV. Creating a database using dbca will create a clean database from the 19.03 home.

In case catalog already contains critical configuration, deleting it is not an option, and the error needs to be resolved with the help of Oracle Support.

Problem 6

Say you get the following error while creating the shard:

```
GDSCTL> create shard -shardgroup primary_shardgroup -destination prsh01
-credential oracred -dbtemplatefile /u01/app/oracle/product/19.3.0/
dbhome_1/assistants/dbca/templates/General_Purpose.dbc
GSM-45029: SQL error
ORA-03710: directory does not exist or is not writeable at destination:
$ORACLE_BASE/fast_recovery_area
ORA-06512: at "GSMADMIN_INTERNAL.DBMS_GSM_POOLADMIN", line 9082
ORA-06512: at "SYS.DBMS_SYS_ERROR", line 86
ORA-06512: at "GSMADMIN_INTERNAL.DBMS_GSM_POOLADMIN", line 6522
ORA-27436: Scheduler agent operation failed with message: Agent Error:
/u01/app/oracle/fast_recovery_area/shard_check.txt (No such file or
directory)
```

Solution

Make sure you are using the correct database creation template containing the desired parameter value for DB_RECOVERY_FILE_DEST; otherwise, create the mentioned directory, like so:

```
# su - oracle
$ export $ORACLE_BASE=/u01/app/oracle
$ mkdir $ORACLE_BASE/fast_recovery_area
```

Problem 7

While creating the shard, say you get the following error:

```
GDSCTL> create shard -shardgroup primary_shardgroup -destination prsh02
-credential oracred -dbtemplatefile /u01/app/oracle/product/19.3.0/
dbhome_1/assistants/dbca/templates/General_Purpose.dbc
GSM-45029: SQL error
ORA-03710: directory does not exist or is not writeable at destination:
$ORACLE_BASE/oradata
ORA-06512: at "GSMADMIN_INTERNAL.DBMS_GSM_POOLADMIN", line 9082
ORA-06512: at "SYS.DBMS_SYS_ERROR", line 86
ORA-06512: at "GSMADMIN_INTERNAL.DBMS_GSM_POOLADMIN", line 6496
ORA-27436: Scheduler agent operation failed with message: Agent Error: /
u01/app/oracle/oradata/shard_check.txt (No such file or directory)
```

Solution

Make sure you are using the correct database template with the correct DB_CREATE_
FILE_DEST parameter; otherwise, create the mentioned directory on the shard server.

Problem 8

Let's say you get this error:

```
GDSCTL> create shard -shardgroup standby_shardgroup -destination stsh01
-credential oracred -dbtemplatefile /u01/app/oracle/product/19.3.0/
dbhome_1/assistants/dbca/templates/CreateShard.dbt
GSM-45029: SQL error
ORA-03857: A listener.ora file already exists in the shard host
Oracle home.
ORA-06512: at "GSMADMIN_INTERNAL.DBMS_GSM_POOLADMIN", line 9082
ORA-06512: at "GSMADMIN_INTERNAL.DBMS_GSM_POOLADMIN", line 7973
ORA-06512: at "SYS.DBMS_SYS_ERROR", line 79
ORA-06512: at "GSMADMIN_INTERNAL.DBMS_GSM_POOLADMIN", line 7969
ORA-06512: at line 1
```

Solution

Remove the `listener.ora` file from the corresponding shard server from the RDBMS home, like so:

[oracle@stsh01 ~]$ rm -rf /u01/app/oracle/product/19.3.0/dbhome_1/network/ admin/listener.ora

Try creating a shard again.

Problem 9

If the deployment fails for whatever reason, you have to clean up all the created resources and redeploy; otherwise, it will try to re-create them and will fail.

```
GDSCTL> deploy
deploy: examining configuration...
deploy: deploying primary shard 'sh21' ...
deploy: network listener configuration successful at destination 'prsh01'
deploy: starting DBCA at destination 'prsh01' to create primary shard
'sh21' ...
deploy: deploying primary shard 'sh22' ...
Remote job failed with error:
EXTERNAL_LOG_ID="job_75283_24",
USERNAME="oracle"
For more details:
  select destination, output from all_scheduler_job_run_details
  where job_name='SHARD_SH22_NETCA'
deploy: NETCA failed at destination 'prsh02'
deploy: waiting for 1 DBCA primary creation job(s) to complete...
deploy: waiting for 1 DBCA primary creation job(s) to complete...
deploy: waiting for 1 DBCA primary creation job(s) to complete...
...
Remote job failed with error:
```
For more details, check the contents of $ORACLE_BASE/cfgtoollogs/dbca/sh21/ customScripts.log on the destination host.

```
deploy: DBCA primary creation job failed at destination 'prsh01' for
shard 'sh21'
Deployment has terminated due to previous errors.
The operation completed successfully
```

Solution

Check the log to identify the reason for the failure. Clean up all the created resources such as the database files using dbca and the network files using netmgr and netca. Only after that can you rerun the deploy command.

Please note that some processes that do not require creation of the resource are resumable.

After correcting the error, try to deploy, and you will see if the process is resumable or if it needs more action from you.

Problem 10

The deploy command fails with the following error:

```
GDSCTL> deploy
Catalog connection is established
deploy: examining configuration...
deploy: deploying standby shard 'sh34' ...
remote scheduler agent not running
Deployment has terminated due to previous errors.
```

Solution

Connect to the shard server and start the agent.

```
[oracle@stsh01 ~]$ schagent -start
Scheduler agent started using port 35516
```

Problem 11

Say you get the following warning:

```
GSM Warnings:
primary_shardgroup sh32:ORA-02625: Failed to add standby shard sh35 to the
broker configuration with error 12541.
ORA-06512: at "SYS.DBMS_GSM_FIXED", line 503
ORA-06512: at "SYS.DBMS_SYS_ERROR", line 95
ORA-06512: at "SYS.DBMS_GSM_FIXED", line 296
ORA-06512: at line 1 (ngsmoci_execute)
```

Solution:

Ora-12541, which is mentioned in the error, means ORA-12541: TNS: no listener. If you have deleted the already deployed listener for some reason, re-create it using netca and name it LISTENER_<shard database name in capital letters>. Or if the listener is just stopped, start it.

Problem 12

Say you get the following warning:

```
[WARNING] [DBT-10328] Specified GDB Name (sh34) may have a potential
conflict with an already existing database on the system.
   ACTION: Specify a different GDB Name that does not conflict with
   existing databases on the system.
[FATAL] [DBT-10317] Specified SID Name (sh34) already exists.
   ACTION: Specify a different SID Name that does not already exist.
```

Solution:

Connect to the shard server and remove the file /u01/app/oracle/product/19.3.0/ dbhome_1/dbs/hc_<sid>.dat, in our case /u01/app/oracle/product/19.3.0/ dbhome_1/dbs/hc_sh34.dat.

Problem 13

Say you get the following warning:

```
SQL> create user app_shard identified by app_shard;
create user app_shard identified by app_shard
*
ERROR at line 1:
ORA-00604: error occurred at recursive SQL level 1
ORA-03745: global service manager not running
ORA-06512: at "GSMADMIN_INTERNAL.DBMS_GSM_UTILITY", line 1665
ORA-06512: at "SYS.DBMS_SYS_ERROR", line 79
ORA-06512: at "GSMADMIN_INTERNAL.DBMS_GSM_UTILITY", line 1561
ORA-06512: at line 1
```

Solution

Connect to the shard server and run gdsctl start gsm.

```
GDSCTL> start gsm
```

Problem 14

Say you get the following:

```
SQL> insert into Customers values(1,'Mari','Kupatadze',utl_raw.cast_to_
raw('hello world'));
insert into Customers values(1,'Mari','Kupatadze',utl_raw.cast_to_
raw('hello world'))
*
ERROR at line 1:
ORA-02519: cannot perform cross-shard operation. Chunk "1" is unavailable
ORA-06512: at "GSMADMIN_INTERNAL.DBMS_GSM_POOLADMIN", line 22404
ORA-06512: at "SYS.DBMS_SYS_ERROR", line 86
ORA-06512: at "GSMADMIN_INTERNAL.DBMS_GSM_POOLADMIN", line 22369
ORA-06512: at "GSMADMIN_INTERNAL.DBMS_GSM_POOLADMIN", line 22421
ORA-06512: at line 1
```

Solution

Use move chunk between the shards.

```
GDSCTL> move chunk -CHUNK 1 -SOURCE sh1 -target sh2

GDSCTL> config chunks
Chunks
------------------------
```

Database	From	To
sh1	2	6
sh2	1	1
sh2	7	12
sh3	2	6
sh4	1	1
sh4	7	12

```
GDSCTL> move chunk -CHUNK 1 -SOURCE sh2 -target sh1

GDSCTL> config chunks
Chunks
------------------------
```

Database	From	To
sh1	1	6
sh2	7	12
sh3	1	6
sh4	7	12

Retry the insert statement.

```
SQL> insert into Customers values(1,'Mari','Kupatadze',utl_raw.cast_to_
raw('hello world'));

SQL> commit;
```

Summary

In this chapter, we gave you an overview of Oracle Global Data Services in the sharding scope. We described the GDSCTL CLI commands related to sharding setup and administration.

The chapter described several methods of sharding, including their characteristics, advantages, and disadvantages.

We also covered all the necessary steps, such as the following:

- Installing the GSM software

- Creating the catalog database

- Setting up the GDS administrator accounts and privileges

- Creating the shard catalog

- Creating the global service manager

- Setting up the TNS entry on the catalog

- Creating the OS credentials

- Registering and starting the scheduler agents on shards

- Creating regions and shard groups

- Setting up valid node checking for registration

- Creating directories on shards

- Creating a shard template for DBCA

- Creating shards

- Reviewing a configuration

- Configuring TNS entries for shards

- Running the deployment

- Reviewing the deployment

- Configuring global services

- Verifying the Data Guard Broker configuration

We also described in detail how to set up sharding in your environment.

Finally, we provided several problems you might encounter and offered solutions to help you troubleshoot your own environment.

In the upcoming chapter, we will delve into sharding within Enterprise Manager. As part of a test, you will transfer a chunk of data from one shard to another. You will then verify the data movement using EMCC and GDSCTL.

CHAPTER 3

Monitoring Oracle GDS and Oracle Sharding

Most administrators prefer using Enterprise Manager to monitor and administer databases. Compared to the command line, the web user interface is a more simple way to monitor databases. In addition, identifying bottlenecks using graphs is easier than checking text or XML versions of log files and comparing logged metrics and values. Graphs help you easily identify a maximum value for the specific threshold and switch to the tuning page.

Enterprise Manager (EM) can also add and monitor the sharding architecture, which will be the main topic of this chapter. We will also explain the installation and configuration steps for EM agents in the sharded environment and guide you through the whole process of autodiscovering the sharded databases and manually adding the sharded catalog database. We will emphasize sections that are related to sharding in the EM web user interface. Finally, you will see the process for moving chunks.

Configuring EM Agents

The lab environment, where agents will be deployed and sharding components will be discovered, is as follows:

- `oem13c`: Oracle Enterprise Manager Cloud Control (OEMCC) 13c server

- `gsmcat`: Shard catalog database (`gsmcatdb`) and shard director

- `prsh01`: Primary shard database server

- `prsh02`: Primary shard database server

© Y V Ravi Kumar, Mariami Kupatadze, Sambaiah Sammeta 2023
Y V Ravi Kumar et al., *Oracle Global Data Services for Mission-critical Systems*,
https://doi.org/10.1007/978-1-4842-9553-3_3

- `stsh01`: Standby read-only shard database server for `prsh01`

- `stsh02`: Standby read-only shard database server for `prsh02`

Note   Make sure all hosts can resolve the hostnames of each other.

Installing Agents on Hosts

Connect to the EM console using the following URL and add all the necessary servers, such as the shard catalog database, primary shards, and standby shards:

```
[oracle@oem13c ~]$ /u01/app/oracle/middleware/bin/emctl status oms -details
...
Console URL: https://oem13c.mycompany.mydomain:7803/em
Upload URL: https://oem13c.mycompany.mydomain:4903/empbs/upload
```

Enter the URL, shown in the previous code, in the browser and log in to the EM console. Then, install the agents on the target hosts by navigating to the menu at the top-right corner of the screen: Setup ➤ Add Target ➤ Add Targets Manually.

In the Add Host Targets section, click Install Agent on Host. Then click the +Add button, enter the hostnames of each target, and choose the correct platform information. Click Next, and fill in values for the following fields:

- Installation base directory: `/u01/app/oracle/em13c`

- Instance directory: `/u01/app/oracle/em13c/agent_inst`

Scroll down and click the plus sign for Named Credentials. Enter the Oracle user credentials. If you don't know the password, you can reset it on the hosts with the `passwd oracle` command. Click the plus sign for Root Credentials, and enter the valid root user information. You can also configure a key-based authentication; for this demo we are using password-based authentication.

Click Next. Review the configuration and run Deploy Agent. Wait for a while. If the warning is the same as in Figure 3-1, ignore it and click the Continue button.

Agent Deployment Summary: ADD_HOST_SYSMAN_Dec_20_2022_7:31:04_AM_UTC

Platform	Host	Initialization	Remote Prerequisite Check	Agent Deployment
Linux x86-64	prsh01.mycompany.mydomain	✓	⚠	○
Linux x86-64	gsmcat.mycompany.mydomain	✓	⚠	○
Linux x86-64	prsh02.mycompany.mydomain	✓	⚠	○
Linux x86-64	stsh01.mycompany.mydomain	✓	⚠	○
Linux x86-64	stsh02.mycompany.mydomain	✓	⚠	○

Agent Deployment Details: prsh01.mycompany.mydomain

| Do you have the privileges to run as root using the Privilege Delegation tool? | ⚠ | The user "oracle" does not have the privileges to run commands as user "root" using the Privilege Delegation tool "/usr/bin/sudo" . | • Ensure user "oracle" has privileges to run commands as user "root" using the Privilege Delegation tool "/usr/bin/sudo".
 • If the Privilege Delegation tool "/usr/bin/sudo" requires a terminal for execution over ssh then set the "oracle.sysman.prov.agentpush.enablePty" property to true in the "/u01/app/oracle/middleware/sysman/prov/agentpush/agentpush.properties" file, which is present on the OMS host.
 • You can also ignore this warning and continue in which case the root.sh, any preinstallation or postinstallation scripts specified with run as root enabled will not be run and you have to run them manually after installation. |

Figure 3-1. *Deployment warnings*

It is expected that the deployment will fail when running the root.sh script, because we have not configured sudo access for the oracle user.

Run the root.sh script on all the targets manually and cancel the session.

[root@**gsmcat** ~]# **/u01/app/oracle/em13c/agent_13.5.0.0.0/root.sh**

[root@**prsh01** ~]# **/u01/app/oracle/em13c/agent_13.5.0.0.0/root.sh**

[root@**prsh02** ~]# **/u01/app/oracle/em13c/agent_13.5.0.0.0/root.sh**

[root@**stsh01** ~]# **/u01/app/oracle/em13c/agent_13.5.0.0.0/root.sh**

[root@**stsh02** ~]# **/u01/app/oracle/em13c/agent_13.5.0.0.0/root.sh**

Make sure that the hosts are added and that the agents are up by selecting Targets ➤ Hosts.

Configuring Autodiscovery

To add the shard catalog database, primary shards, and standby shards, you need to use a smart feature of the EM, dubbed *target autodiscovery*. Select Setup ➤ Add Target ➤ Configure Auto Discovery, and then click the Advanced: Discovery Modules tab. Choose Oracle Database, Listener, and Automatic Storage Management and then click OK.

Wait for a while and go to the section Auto Discovery Results. Select Setup ➤ Add Target ➤ Auto Discovery Results. Select the Targets on Hosts tab, as shown in Figure 3-2.

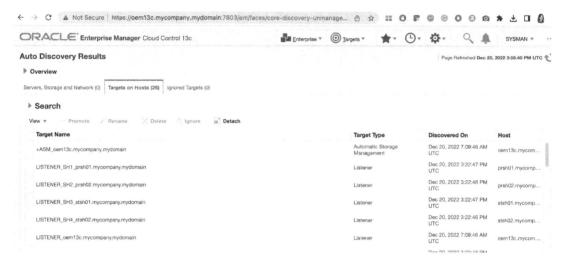

Figure 3-2. *Targets on Hosts tab*

Click the database instance `sh1.mycompany.mydomain` and click the Promote button (Figure 3-3).

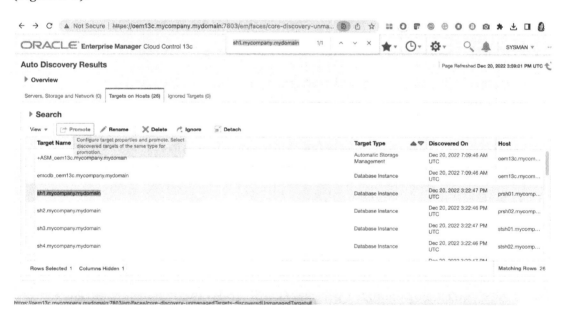

Figure 3-3. *Promoting the targets*

Connect each target, reset the `dbsnmp` password, and unlock the user.

```
SQL> alter user dbsnmp identified by Oracle123;
SQL> alter user dbsnmp account unlock;
```

Return to the web interface, select the target, and enter the password in the Monitoring Password field (Figure 3-4).

Figure 3-4. Promoting the target results

Test the connection. Select Listeners, click Next, and then click Save. Repeat the same steps for other targets. In this testing phase, the catalog database server was not discovered, so we will add it manually.

Select Targets ➤ Databases. Click +Add, click Oracle Database, specify the host, and click Select (Figure 3-5).

Figure 3-5. Selecting the target host

Click Next, select the database and listener, and enter the dbsnmp password in the Monitoring Password field. Then test the connection, click Next, and click Save.

Discovering the Shard Catalog Database in Enterprise Manager

After all the shard and catalog servers are added to EM, we can continue adding the catalog database. In Enterprise Manager Cloud Control, go to Setup ➤ Add Target ➤ Add Target Manually.

Click Add Using Guided Process, search for *Sharded Database*, and click Add (Figure 3-6).

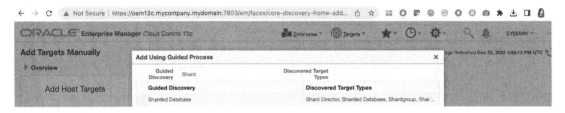

Figure 3-6. *Adding the catalog database*

On the Catalog Database page, click the browse icon next to Catalog Database to locate the shard catalog database (Figure 3-7).

Figure 3-7. *Selecting the catalog database*

Choose the catalog database and click Select. Then connect to the catalog database using SQL*Plus and grant the following role to the dbsnmp user:

```
SQL> grant GDS_CATALOG_SELECT to dbsnmp;
```

Return to the page and fill in the dbsnmp credentials. Then click OK.

On the Sharded Database Components page, you will see a sharded database name, sharded database domain name, sharding type, and shard directors. For shard directors, click Correct, or create new **m**onitoring **c**redentials and click Review and then Submit.

Reviewing Sections Related to Sharding

When sharding targets are added to EM, the following sections will contain links to specific objects. To view sharding architecture–related sections, from the EM console, click Targets and then All Targets.

You'll see Shard Director, Sharded Database, Shardgroup, and Shardspace sections (Figure 3-8).

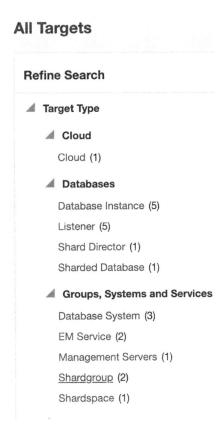

Figure 3-8. *All targets*

Click the Sharded Database link, and choose Target Name (Figure 3-9).

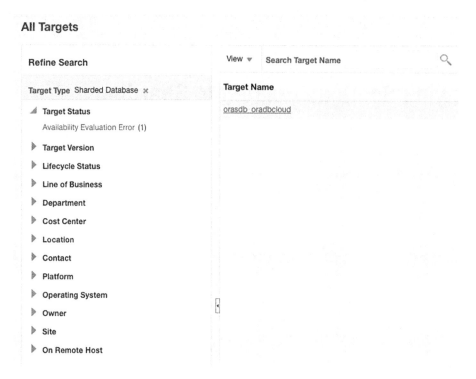

Figure 3-9. *Sharded database*

On the Sharded Database tab, you will see several management tools, such as Add Primary Shards, Add Standby Shards, Deploy Shards, etc. (Figure 3-10).

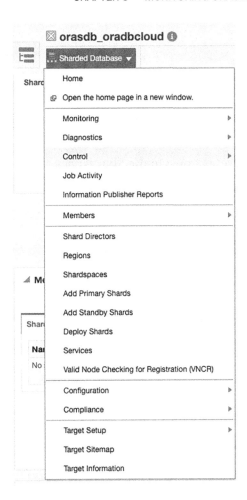

Figure 3-10. *Sharded database control*

Managing Chunks

You are able to manage chunks and more in an Oracle Sharding deployment with Oracle Enterprise Manager Cloud.

To perform a chunk movement operation, select Targets ➤ All Targets. Enter **shardspace** in Search Target Name field (Figure 3-11).

Figure 3-11. *Selecting a shardspace*

Click a value under Target Name. On the Shardspace tab, select Manage Shardgroups (Figure 3-12).

Figure 3-12. *Managing the shardgroups*

Connect to the catalog database and create a new user with the necessary privileges.

```
[oracle@gsmcat ~]$ sqlplus / as sysdba

SQL> alter session enable shard ddl;
SQL> create user shardsys identified by shardsys;
SQL> grant connect, create session, gsmadmin_role to shardsys;
SQL> grant all privileges to shardsys;
SQL> grant select any dictionary to shardsys;
```

Return to the EM console, add the new credentials, and fill in the following fields:

- Username: **shardsys**

- Password: **shardsys**

- Confirm Password: **shardsys**

- Role: **NORMAL**

Test the connection.

In the section shown in Figure 3-13, browse to Shard Director and click OK.

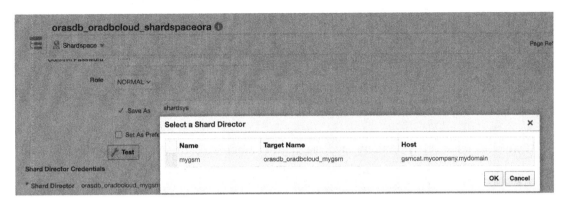

Figure 3-13. *Selecting a shard director*

Click Login. Then select the shardgroup in the list, and click Move Chunk
(Figure 3-14).

Figure 3-14. *Moving a chunk*

Choose the source and destination shards and fill in the necessary values; click OK
when you're done.

- Source Shard: **sh1**

- Destination Shard: **sh2**

- Select ID From Table: **1**

- Start: **Immediately**

Click the link in the Information box at the top of the page to view the provisioning status of the chunk movement (Figure 3-15).

Figure 3-15. *Information box*

If we click `gsmcat.mycompany.mydomain` and select "Execute GDSCTL script," we will see that EM has run the command shown in Figure 3-16 in the background.

Figure 3-16. *GDSCTL command log*

If you connect to the catalog database and see the chunk distribution, you will find out that chunk 1 moved to the sh2 shard, which was also synchronized with its standby database sh4.

```
GDSCTL> config chunks
Chunks
-----------------------
Catalog connection is established
```

Database	From	To
--------	----	--
sh1	2	6
sh2	**1**	**1**
sh2	7	12
sh3	2	6
sh4	**1**	**1**
sh4	7	12

Troubleshooting

This section offers concise and practical guidance to help you quickly diagnose and resolve common issue that may arise while setting up/installing the product.

Problem

Here is the error:

ERROR: NMO not setuid-root (Unix-only)

Reason

The owner of the nmo, nmb, and nmo executables is not the root user.

Solution

Run the root.sh script.

Check the current permissions.

```
[root@gsmcat sbin]# ll
total 18832
-rwx--x--x 1 oracle oinstall   52748 Mar 21  2021 nmb.0
-rwx--x--x 1 oracle oinstall   50147 Mar 21  2021 nmgsshe.0
-rwx--x--x 1 oracle oinstall  105619 Mar 21  2021 nmhs.0
-rwx--x--x 1 oracle oinstall 4786506 Mar 21  2021 nmo.0
-rwx--x--x 1 oracle oinstall 4703266 Mar 21  2021 nmoconf
```

```
-rwx--x--x 1 oracle oinstall 4708170 Mar 21   2021 nmopdpx.0
-rwx--x--x 1 oracle oinstall 4708170 Mar 21   2021 nmosudo.0
-rwx------ 1 oracle oinstall  104376 Mar 21   2021 nmr.0
-rwx------ 1 oracle oinstall   34250 Mar 21   2021 nmrconf
-rw-r----- 1 oracle oinstall   10310 Dec 16   2020 nmr_macro_list
```

Run root.sh.

```
[root@gsmcat agent_13.5.0.0.0]# ./root.sh
```

Double-check that the permissions are changed.

```
[root@gsmcat sbin]# ll
total 37804
-rwsr-x--- 1 root    oinstall   52748 Dec 20 16:30 nmb
-rwx--x--x 1 oracle oinstall   52748 Mar 21   2021 nmb.0
-rwxr-xr-x 1 root    oinstall   50147 Dec 20 16:30 nmgsshe
-rwx--x--x 1 oracle oinstall   50147 Mar 21   2021 nmgsshe.0
-rwsr-x--- 1 root    oinstall  105619 Dec 20 16:30 nmhs
-rwx--x--x 1 oracle oinstall  105619 Mar 21   2021 nmhs.0
-rwsr-x--- 1 root    oinstall 4786506 Dec 20 16:30 nmo
-rwx--x--x 1 oracle oinstall 4786506 Mar 21   2021 nmo.0
-rwx--x--x 1 oracle oinstall 4703266 Mar 21   2021 nmoconf
-rwx--x--x 1 root    root    4786506 Dec 20 16:30 nmo.new.bak
-rwxr-xr-x 1 root    oinstall 4708170 Dec 20 16:30 nmopdpx
-rwx--x--x 1 oracle oinstall 4708170 Mar 21   2021 nmopdpx.0
-rw-r----- 1 root    oinstall     188 Dec 20 16:30 nmo_public_key.txt
-rwxr-xr-x 1 root    oinstall 4708170 Dec 20 16:30 nmosudo
-rwx--x--x 1 oracle oinstall 4708170 Mar 21   2021 nmosudo.0
-rwsr-x--- 1 root    oinstall  104376 Dec 20 16:30 nmr
-rwx------ 1 oracle oinstall  104376 Mar 21   2021 nmr.0
-rwx------ 1 oracle oinstall   34250 Mar 21   2021 nmrconf
-rw-r----- 1 root    oinstall   10310 Dec 16   2020 nmr_macro_list
-rwx------ 1 root    root     104376 Dec 20 16:30 nmr.new.bak
```

Summary

Enterprise Manager is a powerful tool for deploying, administering, and monitoring almost all kinds of Oracle architecture.

In this chapter, we added the sharding architecture along with one catalog database, one GSM, and two primaries with standby shards. We gave an overview of the sharding-related sections in the console, and for testing purposes, we moved a chunk from one shard to another. We verified the successful movement of the chunk with EMCC and GDSCTL.

In the next chapter, we will show you how to download and install the Oracle global service manager for Linux servers.

CHAPTER 4

Installing a Global Service Manager

In this chapter, we will show you how to download and install an Oracle global service manager (GSM) on Linux servers.

Setting Up the Environment

For this chapter, and the entire book, we are going to use the setup shown in Figure 4-1, which has a single instance for both the primary and standby databases. We have installed Oracle 19c (19.3.0) on both the primary and physical standby database servers and applied October 2022 PSU. All these servers have Oracle Enterprise Linux 7.1 as the operating system.

© Y V Ravi Kumar, Mariami Kupatadze, Sambaiah Sammeta 2023
Y V Ravi Kumar et al., *Oracle Global Data Services for Mission-critical Systems*,
https://doi.org/10.1007/978-1-4842-9553-3_4

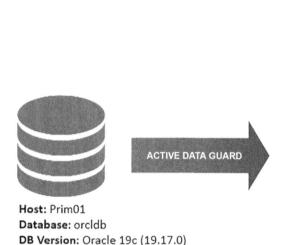

Host: stbyh01
Database: orcldbp
DB Version: Oracle 19c (19.17.0)
GSM version: 19c

Host: Prim01
Database: orcldb
DB Version: Oracle 19c (19.17.0)
GSM version: 19c

Host: cstbyh01
Database: orcldbs
DB Version: Oracle 19c (19.17.0)
GSM version: 19c

Figure 4-1. *Configurations and components of all three environments*

The following is the primary database server:

```
Primary DB server    : prim01.localdomain
OS version           : Oracle Enterprise Linux 7.1 64 bit
Oracle Home          : /u01/app/oracle/product/19.3.0.0/dbhome_1
Database Version     : 19.3.0.0 with October 2022 Database Bundle Patch
```

```
[oracle@ prim01 ~]$ export ORACLE_HOME=/u01/app/oracle/product/19.3.0.0/
dbhome_1
[oracle@ prim01 ~]$ export PATH=$ORACLE_HOME/bin:$PATH

[oracle@prim01 ~]$ $ORACLE_HOME/OPatch/opatch lspatches
34419443;Database Release Update : 19.17.0.0.221018 (34419443)
29585399;OCW RELEASE UPDATE 19.3.0.0.0 (29585399)

OPatch succeeded.
```

We will utilize two physical standby databases for this exercise.

First Physical Standby Database Server

The physical standby database environment is the same version as the primary database, i.e., Oracle 19c (19.9.0) database binaries patched with the Oct 2022 patch set update (PSU).

```
First Standby server  : stbyh01.localdomain
OS version            : Oracle Enterprise Linux 7.1 64 bit
Oracle Home           : /u01/app/oracle/product/19.3.0.0/dbhome_1
Database Version      : 19.3.0.0 with October 2020 Database Bundle Patch

[oracle@stbyh01 ]$ export ORACLE_HOME=/u01/app/oracle/product/19.3.0.0/
dbhome_1
[oracle@stbyh01 ]$ export PATH=$ORACLE_HOME/bin:$PATH

[oracle@stbyh01 ~]$ $ORACLE_HOME/OPatch/opatch lspatches
34419443;Database Release Update : 19.17.0.0.221018 (34419443)
29585399;OCW RELEASE UPDATE 19.3.0.0.0 (29585399)

OPatch succeeded.
[oracle@stbyh01 ~]
```

Second Physical Standby Database Server

The physical standby database environment has the same version as the primary database, i.e., Oracle 19c (19.3.0) database binaries patched with the Oct 2022 PSU.

```
Second Standby server : cstbyh01.localdomain
OS version            : Oracle Enterprise Linux 7.1 64 bit
Oracle Home           : /u01/app/oracle/product/19.3.0.0/dbhome_1
Database Version      : 19.3.0.0 with October 2020 Database Bundle Patch

[oracle@cstbyh01 ]$ export ORACLE_HOME=/u01/app/oracle/product/19.3.0.0/
dbhome_1
[oracle@cstbyh01 ]$ export PATH=$ORACLE_HOME/bin:$PATH
```

```
[oracle@stbyh01 ~]$ $ORACLE_HOME/OPatch/opatch lspatches
34419443;Database Release Update : 19.17.0.0.221018 (34419443)
29585399;OCW RELEASE UPDATE 19.3.0.0.0 (29585399)

OPatch succeeded.
[oracle@cstbyh01 ~]
```

Prerequisites

Before you install any software, you should always review the software, hardware, operating system, and network requirements needed for that specific software. We will now cover the requirements you need to meet before installing Oracle Global Data Services (GDS).

Linux Package Requirements

The following Linux packages must be installed on the server where you want to install the GSM software:

- Linux system kernel version 2.6.18 or later

- Package gcc-4.1.2 (x86_64)

- Package libaio-0.3.106 (x86_64)

- Package libaio-devel-0.3.106 (x86_64)

- Package libstdc++-4.1.2 (x86_64)

- Package sysstat-7.0.2

- Package compat-libstdc++-33-3.2.3 (x86_64)

- Package libgcc-4.1.2 (x86_64)

- Package libstdc++-devel-4.1.2 (x86_64)

- Package glibc-devel-2.5 (x86_64)

- Package gcc-c++-4.1.2 (x86_64)

- Package glibc-2.5-58 (x86_64)

- Package `ksh-...`

- Package `make-3.81`

- Package `binutils-2.17.50.0.6`

Space Requirements

These are the space requirements:

- At least 1.5GB of free disk space

- At least 256MB of total physical memory

- At least 20MB of available physical memory

- At least 6GB of total swap space

Ports Requirements

All the databases that are part of the Global Data Services configuration must be able to reach all the GSM's listener and ONS ports. For this to happen, all the GSM listener ports must also be opened so that connections coming from the GDS pool databases, GDS catalog database, external client tier, and other global service managers can happen without any issues. The default TNS listener port for each of the GDS pool databases must be opened in both directions to GSMs and the GDS catalog. If a GSM must be installed on a separate machine, then you must open the port on that machine (in both directions) so that the GSM will be able to connect to all the databases that are part of the GSM configuration.

Downloading the Global Service Manager Software

The GSM is the central component of the GDS framework. The GSM software is available as a separate download, available here:

    https://edelivery.Oracle.com

Once you log in to the download page, you can search for *Oracle Database Global Service Manager*, as shown in Figure 4-2.

Figure 4-2. *Downloading the Oracle GSM*

As you can see, currently the Oracle GSM is available in versions 12.1.0.1.0 to 19.3.0.0.0. In this book, we will be downloading and installing version 19.3.0.0.0.

Once you have selected the version, you can select the required platform, as shown in Figure 4-3.

Figure 4-3. *Picking the Oracle global service manager platform*

As shown in Figure 4-4, we downloaded Oracle Database Global Service Manager 19.3.0.0.0 for the Linux x86_64 platform.

Figure 4-4. *Downloading the Oracle Global Service manager*

Once you have downloaded the software to the local machine, you can copy it (using `winscp`) to the target server where you will be installing the GSM and stage it in some location. In our case, we are staging it to `/u01/software`.

```
[oracle@prim01 software]$ ls -ltr
total 937396
-rwxr-x---. 1 Oracle dba 959891519 Nov 16 14:10 V982067-01.zip
[oracle@prim01 software]$
```

Unzipping the Global Data Service Manager Binaries

From the directory `/u01/software`, unzip the global service manager `V982067-01.zip` file. This will unzip it into a new directory named `gsm`.

```
[oracle@prim01 software]$ cd gsm
[oracle@prim01 gsm]$ ls -ltr
total 24
-rwxrwxr-x  1 Oracle oinstall  500 Feb  6  2013 welcome.html
-rwxr-xr-x  1 Oracle oinstall 8851 Apr 17  2019 runInstaller
drwxr-xr-x  4 Oracle oinstall 4096 Apr 17  2019 install
drwxrwxr-x  2 Oracle oinstall   29 Apr 17  2019 response
drwxr-xr-x 15 Oracle oinstall 4096 Apr 17  2019 stage
[oracle@prim01 gsm]$
```

Installing the Oracle Global Data Service Manager

The Oracle GSM software must be installed in the new Oracle home directory. Once you have downloaded the software, you need to unzip it and install it by running the script `runInstaller` to invoke the Oracle universal installer just like you installed the Oracle database binaries. The GSM software can be installed on a system where you already have other Oracle products installed as there are no dependencies with other installed Oracle products. You can install more than one global service manager binary in the same system provided that each global service manager has its own separate Oracle home directory. To provide high availability for the global service manager, Oracle recommends installing multiple (normally three) global service managers for each GDS region.

In the Real Application Cluster (RAC), you must install the global service manager in each of the hosts in the cluster. Currently, Oracle doesn't support installing global service managers on multiple hosts; you have to install them separately.

You can use the same operating system user that you typically use to install Oracle database software to install the global service manager, or you can create a separate operating system user to install and maintain the global service manager binaries. This user account is known as the *GDS administrator*. The GDS administrator is not only responsible for installing/maintaining and administering the global service manager but also responsible for administering the GDS catalog, regions, and gdspool.

Creating the Oracle Home Directory for the Global Service Manager

Create the home directory for the GSM software in all the nodes of both the primary and standby databases.

```
@Primary database server
[oracle@prim01 ~]$ mkdir -p /u01/app/oracle/product/19.3.0.0/gsmhome_1

@Physical Standby servers
[oracle@stbyh01 ~]$ mkdir -p /u01/app/oracle/product/19.3.0.0/gsmhome_1
[oracle@cstbyh01 ~]$ mkdir -p /u01/app/oracle/product/19.3.0.0/gsmhome_1
```

Invoking the Oracle Universal Installer

Before invoking the Oracle universal installer, make sure that the DISPLAY environment variable on the Linux machine is working. You may need to set the DISPLAY environment variable and test the GUI to make sure it works. Once the display works, log in to the server as the GDS administrator operating system user and invoke the Oracle universal installer by running the command .runInstaller from the directory where the binaries have been unzipped, as shown in Figure 4-5.

```
[oracle@prim01 gsm]$ ls -ltr
total 24
-rwxrwxr-x  1 oracle oinstall   500 Feb  6  2013 welcome.html
-rwxr-xr-x  1 oracle oinstall  8851 Apr 17  2019 runInstaller
drwxr-xr-x  4 oracle oinstall  4096 Apr 17  2019 install
drwxrwxr-x  2 oracle oinstall    29 Apr 17  2019 response
drwxr-xr-x 15 oracle oinstall  4096 Apr 17  2019 stage
[oracle@prim01 gsm]$
[oracle@prim01 gsm]$ ./runInstaller
Starting Oracle Universal Installer...

Checking Temp space: must be greater than 551 MB.   Actual 1459 MB    Passed
Checking monitor: must be configured to display at least 256 colors.   Actual 16777216    Passed
Preparing to launch Oracle Universal Installer from /tmp/OraInstall2022-11-16_02-24-01PM. Please wait ...[oracle@prim01 gsm]$ 
```

Figure 4-5. *Invoking the Oracle universal installer*

On the next screen, shown in Figure 4-6, give the location for the Oracle base and Oracle home directory. See also Figure 4-7, Figure 4-8, and Figure 4-9.

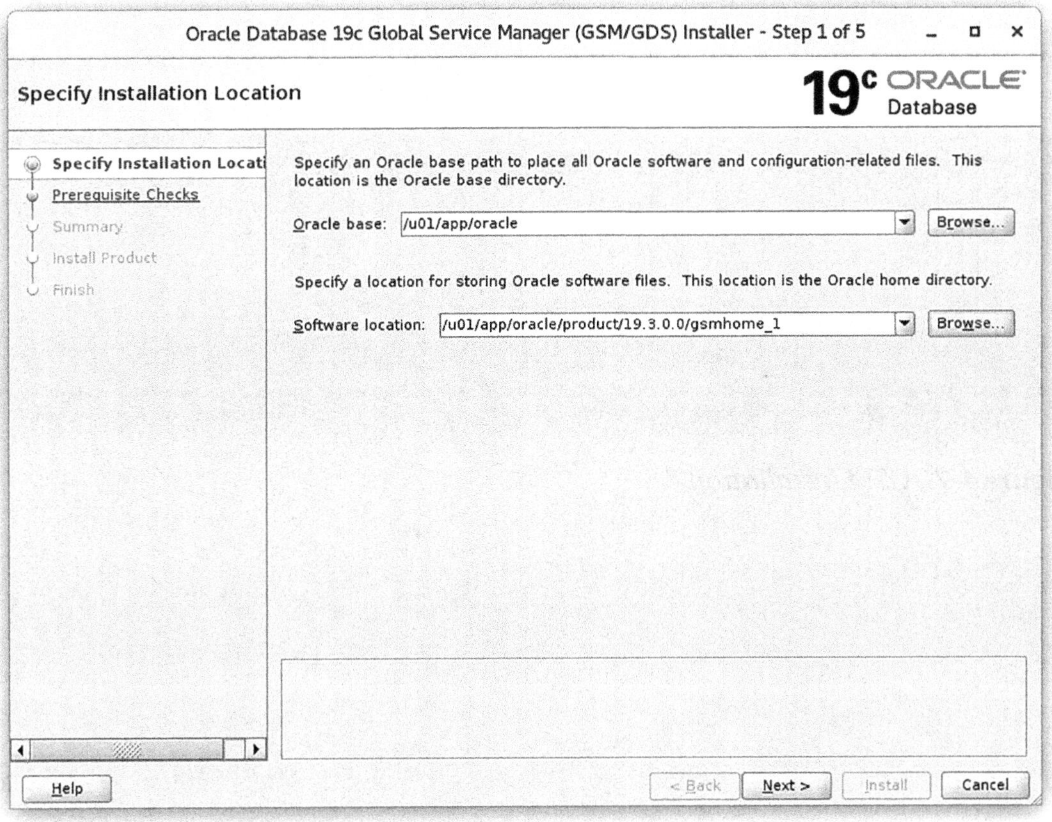

Figure 4-6. *GSM installation, software location*

On the next screen, shown in Figure 4-7, give the location of the Inventory Directory.

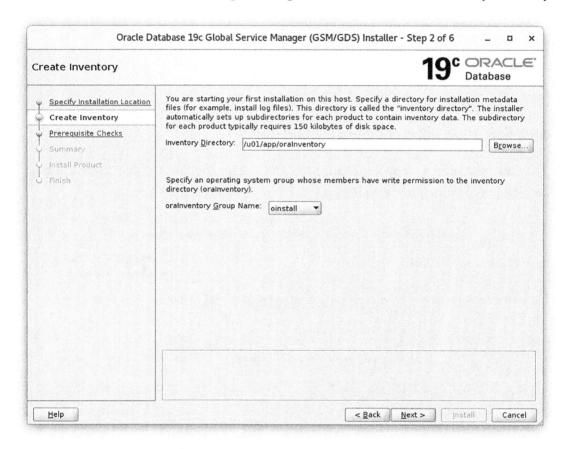

Figure 4-7. *GSM installation*

On the next screen, Figure 4-8, we can see the the summary of the GSM installation.

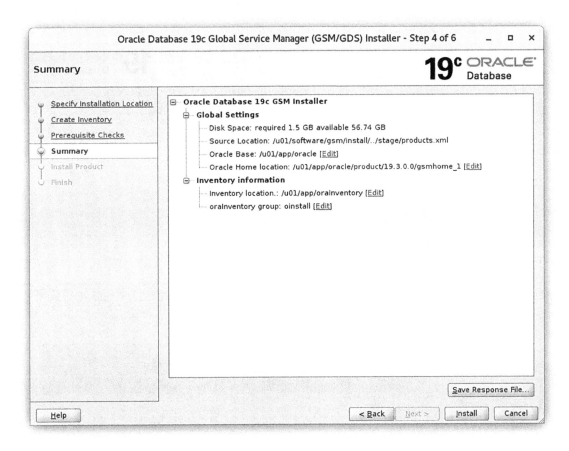

Figure 4-8. *GSM installation, summary*

On the next screen, Figure 4-9 we can see the progress of the GSM installation.

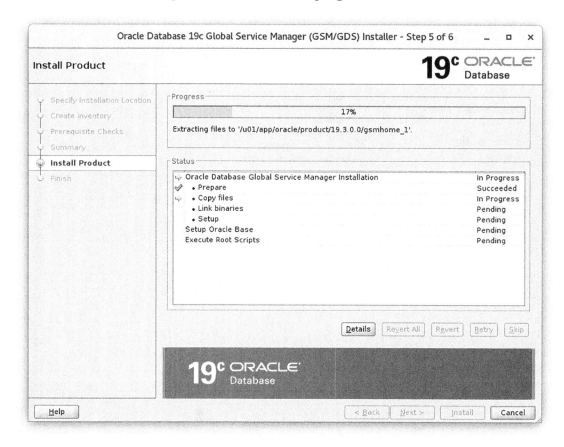

Figure 4-9. *GSM installation in progress*

The installation goes quickly and will provide an option to run the root.sh script
(shown in Figure 4-10) that needs to be run as the superuser root.

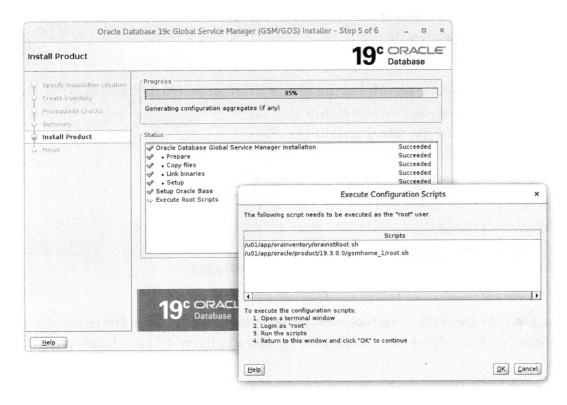

Figure 4-10. *GSM, root script*

To run the orainstRoot.sh script, open a new terminal, log in as the root user, and run it as shown here:

```
[root@prim01 ~]# /u01/app/oraInventory/orainstRoot.sh
Changing permissions of /u01/app/oraInventory.
Adding read,write permissions for group.
Removing read,write,execute permissions for world.

Changing groupname of /u01/app/oraInventory to oinstall.
The execution of the script is complete.
[root@prim01 ~]#
```

Once the orainstRoot.sh script execution completes, run the root.sh script in the same window as the root user.

```
[root@prim01 ~]# /u01/app/oracle/product/19.3.0.0/gsmhome_1/root.sh
Performing root user operation.
```

109

The following environment variables are set as:
    ORACLE_OWNER= Oracle
    ORACLE_HOME= /u01/app/oracle/product/19.3.0.0/gsmhome_1

Enter the full pathname of the local bin directory: [/usr/local/bin]:
    Copying dbhome to /usr/local/bin ...
    Copying oraenv to /usr/local/bin ...
    Copying coraenv to /usr/local/bin ...

Creating /etc/oratab file...
Entries will be added to the /etc/oratab file as needed by
Database Configuration Assistant when a database is created
Finished running generic part of root script.
Now product-specific root actions will be performed.
[root@prim01 ~]#

Once the execution of the root.sh script completes, go back to the first terminal where the GUI is still running and click OK (as shown in Figure 4-11 and Figure 4-12).

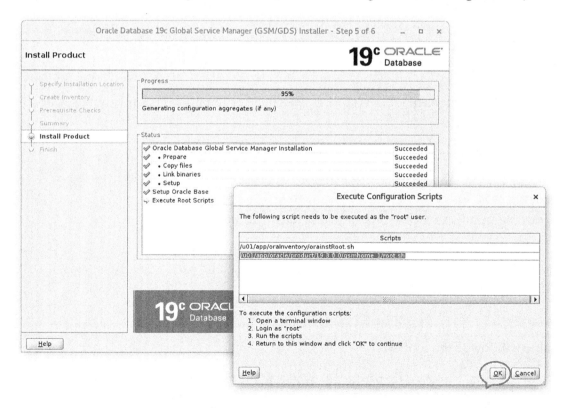

Figure 4-11. *GSM, root completion*

This completes the installation of the GSM. As mentioned earlier in this chapter, the GSM can be installed on the same machine as the Oracle databases are running or on a completely separate machine. If the GDS configuration supports more databases, to avoid the performance issues, it is recommended to install the GSM on a separate dedicated server. If it's a RAC cluster, you will have to install the GSM individually on each host, which helps provide high availability for the GSM.

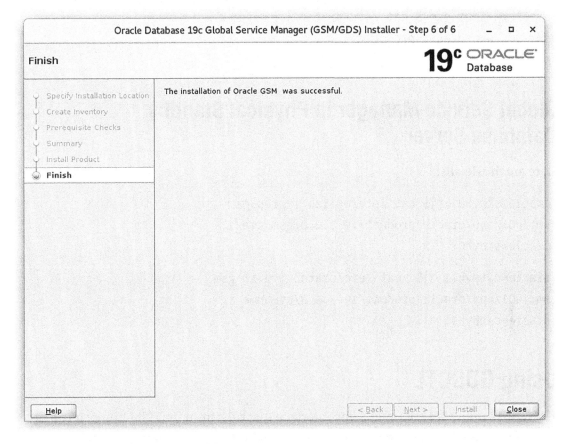

Figure 4-12. *GSM, istallation completion*

In our case, we installed one GSM in each of the primary database servers and two global service managers in each of the physical standby database servers. Because we created multiple regions, we have assigned one GSM for each region.

Once the installation completes, set the required environment variables such as ORACLE_HOME and $ORACLE_HOME/bin to the PATH environment variable, and set the TNS_ADMIN environment variable to $ORACLE_HOME/network/admin. Or you can simply add the Oracle home directory for each GSM to /etc/oratab and run oraenv to source the environment whenever we want to use it.

The following are the details of the GSM installed in our setup, which we are going to use for the entire book.

Global Service Manager in Primary Database Server

Here are the details:

```
[oracle@prim01 gsm]$ cat /etc/oratab | grep gsm
gsm:/u01/app/oracle/product/19.3.0.0/gsmhome_1
[oracle@prim01 gsm]$
```

Global Service Manager in Physical Standby Database Server

Here are the details:

```
[oracle@stbyh01 ~]$ cat /etc/oratab | grep gsm
gsm:/u01/app/oracle/product/19.3.0.0/gsmhome_1
[oracle@stbyh01 ~]$

[oracle@cstbyh01 ~]$  cat /etc/oratab | grep gsm
gsm:/u01/app/oracle/product/19.3.0.0/gsmhome_1
[oracle@cstbyh01 ~]$
```

Using GDSCTL

The GDSCTL utility is a command-line interface that runs from the GSM home. It can be invoked by sourcing the environment to the GSM location and running the command gdsctl at the operating system prompt, as shown here:

```
[oracle@prim01 ~]$ . oraenv
ORACLE_SID = [oracle] ? gsm
The Oracle base has been set to /u01/app/oracle
[oracle@prim01 ~]$ echo $ORACLE_HOME
```

```
/u01/app/oracle/product/19.3.0.0/gsmhome_1
[oracle@prim01 ~]$ gdsctl  ←
GDSCTL: Version 19.0.0.0.0 - Production on Wed Nov 16 14:40:35 CST 2022

Copyright (c) 2011, 2019, Oracle.  All rights reserved.

Welcome to GDSCTL, type "help" for information.

Warning:  GSM  is not set automatically because gsm.ora does not contain
GSM entries. Use "set  gsm" command to set GSM for the session.
Current GSM is set to GSMORA
GDSCTL>
```

This command will display the GDSCTL prompt; you can run all the related GDS commands from here. Also, from the previous output, you can even see the version of the GDS manager from which the GDSCTL is currently running. You see a warning message because you didn't create any ORA file yet; you can ignore it for now. The gsm. ora file gets created in the $GSM_HOME/network/admin directory when you create the GSM. GDSCTL is invoked from the GSM home, and it checks for the gsm.ora file in the GSM home to resolve the global service home.

Summary

In this chapter, you learned what a GSM is, where to download its software, and how to install it on a Linux machine. In the next chapter, you will see how to configure a GSM and its various components.

CHAPTER 5

Configuring and Administering Oracle GDS

In this chapter, you will learn how to configure the various Global Data Services (GDS) components and learn how to administer GDS, which includes learning how to add a global service manager (GSM), how to create and connect to the catalog database, how to add a gdspool and regions to the GDS configuration, how to add databases to the GDS configuration, and how to manage the GDS configurations.

Specifically, in this chapter, we will cover the following topics:

- How to use GDSTL

- How to add a new GSM and start it

- How to create the GDS catalog database

- How to configure GDS admin accounts in both the GDS catalog and the GDS pool databases

- How to add a region to the GDS configuration

- How to add a gdspool

- How to add databases to the GDS configuration

- How to add a Data Guard broker configuration to the GDS configuration

© Y V Ravi Kumar, Mariami Kupatadze, Sambaiah Sammeta 2023
Y V Ravi Kumar et al., *Oracle Global Data Services for Mission-critical Systems*,
https://doi.org/10.1007/978-1-4842-9553-3_5

Setting Up the Environment

Before doing anything else, it's essential that you make sure your environment is properly set up. Our setup includes a single-instance primary database and two single-instance physical standby databases. We have installed Oracle 19c (19.3.0) on both the primary and physical standby database servers and applied the October 2022 patch set update (PSU).

Primary Database Version and the Patch Set

Here are the details:

```
Primary DB server     : prim01.localdomain
OS version            : Oracle Enterprise Linux 7.1 64 bit
Oracle Home           : /u01/app/oracle/product/19.3.0.0/dbhome_1
Database Version       : 19.3.0.0 with October 2022 Database Bundle Patch
```

```
[oracle@ prim01 ~]$ export ORACLE_HOME=/u01/app/oracle/product/19.3.0.0/dbhome_1
[oracle@ prim01 ~]$ export PATH=$ORACLE_HOME/bin:$PATH

[oracle@prim01 ~]$ $ORACLE_HOME/OPatch/opatch lspatches
34419443;Database Release Update : 19.17.0.0.221018 (34419443)
29585399;OCW RELEASE UPDATE 19.3.0.0.0 (29585399)

OPatch succeeded.
```

The primary database name is orcldb, and it's located in the east region. Here are its details:

```
SQL> @/home/oracle/database_info.sql
```

DATABASE_HOST	DB_NAME	DB_UNIQUE_NAME	DATABASE_ROLE	OPEN_MODE	STARTUP_TIME
prim01.localdomain	orcldb	orcldb	PRIMARY	READ WRITE	25-OCT-22

Physical Standby Database Server

We have two physical standby databases configured, and they run on two different database servers.

First Physical Standby Database Server

The first physical standby database environment is the same version as the primary database, i.e., Oracle 19c (19.3.0) database binaries patched with the Oct 2022 PSU.

```
First Standby server  : stbyh01.localdomain
OS version            : Oracle Enterprise Linux 7.1 64 bit
Oracle Home           : /u01/app/oracle/product/19.3.0.0/dbhome_1
Database Version      : 19.3.0.0 with October 2020 Database Bundle Patch
```

```
[oracle@stbyh01 ]$ export ORACLE_HOME=/u01/app/oracle/product/19.3.0.0/dbhome_1
[oracle@stbyh01 ]$ export PATH=$ORACLE_HOME/bin:$PATH

[oracle@stbyh01 ~]$ $ORACLE_HOME/OPatch/opatch lspatches
34419443;Database Release Update : 19.17.0.0.221018 (34419443)
29585399;OCW RELEASE UPDATE 19.3.0.0.0 (29585399)

OPatch succeeded.
[oracle@stbyh01 ~]
```

The first physical standby database name is orcldbp, and this standby database is in the south region.

```
SQL> @/home/oracle/database_info.sql
```

DATABASE_HOST	DB_NAME	DB_UNIQUE_NAME	DATABASE_ROLE	OPEN_MODE	STARTUP_TIME
stbyh01.localdomain	orcldb	orcldbp	PHYSICAL STANDBY	READ ONLY WITH APPLY	26-OCT-22

Second Physical Standby Database Server

The second physical standby database environment is also the same version as the primary database, i.e., Oracle 19c (19.9.0) database binaries patched with the Oct 2022 PSU.

```
Second Standby server : cstbyh01.localdomain
OS version             : Oracle Enterprise Linux 7.1 64 bit
Oracle Home            : /u01/app/oracle/product/19.3.0.0/dbhome_1
Database Version       : 19.3.0.0 with October 2020 Database Bundle Patch
```

```
[oracle@cstbyh01 ]$ export ORACLE_HOME=/u01/app/oracle/product/19.3.0.0/dbhome_1
[oracle@cstbyh01 ]$ export PATH=$ORACLE_HOME/bin:$PATH

[oracle@stbyh01 ~]$ $ORACLE_HOME/OPatch/opatch lspatches
34419443;Database Release Update : 19.17.0.0.221018 (34419443)
29585399;OCW RELEASE UPDATE 19.3.0.0.0 (29585399)
```

```
OPatch succeeded.
[oracle@cstbyh01 ~]
```

The name of our second physical standby database is orcldbs, and this standby database is in the north region.

```
SQL> @/home/oracle/database_info.sql

DATABASE_HOST       DB_NAME DB_UNIQUE_NAME DATABASE_ROLE   OPEN_MODE            STARTUP_TIME
------------------- ------- -------------- --------------- -------------------- ------------
cstbyh01.localdomain orcldb  orcldbs                PHYSICAL STANDBY READ ONLY WITH APPLY 26-OCT-22
```

We have created two scripts that we can use to check the database configuration. We will be using these two scripts throughout the book.

The SQL script called database_info.sql will pull the current database details such as the mode and role of the database.

Script : database_info.sql

```
set lines 190
col DATABASE_HOST for a31;
col DATABASE_ROLE for a11
col OPEN_MODE for a11;
col HOST_NAME for a15;

col STARTUP_TIME for a21
```

SELECT in.HOST_NAME "DATABASE_HOST" ,db.name "DB_NAME",db.db_unique_name "DB_UNIQUE_NAME" , db.DATABASE_ROLE " DATABASE_ROLE", db.OPEN_MODE " OPEN_MODE ", STARTUP_TIME from GV$DATABASE db, gv$instance in where in.INST_ID=db.INST_ID;

The second script, called `standby_lag.sql`, will check the current lag on the standby database and display the standby database role and mode information as well. Please note that this script has three different SQL commands, First SQL command will get the details of the physical standby database, second SQL command will check if the managed recovery process (mrp) is running or not and the third SQL command will check for the lag information in the physical standby database.

Script : standby_lag.sql

```
set lines 190
col DATABASE_HOST for a31;
col DATABASE_ROLE for a11
col OPEN_MODE for a11;
col HOST_NAME for a15;
col STARTUP_TIME for a21
```

SELECT in.HOST_NAME "DATABASE_HOST" ,db.name "DB_NAME",db.db_unique_name "DB_UNIQUE_NAME" , db.DATABASE_ROLE " DATABASE_ROLE", db.OPEN_MODE " OPEN_MODE ", STARTUP_TIME from GV$DATABASE db, gv$instance in where in.INST_ID=db.INST_ID;

select inst_id,process, status, thread#, sequence#, block#, blocks
from gv$managed_standby
where process='MRPO';

select ar.thread#, (select max (sequence#)
from v$archived_log

where archived='YES' and thread#=ar.thread#) archived,max(ar.sequence#)
applied,
(select max(sequence#) from v$archived_log where archived='YES' and
thread#=ar.thread#)-max(ar.sequence#)gap
 from v$archived_log ar where ar.applied='YES' group by ar.thread# order by
thread#;

About GDSCTL

This GDSCTL utility is a command-line tool used to configure and manage the global database service configuration. GDSCTL is invoked from the GSM home, and it checks for the gsm.ora file to resolve the global service home.

Connecting to the GDSCTL Utility

There are two ways to source the GSM environment. Either you can do it by adding the GSM home to /etc/oratab, running .oraenv, and setting the GSM, which is similar to what we do to connect to the Oracle database, or you can export the ORACLE_HOME and PATH variables and set them to point to the GSM home where the GSM software is installed. Once the environment is sourced, you just need to enter the GDSCTL command at the operating system prompt. This will start GDSCTL and display the GDSCTL command prompt from where you can run the commands.

Let's first try the option where we can connect to the GDSCTL utility by exporting the ORACLE_HOME and PATH variables.

```
[oracle@prim01 ~]$ export ORACLE_HOME=/u01/app/oracle/product/19.3.0.0/
gsmhome_1
[oracle@prim01 ~]$ export PATH=$ORACLE_HOME/bin:$PATH
[oracle@prim01 ~]$ gdsctl
GDSCTL: Version 19.0.0.0.0 - Production on Wed Oct 26 15:36:05 CDT 2022

Copyright (c) 2011, 2019, Oracle.  All rights reserved.

Welcome to GDSCTL, type "help" for information.

Warning:  GSM  is not set automatically because gsm.ora does not contain
GSM entries. Use "set  gsm" command to set GSM for the session.
```

```
Current GSM is set to GSMORA
GDSCTL>
```

Let's now see the second option where we add the GSM home location to oratab and then run .oraenv to source the GSM home and run GDSCTL.

```
[oracle@prim01 ~]$ cat /etc/oratab | grep gsm
gsm:/u01/app/oracle/product/19.3.0.0/gsmhome_1
[oracle@prim01 ~]$ . oraenv
ORACLE_SID = [catgds] ? gsm
The Oracle base remains unchanged with value /u01/app/oracle
[oracle@prim01 ~]$ gdsctl
GDSCTL: Version 19.0.0.0.0 - Production on Wed Oct 26 15:37:45 CDT 2022

Copyright (c) 2011, 2019, Oracle.  All rights reserved.

Welcome to GDSCTL, type "help" for information.

Warning:  GSM  is not set automatically because gsm.ora does not contain
GSM entries. Use "set  gsm" command to set GSM for the session.
Current GSM is set to GSMORA
GDSCTL>
```

Many GDSCTL commands require connecting to the GDS catalog before running them. For example, if you want to add any of the GDS components such as a GSM, gdspool, and so on, you must first connect to the GDS catalog from the GDSCTL command prompt by using the connect command and then run the commands to add the GDS components. You will learn more about this later in the chapter.

To get to know all the commands that GDSCTL supports, you can use the help command in GDSCTL, which displays all the available commands. If you want help with any specific GDSCTL command, you can use the help command followed by a specific command name, and it will give details of that specific command including the correct syntax to use. For example, if you want to know the command to add a GDS region, you can use the help command, as shown here:

```
GDSCTL> help add region
Syntax
ADD REGION -region region_name_list [-buddy region_name]
```

Purpose
Adds GDS regions.

Usage Notes
Note, a default GDS region "REGIONORA" will be created during GDS catalog
creation if -region option was not used

Keywords and Parameters
buddy: buddy GDS region name.
region: a comma-delimited list of region names.

Examples
GDSCTL> add region -region west, east

GDSCTL>

Overview of the GDS Catalog

A GDS catalog is a repository that is created in a separate Oracle database. This
repository stores the metadata information for a single GDS configuration and all its
provided services. Each catalog is associated with only one GDS configuration. The
minimum version of Oracle Database that can be used to create the GDS catalog is
12.1. This catalog database can reside on the same servers where the global database
configuration database resides, or it can run on a completely different server. Since this
catalog database is the central repository for the entire GDS configuration, it is advisable
to create this database on a separate host and use Oracle high-availability features such
as Oracle RAC and Oracle Data Guard to protect the catalog database from a single point
of failure.

In our case, we created a `catgds` database on the same server, called `prim01`, where
our primary database is running. We will use this database to create the GDS catalog
later in the chapter. We also created a physical standby database for the catalog database
with the name `catgdsdr` on the server `stbyh01.localdomain`. The following is the
catalog database information.

Primary Catalog Database Details

Here are the details:

```
SQL> @/home/oracle/database_info.sql
```

DATABASE_HOST	DB_NAME	DB_UNIQUE_NAME	DATABASE_ROLE	OPEN_MODE	STARTUP_TIME
prim01.localdomain	catgds	catgds	PRIMARY	READ WRITE	26-OCT-22

Standby Catalog Database Details

Here are the details:

```
SQL> @/home/oracle/database_info.sql
```

DATABASE_HOST	DB_NAME	DB_UNIQUE_NAME	DATABASE_ROLE	OPEN_MODE	STARTUP_TIME
stbyh01.localdomain	catgds	catgdsdr	PHYSICAL STANDBY	READ ONLY WITH APPLY	26-OCT-22

The following is the TNS entry for the primary catalog database in our environment. This entry needs to be added to the tnsnames.ora file of ORACLE_HOME in all the database servers where the gdspool databases and GSMs are running.

```
CATGDS =
  (DESCRIPTION =
    (ADDRESS = (PROTOCOL = TCP)(HOST = prim01.localdomain)(PORT = 1521))
    (CONNECT_DATA =
      (SERVER = DEDICATED)
      (SERVICE_NAME = catgds)
    )
  )
```

Creating the GDS Catalog

In this section, you will learn how to create the GDS catalog in the database catgds. This catalog is created and managed by a GDS administrator. The GDS administrator who creates the GDS catalog must have a dedicated user account in the catalog database and should have the gsmadmin_role role granted to it. Even though the GDS administrator has a user account in the catalog database, Oracle strongly recommends not connecting to the catalog database directly using this account. Instead, Oracle recommends that the GDS administrator use the GDSCTL utility to communicate with the catalog and to create, configure, and manage the GDSs.

Let's create a user account that can be used by the GDS administrator. We will create a user with the name gsmadm in the catalog database and then grant the gsmadmin_role role to this user.

```
SQL> create user gsmadm identified by welcome;

User created.

SQL> grant gsmadmin_role to gsmadm;

Grant succeeded.

SQL> select username,account_status from dba_users where username in
('GSMADM');

USERNAME            ACCOUNT_STATUS
------------------- --------------------------------
GSMADM              OPEN

SQL>
```

Let's see how we can now create the catalog in the catalog database catgds by using the previous user account and by using the GDSCTL utility.

As mentioned earlier, all the gdspool databases should be able to connect to the GDS catalog database. So, before we create the catalog, we should make sure that we are able to do tnsping to the catalog database from all the servers where the gdspool databases and the GSMs are running. In our case, we will test this from the primary and both the standby database servers.

```
[oracle@prim01 admin]$ tnsping catgds

TNS Ping Utility for Linux: Version 19.0.0.0.0 - Production on 26-OCT-2022
15:34:13

Copyright (c) 1997, 2022, Oracle.  All rights reserved.

Used parameter files:
/u01/app/oracle/product/19.3.0.0/dbhome_1/network/admin/sqlnet.ora

Used TNSNAMES adapter to resolve the alias
Attempting to contact (DESCRIPTION = (ADDRESS = (PROTOCOL = TCP)(HOST =
prim01.localdomain)(PORT = 1521)) (CONNECT_DATA = (SERVER = DEDICATED)
(SERVICE_NAME = catgds)))
OK (0 msec)
[oracle@prim01 admin]$

[oracle@stbyh01 dbs]$ tnsping catgds

TNS Ping Utility for Linux: Version 19.0.0.0.0 - Production on 26-OCT-2022
15:33:55

Copyright (c) 1997, 2022, Oracle.  All rights reserved.

Used parameter files:

Used TNSNAMES adapter to resolve the alias
Attempting to contact (DESCRIPTION = (ADDRESS = (PROTOCOL = TCP)(HOST =
prim01.localdomain)(PORT = 1521)) (CONNECT_DATA = (SERVER = DEDICATED)
(SERVICE_NAME = catgds)))
OK (0 msec)
[oracle@stbyh01 dbs]$

[oracle@cstbyh01 admin]$ tnsping catgds

TNS Ping Utility for Linux: Version 19.0.0.0.0 - Production on 26-OCT-2022
15:33:37

Copyright (c) 1997, 2022, Oracle.  All rights reserved.

Used parameter files:
```

```
Used TNSNAMES adapter to resolve the alias
Attempting to contact (DESCRIPTION = (ADDRESS = (PROTOCOL = TCP)(HOST =
prim01.localdomain)(PORT = 1521)) (CONNECT_DATA = (SERVER = DEDICATED)
(SERVICE_NAME = catgds)))
OK (0 msec)
[oracle@cstbyh01 admin]$
```

To create the catalog, we will use the create catalog command at the GDSCTL command prompt. When using this command, we need to provide the host and port details of the database in which this GDS catalog is going to get created, and we also need to provide the GDS administrator account details. The following is the syntax for creating the catalog:

```
GDSCTL > create gdscatalog -database server:1521:catalog_db -user gsm_admin
```

We will connect to the GDSCTL utility from the GSM home in the primary database host and create the GDS catalog.

```
[oracle@prim01 ~]$ . oraenv
ORACLE_SID = [oracle] ? gsm
[oracle@prim01 ~]$ gdsctl
GDSCTL: Version 19.0.0.0.0 - Production on Wed Oct 26 15:51:21 CDT 2022

Copyright (c) 2011, 2019, Oracle.  All rights reserved.

Welcome to GDSCTL, type "help" for information.

Warning:  GSM  is not set automatically because gsm.ora does not contain
GSM entries. Use "set  gsm" command to set GSM for the session.
Current GSM is set to GSMORA
GDSCTL> create catalog -database prim01:1521/CATGDS -user gsmadm/welcome;
Catalog is created
GDSCTL>
```

As you can see, we used the GDS administrator user (gsmadm in this case) to create the GDS catalog. Once the catalog is created, let's see how the GDS administrator can connect to the catalog from the GDSCTL command-line utility. The following is the syntax for connecting to the catalog. We need to provide the GDS administrator username/ password and the catalog database hostname and port details in this command.

```
GDSCTL > connect [username/password]@[host/scan_name]:port/catalog_
database_name
```

In our case, we can connect to the catalog database as shown here:

```
[oracle@prim01 ~]$ . oraenv
ORACLE_SID = [catgds] ? gsm
The Oracle base remains unchanged with value /u01/app/oracle
[oracle@prim01 ~]$ gdsctl
GDSCTL: Version 19.0.0.0.0 - Production on Wed Oct 26 15:49:07 CDT 2022

Copyright (c) 2011, 2019, Oracle.  All rights reserved.

Welcome to GDSCTL, type "help" for information.

Warning:  GSM  is not set automatically because gsm.ora does not contain
GSM entries. Use "set  gsm" command to set GSM for the session.
Current GSM is set to GSMORA
GDSCTL> connect gsmadm/welcome@prim01:1521/CATGDS;
Catalog connection is established
GDSCTL>
```

The GDS administrator, once it connects to the catalog, can make any of the required changes to the GDS configuration in the catalog, and all the GSMs that are running on different servers are notified about these changes. Once a GSM receives the configuration updates from the catalog, it then connects to the configured pool databases and implements those changes. To support this process, all the GSMs must be able to connect to the catalog and to the configured databases. For this, the Oracle default user account gsmcatuser will be used.

About the GSMCATUSER Account

Every GSM in the GDS configuration connects to the catalog database using a precreated user account, GSMCATUSER, through a direct Oracle Net services connection. This is a default user account that is created in the Oracle database (since the 12c version) during its installation. This user account will be locked by default. To register the GSM to the catalog, we must unlock it and change its password. We can log in to the catalog database as the database administrator (DBA) and perform this step.

```
[oracle@prim01 ~]$ . oraenv
ORACLE_SID = [gsm] ? catgds
The Oracle base remains unchanged with value /u01/app/oracle
[oracle@prim01 ~]$ sqlplus / as sysdba

SQL*Plus: Release 19.0.0.0.0 - Production on Wed Oct 26 15:38:37 2022
Version 19.17.0.0.0

Copyright (c) 1982, 2022, Oracle.  All rights reserved.

Connected to:
Oracle Database 19c Enterprise Edition Release 19.0.0.0.0 - Production
Version 19.17.0.0.0

SQL> @/home/oracle/database_info.sql
```

```
DATABASE_HOST        DB_NAME  DB_UNIQUE_NAME  DATABASE_ROLE  OPEN_MODE   STARTUP_TIME
-------------------- -------  --------------- -------------  ----------- ----------------
prim01.localdomain   catgds   catgds          PRIMARY        READ WRITE  26-OCT-22
```

Check the account status of the user account gsmcatuser.

```
SQL>  col username for a19
SQL>  select username,account_status from dba_users where
username='GSMCATUSER';
```

```
USERNAME            ACCOUNT_STATUS
------------------- ---------------------------------
GSMCATUSER          LOCKED
```

Change the password for the user, gsmcatuser.

```
SQL> alter user gsmcatuser identified by welcome;

User altered.
```

Unlock the user account gsmcatuser.

```
SQL> alter user gsmcatuser account unlock;

User altered.
```

Check the account status of user account gsmcatuser.

```
SQL> select username,account_status from dba_users where username in
('GSMCATUSER');

USERNAME            ACCOUNT_STATUS
------------------  -------------------
GSMCATUSER          OPEN
```

Registering the GSM to the GDS Catalog

You will now learn how you can register the GSM to the GDS catalog. As mentioned earlier, in our case, we have three GSMs. The first one is running on the server prim01, and the other two GSMs are running from two different standby database servers, stby01 and cstby01.

Here are the first GSM's details:

```
gsm name          : gsmeast
Host running on : prim01
Oracle home       : /u01/app/oracle/product/19.3.0.0/gsmhome_1
```

Here are the second GSM's details:

```
gsm name          : gsmnorth
Host running on : stbyh01
Oracle home       : /u01/app/oracle/product/19.3.0.0/gsmhome_1
```

Here are the third GSM's details:

```
gsm name          : gsmsouth
Host running on : cstbyh01
Oracle home       : /u01/app/oracle/product/19.3.0.0/gsmhome_1
```

Now, let's add all three GSMs to the GDS catalog one by one. For this, we will use the add gsm command from the GDSCTL command-line utility. The following is the syntax for adding the GSM:

```
GDSCTL> add gsm -gsm gsm_name -listener listener_port -catalog catalog_
host:port/db_name
```

We need to provide the name of the GSM that we are going to register, the port of the GSM listener where it will be listening to the client connections, and the catalog database details that include the catalog hostname, database name, and port. When we run this command, GDSCTL will establish the connection to the GDS catalog and connect to the catalog as the GSMCATUSER user.

Add the first GSM with the name gsmeast. This GSM is configured to run from the server prim01 where our primary database resides.

```
[oracle@prim01 ~]$ gdsctl
GDSCTL: Version 19.0.0.0.0 - Production on Wed Oct 26 16:00:17 CDT 2022

Copyright (c) 2011, 2019, Oracle.  All rights reserved.

Welcome to GDSCTL, type "help" for information.

Warning:  GSM  is not set automatically because gsm.ora does not contain
GSM entries. Use "set  gsm" command to set GSM for the session.
Current GSM is set to GSMORA
GDSCTL>
```

Connect to the catalog database.

```
GDSCTL> connect gsmadm/welcome@prim01:1521/CATGDS;
Catalog connection is established
```

Add the GSM with the name gsmeast, as shown here:

```
GDSCTL> add gsm -gsm gsmeast -listener 1581 -catalog prim01:1521/CATGDS;
"gsmcatuser" password:
GSM successfully added
GDSCTL>
```

As you can see, when the preceding add gsm command executed, it asked for the password of the user account gsmcatuser, and once we provide its password, it will connect to the GDS catalog as the gsucatuser user. Then the command will register a new GSM with the name gsmeast and create a GSM listener, which runs on port 1581 on the server prim01. As soon as we add the GSM to the catalog, its entries are added to the gsm.ora and tnsnames.ora files of the GSM at the following location:

```
[oracle@prim01 admin]$ pwd
/u01/app/oracle/product/19.3.0.0/gsmhome_1/network/admin
[oracle@prim01 admin]$ ls -ltr
total 12
-rw-r--r--. 1 oracle oinstall 1536 Feb 13  2018 shrept.lst
drwxr-xr-x. 2 oracle oinstall   79 Oct 26 13:14 samples
-rw-------. 1 oracle oinstall    0 Oct 26 16:12 gsmwallet.lck
drwxr-xr-x. 2 oracle oinstall   90 Oct 26 16:12 gsmwallet
-rw-r--r--. 1 oracle oinstall  501 Oct 26 16:12 gsm.ora
-rw-r--r--. 1 oracle oinstall  507 Oct 26 16:12 tnsnames.ora
[oracle@prim01 admin]$

[oracle@prim01 admin]$ cat gsm.ora

# gsm.ora Network Configuration File: /u01/app/oracle/product/19.3.0.0/
gsmhome_1/network/admin/gsm.ora
# Generated by Oracle configuration tools.

SQLNET.WALLET_OVERRIDE = TRUE

GSMEAST =
  (configuration =
    (listener =
      (ADDRESS = (HOST = prim01.localdomain)(PORT = 1581)(PROTOCOL = tcp))
    )
    (cloud = oradbcloud)
  )

WALLET_LOCATION =
  (SOURCE =
    (METHOD = FILE)
```

```
      (METHOD_DATA =
        (DIRECTORY = /u01/app/oracle/product/19.3.0.0/gsmhome_1/network/
        admin/gsmwallet)
      )
    )

[oracle@prim01 admin]$ cat tnsnames.ora
# tnsnames.ora Network Configuration File: /u01/app/oracle/
product/19.3.0.0/gsmhome_1/network/admin/tnsnames.ora
# Generated by Oracle configuration tools.

GSMEAST =
  (DESCRIPTION =
    (ADDRESS = (HOST = prim01.localdomain)(PORT = 1581)(PROTOCOL = tcp))
    (CONNECT_DATA =
      (SERVICE_NAME = GDS$CATALOG.oradbcloud)
    )
  )

GSMEAST_CATALOG =
  (DESCRIPTION =
    (address = (protocol = tcp)(host = prim01)(port = 1521))
    (CONNECT_DATA =
      (SERVICE_NAME = GDS$CATALOG.oradbcloud)
    )
  )

[oracle@prim01 admin]$
```

We will register the second GSM with the name gsmnorth, and for this one we will add it on the first physical standby database server, stbyh01. We will run this from the server stbyh01 where we want this GSM to run.

```
[oracle@stbyh01 ~]$ . oraenv
ORACLE_SID = [gsm] ?
The Oracle base remains unchanged with value /u01/app/oracle
[oracle@stbyh01 ~]$ echo $ORACLE_HOME
/u01/app/oracle/product/19.3.0.0/gsmhome_1
```

```
[oracle@stbyh01 ~]$ gdsctl
GDSCTL: Version 19.0.0.0.0 - Production on Wed Oct 26 16:19:56 CDT 2022

Copyright (c) 2011, 2019, Oracle.  All rights reserved.

Welcome to GDSCTL, type "help" for information.

Warning:  GSM  is not set automatically because gsm.ora does not contain
GSM entries. Use "set  gsm" command to set GSM for the session.
Current GSM is set to GSMORA
GDSCTL>
```

Connect to the catalog database.

```
GDSCTL> connect gsmadm/welcome@prim01:1521/CATGDS;
Catalog connection is established
```

Add the GSM with the name gsmnorth, as shown here:

```
GDSCTL> add gsm -gsm gsmnorth -listener 1582 -catalog prim01:1521/CATGDS
"gsmcatuser" password:
GSM successfully added
GDSCTL>
```

The preceding command will add a new GDS with the name gsmnorth and will create a GSM listener to run on port 1582.

Adding the third GSM with the name gsmsouth. This GSM will be running from the second standby database server, cstbyh01.

```
[oracle@cstbyh01 ~]$ . oraenv
ORACLE_SID = [orcldbs] ? gsm
The Oracle base remains unchanged with value /u01/app/oracle
[oracle@cstbyh01 ~]$ gdsctl
GDSCTL: Version 19.0.0.0.0 - Production on Wed Oct 26 17:38:58 CDT 2022

Copyright (c) 2011, 2019, Oracle.  All rights reserved.

Welcome to GDSCTL, type "help" for information.

Warning:  GSM  is not set automatically because gsm.ora does not contain
GSM entries. Use "set  gsm" command to set GSM for the session.
```

```
Current GSM is set to GSMORA
GDSCTL>
```

Connect to the catalog database.

```
GDSCTL> connect gsmadm/welcome@prim01:1521/CATGDS;
Catalog connection is established
GDSCTL>
```

Add the GSM with the name gsmsouth, as shown here:

```
GDSCTL> add gsm -gsm gsmsouth -listener 1583 -catalog prim01:1521/CATGDS
"gsmcatuser" password:
GSM successfully added
GDSCTL>
```

The preceding command will add a new GDS with the name gsmsouth and will create a GSM listener to listen for the client connections on port 1583.

Starting All the Global Service Managers

Once we complete adding the GSMs to the GDSs configuration, we can now start all the GSMs one by one. When we start a GSM, it will also start the listener that's associated with a specific GSM.

Starting gsmeast

From the host prim01, connect to GDSCTL from the GSM Oracle home and start the GSM called gsmeast.

```
GDSCTL> start gsm -gsm GSMEAST;
GSM is started successfully
GDSCTL>
```

Once the GSM is started, we can check its status by running the command status from the GDSCTL prompt, as shown here:

```
GDSCTL> status
Alias                      GSMEAST
Version                    19.0.0.0.0
```

Start Date	26-OCT-2022 17:40:55
Trace Level	off
Listener Log File	/u01/app/oracle/diag/gsm/prim01/gsmeast/ alert/log.xml
Listener Trace File	/u01/app/oracle/diag/gsm/prim01/gsmeast/trace/ ora_4666_140598579297344.trc
Endpoint summary	(ADDRESS=(HOST=prim01.localdomain)(PORT=1581) (PROTOCOL=tcp))
GSMOCI Version	3.0.180702
Mastership	Y
Connected to GDS catalog	Y
Process Id	4669
Number of reconnections	0
Pending tasks. Total	0
Tasks in process. Total	0
Regional Mastership	TRUE
Total messages published	0
Time Zone	-05:00
Orphaned Buddy Regions: None	
GDS region	regionora

```
GDSCTL>
```

From the previous output, we can see all the details of the GSM including the GSM version, the listener it started, the default region (regionora) associated to it, and a few other details. We can change the default region of the GSM once we add new regions.

Let's start the GSM gsmnorth on the server stbyh01. Log in to GDSCTl on stbyh01 and start the GSM.

```
[oracle@stbyh01 ~]$ . oraenv
ORACLE_SID = [orcldbp] ? gsm
The Oracle base remains unchanged with value /u01/app/oracle
[oracle@stbyh01 ~]$ gdsctl
GDSCTL: Version 19.0.0.0.0 - Production on Wed Oct 26 17:41:06 CDT 2022
```

Welcome to GDSCTL, type "help" for information.

Current GSM is set to GSMNORTH
GDSCTL> start gsm -gsm GSMNORTH;
GSM is started successfully
GDSCTL>

We can check the status of GSM gsmnorth.

```
GDSCTL> status
Alias                     GSMNORTH
Version                   19.0.0.0.0
Start Date                26-OCT-2022 17:41:15
Trace Level               off
Listener Log File         /u01/app/oracle/diag/gsm/stbyh01/gsmnorth/
                          alert/log.xml
Listener Trace File       /u01/app/oracle/diag/gsm/stbyh01/gsmnorth/trace/
                          ora_4225_139726813695040.trc
Endpoint summary          (ADDRESS=(HOST=stbyh01.localdomain)(PORT=1582)
                          (PROTOCOL=tcp))
GSMOCI Version            3.0.180702
Mastership                N
Connected to GDS catalog  Y
Process Id                4228
Number of reconnections   0
Pending tasks.    Total   0
Tasks in  process. Total  0
Regional Mastership       FALSE
Total messages published  0
Time Zone                 -05:00
Orphaned Buddy Regions:
    None
GDS region                regionora

GDSCTL>
```

We can now start the GSM gsmsouth. Log in to GDSCTl on the server cstbyh01 and start the GSM.

```
[oracle@cstbyh01 ~]$ . oraenv
ORACLE_SID = [gsm] ?
The Oracle base remains unchanged with value /u01/app/oracle
[oracle@cstbyh01 ~]$ gdsctl
GDSCTL: Version 19.0.0.0.0 - Production on Wed Oct 26 17:42:57 CDT 2022

Copyright (c) 2011, 2019, Oracle.  All rights reserved.

Welcome to GDSCTL, type "help" for information.

Current GSM is set to GSMSOUTH
GDSCTL> start gsm -gsm GSMSOUTH;
GSM is started successfully
GDSCTL>
```

Check the status of the GSM called gsmsouth.

```
GDSCTL> status gsm -gsm GSMSOUTH;
Alias                      GSMSOUTH
Version                    19.0.0.0.0
Start Date                 26-OCT-2022 17:43:05
Trace Level                off
Listener Log File          /u01/app/oracle/diag/gsm/cstbyh01/gsmsouth/
                           alert/log.xml
Listener Trace File        /u01/app/oracle/diag/gsm/cstbyh01/gsmsouth/trace/
                           ora_4250_140570175908928.trc
Endpoint summary           (ADDRESS=(HOST=cstbyh01.localdomain)(PORT=1583)
                           (PROTOCOL=tcp))
GSMOCI Version             3.0.180702
Mastership                 N
Connected to GDS catalog   Y
Process Id                 4253
Number of reconnections    0
Pending tasks.     Total   0
Tasks in  process. Total   0
```

```
Regional Mastership       FALSE
Total messages published  0
Time Zone                 -05:00
Orphaned Buddy Regions:
     None
GDS region                regionora

GDSCTL>
```

In addition to the status command, we can check the configuration of any GSM by running the config gsm command. From the GSM running on prim01, we can check the configuration of all the GSMs, as shown here:

```
[oracle@prim01 ~]$ gdsctl
GDSCTL: Version 19.0.0.0.0 - Production on Wed Oct 26 17:46:04 CDT 2022

Copyright (c) 2011, 2019, Oracle.  All rights reserved.

Welcome to GDSCTL, type "help" for information.

Current GSM is set to GSMEAST
GDSCTL> config gsm -gsm GSMEAST
Catalog connection is established
Name: gsmeast
Endpoint 1: (ADDRESS=(HOST=prim01.localdomain)(PORT=1581)(PROTOCOL=tcp))
Local ONS port: 6123
Remote ONS port: 6234
ORACLE_HOME path: /u01/app/oracle/product/19.3.0.0/gsmhome_1
GSM Host name: prim01.localdomain
Region: regionora

Buddy
-----------------------

GDSCTL> config gsm -gsm GSMNORTH
Name: gsmnorth
Endpoint 1: (ADDRESS=(HOST=stbyh01.localdomain)(PORT=1582)(PROTOCOL=tcp))
Local ONS port: 6123
Remote ONS port: 6234
```

```
ORACLE_HOME path: /u01/app/oracle/product/19.3.0.0/gsmhome_1
GSM Host name: stbyh01.localdomain
Region: regionora

Buddy
------------------------

GDSCTL> config gsm -gsm GSMSOUTH
Name: gsmsouth
Endpoint 1: (ADDRESS=(HOST=cstbyh01.localdomain)(PORT=1583)(PROTOCOL=tcp))
Local ONS port: 6123
Remote ONS port: 6234
ORACLE_HOME path: /u01/app/oracle/product/19.3.0.0/gsmhome_1
GSM Host name: cstbyh01.localdomain
Region: regionora

Buddy
------------------------

GDSCTL>
```

We can also check if the GSM is up and running by running the ps -ef| grep gsm command at the operating system level.

```
[oracle@prim01 admin]$ ps -ef| grep gsm
oracle    4666    1  0 17:40 ?        00:00:00
/u01/app/oracle/product/19.3.0.0/gsmhome_1/bin/gsmmon GSMEAST -inherit
oracle    4669    1  0 17:40 ?        00:00:00
/u01/app/oracle/product/19.3.0.0/gsmhome_1/bin/gsmoci ifile=/u01/
app/oracle/product/19.3.0.0/gsmhome_1/network/admin/gsm.ora GSMEAST
SNLSM:4ab30000 -inherit
oracle    4681    1  0 17:40 ?        00:00:00
/u01/app/oracle/product/19.3.0.0/gsmhome_1/bin/tnslsnr
ifile=/u01/app/oracle/product/19.3.0.0/gsmhome_1/network/admin/gsm.ora
GSMEAST SNLSM:4ab30000 -inherit -mode gsm
oracle    4683    1  0 17:40 ?        00:00:00
/u01/app/oracle/product/19.3.0.0/gsmhome_1/bin/gsmping
```

```
ifile=/u01/app/oracle/product/19.3.0.0/gsmhome_1/network/admin/gsm.ora
GSMEAST SNLSM:4ab30000 -inherit
oracle    4685    1  0 17:40 ?         00:00:00
/u01/app/oracle/product/19.3.0.0/gsmhome_1/bin/gsmopxy
ifile=/u01/app/oracle/product/19.3.0.0/gsmhome_1/network/admin/gsm.ora
GSMEAST SNLSM:4ab30000 -inherit
oracle    4687    1  0 17:40 ?         00:00:00
/u01/app/oracle/product/19.3.0.0/gsmhome_1/bin/gsmonsc
ifile=/u01/app/oracle/product/19.3.0.0/gsmhome_1/network/admin/gsm.ora
GSMEAST SNLSM:4ab30000 -inherit
oracle    4691    1  0 17:40 ?         00:00:00
/u01/app/oracle/product/19.3.0.0/gsmhome_1/bin/ons
oracle    4951 2710  0 17:44 pts/0     00:00:00 grep --color=auto gsm
[oracle@prim01 admin]$
```

We have started all three GSMs. We can now add other components of the GSM configuration.

Also, so far, we saw how to run the commands from the GDSCTL command prompt. We can also run the same GDSCTL commands from the operating system prompt as shown next. This is just another way to run the commands. In the following example, the gdsctl command will connect to the catalog database and get the status of the GSM named gsmnorth.

```
[oracle@stbyh01 ~]$ gdsctl status  gsm -gsm gsmnorth -catalog gsmadm/
welcome@prim01:1521/CATGDS
Alias                   GSMNORTH
Version                 19.0.0.0.0
Start Date              26-OCT-2022 17:41:15
Trace Level             off
Listener Log File       /u01/app/oracle/diag/gsm/stbyh01/gsmnorth/
                        alert/log.xml
Listener Trace File     /u01/app/oracle/diag/gsm/stbyh01/gsmnorth/trace/
                        ora_4225_139726813695040.trc
Endpoint summary        (ADDRESS=(HOST=stbyh01.localdomain)(PORT=1582)
                        (PROTOCOL=tcp))
GSMOCI Version          3.0.180702
```

```
Mastership                  N
Connected to GDS catalog    Y
Process Id                  4228
Number of reconnections     0
Pending tasks.     Total    0
Tasks in  process. Total    0
Regional Mastership         FALSE
Total messages published    0
Time Zone                   -05:00
Orphaned Buddy Regions:
    None
GDS region                  regionora

[oracle@stbyh01 ~]$
```

Adding a GDS Pool to the GDS Configuration

As you know, the GDS pool is nothing but a subset of the databases within the GDS configuration, which provides a unique set of global services. When we set up a GSM and create the GDSs catalog, a default GDS pool, DBPOOLORA, was created. If we need more GSD pools, we can add them to the GDS configuration using the following command:

```
GDSCTL> add gdspool -dbpool database_pool_list [-users user_list]
```

By default, when we add a gdspool to the GDS configuration, it is managed by default by the GDS administrator, which in our case is gsmcatuser. But if we want a different user to manage the gdspool, we can use the previously mentioned -user option when we add the gdspool. In our case, we will use gsmcatuser to manage the configuration.

For our setup, we will create two gdspools with the names sales and hr. GDS pool names must be unique in the GDS configuration. We will connect to GDSCTL from the primary database server and add the gdspools sales and hr, as shown here:

```
[oracle@prim01 ~]$ . oraenv
ORACLE_SID = [oracle] ? gsm
The Oracle base has been set to /u01/app/oracle
[oracle@prim01 ~]$ gdsctl
GDSCTL: Version 19.0.0.0.0 - Production on Wed Oct 26 17:48:32 CDT 2022
```

```
Copyright (c) 2011, 2019, Oracle.  All rights reserved.

Welcome to GDSCTL, type "help" for information.

Current GSM is set to GSMEAST
GDSCTL> add gdspool -gdspool SALES
Catalog connection is established
The operation completed successfully
GDSCTL> add gdspool -gdspool HR
The operation completed successfully
GDSCTL>
```

We can check the configuration of the gdspools using the `config gdspool` command.

```
GDSCTL> config gdspool
Name                                Broker                  Sharded
----                                ------                  -------
dbpoolora                           No                      No
hr                                  No                      No
sales                               No                      No

GDSCTL>
```

The previous output shows that this GDS configuration has three gdspools: the default gdspool `dbpoolora` and `sales` and `hr` that we just created.

Adding Regions to the GDS Configuration

By default, when we create a GDS catalog, a default GDS region called `regionora` is created. We can add more regions to the GDS configuration as per our requirements. Like the gdspool name, the name of the region must be unique to the global service configuration. We must connect to the GDS catalog and add the GSM regions as shown here:

```
GDSCTL> connect gsmadm/welcome@prim01:1521/CATGDS;
Catalog connection is established

GGDSCTL> add region -region east
The operation completed successfully
GGDSCTL> add region -region south
```

```
The operation completed successfully
GDSCTL> add region -region north
The operation completed successfully
```

The preceding example created three regions with the names east, north, and south. We can check the current regions in the GDS configuration by running the config region command, as shown here:

```
GDSCTL> config region
Name                          Buddy
-------                       -------
east
north
regionora
south
```

From the previous output, we can see that we have a total of four regions in this GDS configuration. We also see a Buddy column, which is a kind of failover region. We will discuss more about this later in the book.

As mentioned, regionora is the default region that gets assigned to each of the GSMs. Since we created three new regions, let's see how to assign these regions to the GSMs. We can assign a specific region to a specific GSM using the modify gsm command from GDSCTL.

From the gsmeast node of the GSM, first check the current status of the GSM, which shows the default assigned, and then we will modify the GSM to assign it to a new region.

```
[oracle@prim01 ~]$
[oracle@prim01 ~]$ gdsctl
GDSCTL: Version 19.0.0.0.0 - Production on Thu Oct 27 19:04:42 CDT 2022

Copyright (c) 2011, 2019, Oracle.  All rights reserved.

Welcome to GDSCTL, type "help" for information.

Current GSM is set to GSMEAST
GDSCTL> connect gsmadm/welcome@prim01:1521/CATGDS;
Catalog connection is established
```

```
GDSCTL> status  gsm -gsm gsmeast
Alias                      GSMEAST
Version                    19.0.0.0.0
Start Date                 27-OCT-2022 17:25:48
Trace Level                off
Listener Log File          /u01/app/oracle/diag/gsm/prim01/gsmeast/
                           alert/log.xml
Listener Trace File        /u01/app/oracle/diag/gsm/prim01/gsmeast/trace/
                           ora_4647_140358465875008.trc
Endpoint summary           (ADDRESS=(HOST=prim01.localdomain)(PORT=1581)
                           (PROTOCOL=tcp))
GSMOCI Version             3.0.180702
Mastership                 Y
Connected to GDS catalog   Y
Process Id                 4649
Number of reconnections    0
Pending tasks.    Total    0
Tasks in  process. Total   0
Regional Mastership        TRUE
Total messages published   6
Time Zone                  -05:00
Orphaned Buddy Regions:
   None
GDS region                 regionora

GDSCTL> modify gsm -gsm gsmeast -region east;
GSM modified
GDSCTL> status  gsm -gsm gsmeast

Alias                      gsmeast
Version                    19.0.0.0.0
Start Date                 27-OCT-2022 19:05:08
Trace Level                off
```

```
Listener Log File          /u01/app/oracle/diag/gsm/prim01/gsmeast/
                           alert/log.xml
Listener Trace File        /u01/app/oracle/diag/gsm/prim01/gsmeast/trace/
                           ora_11036_139777818475584.trc
Endpoint summary           (ADDRESS=(HOST=prim01.localdomain)(PORT=1581)
                           (PROTOCOL=tcp))
GSMOCI Version             3.0.180702
Mastership                 Y
Connected to GDS catalog   Y
Process Id                 11039
Number of reconnections    0
Pending tasks.     Total   0
Tasks in  process. Total   0
Regional Mastership        TRUE
Total messages published   0
Time Zone                  -05:00
Orphaned Buddy Regions:
     None
GDS region                 east        <=======
GDSCTL>
```

From the gsmnorth node of the GSM, modify the GSM named gsmnorth, as shown here:

```
[oracle@stbyh01 admin]$ gdsctl
GDSCTL: Version 19.0.0.0.0 - Production on Thu Oct 27 19:05:30 CDT 2022

Copyright (c) 2011, 2019, Oracle.  All rights reserved.

Welcome to GDSCTL, type "help" for information.

Current GSM is set to GSMNORTH
GDSCTL> connect gsmadm/welcome@prim01:1521/CATGDS;
Catalog connection is established
```

```
GDSCTL> status gsm -gsm gsmnorth
Alias                     GSMNORTH
Version                   19.0.0.0.0
Start Date                27-OCT-2022 17:25:55
Trace Level               off
Listener Log File         /u01/app/oracle/diag/gsm/stbyh01/gsmnorth/
                          alert/log.xml
Listener Trace File       /u01/app/oracle/diag/gsm/stbyh01/gsmnorth/trace/
                          ora_4159_140228367899712.trc
Endpoint summary          (ADDRESS=(HOST=stbyh01.localdomain)(PORT=1582)
                          (PROTOCOL=tcp))
GSMOCI Version            3.0.180702
Mastership                Y
Connected to GDS catalog  Y
Process Id                4161
Number of reconnections   0
Pending tasks.    Total   0
Tasks in  process. Total  0
Regional Mastership       FALSE
Total messages published  0
Time Zone                 -05:00
Orphaned Buddy Regions:
  None
GDS region                regionora

GDSCTL> modify gsm -gsm gsmnorth -region north        ⬅
GSM modified

GDSCTL>  status gsm -gsm gsmnorth
Alias                     gsmnorth
Version                   19.0.0.0.0
Start Date                27-OCT-2022 19:06:01
Trace Level               off
Listener Log File         /u01/app/oracle/diag/gsm/stbyh01/gsmnorth/
                          alert/log.xml
```

```
Listener Trace File      /u01/app/oracle/diag/gsm/stbyh01/gsmnorth/trace/
                         ora_22969_140311640628288.trc
Endpoint summary         (ADDRESS=(HOST=stbyh01.localdomain)(PORT=1582)
                         (PROTOCOL=tcp))
GSMOCI Version           3.0.180702
Mastership               N
Connected to GDS catalog  Y
Process Id               22972
Number of reconnections  0
Pending tasks.    Total  0
Tasks in  process. Total 0
Regional Mastership      TRUE
Total messages published 0
Time Zone                -05:00
Orphaned Buddy Regions:
  None
GDS region               north

GDSCTL
```

From the gsmsouth node of the GSM, modify the GSM as shown here:

```
[oracle@cstbyh01 admin]$ gdsctl
GDSCTL: Version 19.0.0.0.0 - Production on Thu Oct 27 19:06:18 CDT 2022

Copyright (c) 2011, 2019, Oracle.  All rights reserved.

Welcome to GDSCTL, type "help" for information.

Current GSM is set to GSMSOUTH
GDSCTL> status gsm -gsm gsmsouth
Alias                    GSMSOUTH
Version                  19.0.0.0.0
Start Date               27-OCT-2022 17:26:00
Trace Level              off
Listener Log File        /u01/app/oracle/diag/gsm/cstbyh01/gsmsouth/
                         alert/log.xml
```

```
Listener Trace File        /u01/app/oracle/diag/gsm/cstbyh01/gsmsouth/trace/
                           ora_3929_140465921510464.trc
Endpoint summary           (ADDRESS=(HOST=cstbyh01.localdomain)(PORT=1583)
                           (PROTOCOL=tcp))
GSMOCI Version             3.0.180702
Mastership                 N
Connected to GDS catalog   Y
Process Id                 3932
Number of reconnections    0
Pending tasks.     Total   0
Tasks in  process. Total   0
Regional Mastership        FALSE
Total messages published   0
Time Zone                  -05:00
Orphaned Buddy Regions:
  None
GDS region                 regionora

GDSCTL> modify gsm -gsm gsmsouth -region south
Catalog connection is established

GSM modified

GDSCTL>   status gsm -gsm gsmsouth
Alias                      gsmsouth
Version                    19.0.0.0.0
Start Date                 27-OCT-2022 19:06:48
Trace Level                off
Listener Log File          /u01/app/oracle/diag/gsm/cstbyh01/gsmsouth/
                           alert/log.xml
Listener Trace File        /u01/app/oracle/diag/gsm/cstbyh01/gsmsouth/trace/
                           ora_22756_140376848170048.trc
Endpoint summary           (ADDRESS=(HOST=cstbyh01.localdomain)(PORT=1583)
                           (PROTOCOL=tcp))
GSMOCI Version             3.0.180702
Mastership                 N
```

```
Connected to GDS catalog   Y
Process Id                 22759
Number of reconnections    0
Pending tasks.     Total   0
Tasks in  process. Total   0
Regional Mastership        TRUE
Total messages published   0
Time Zone                  -05:00
Orphaned Buddy Regions:
  None
GDS region south
```

GDSCTL>

Since we removed the default region from all the GSMs, we can remove the default region regionora if we want. For this, we can use the remove region command from the GDSCTL prompt.

```
GDSCTL> config region
Name                        Buddy
----                        -----
east
north
regionora
south

GDSCTL> remove region -region regionora
The operation completed successfully
GDSCTL> config region
Name                        Buddy
----                        -----
east
north
south

GDSCTL>
```

Adding Databases to the GDS Configuration

To create and start any GDS services, we first need to add the database to the GDS configuration. The database that is being added to the GDS pool must use the spfile, and it should also have a scan set up if the database is a Real Application Cluster (RAC) database. In our case, all the primary and standby databases are single-instance databases and are using an spfile. We will be dealing with RAC databases in a later chapter.

About the GSMUSER Account

Every GDS manager connects to the GDS pool using the account GSMUSER, which is created by default starting from Oracle 12c. However, this user account will be locked by default, so we must unlock the account and change its password.

Connect to the primary database and run the following commands:

```
Connect to the primary database and ensure the account "GSMUSER" is
available and accessible.

[oracle@prim01 ~]$ sqlplus / as sysdba

SQL*Plus: Release 19.0.0.0.0 - Production on Thu Oct 27 17:32:10 2022
Version 19.17.0.0.0

Copyright (c) 1982, 2022, Oracle.  All rights reserved.

Connected to:
Oracle Database 19c Enterprise Edition Release 19.0.0.0.0 - Production
Version 19.17.0.0.0

SQL> @/home/oracle/database_info.sql

DATABASE_HOST        DB_NAME DB_UNIQUE_NAME   DATABASE_ROLE OPEN_MODE    STARTUP_TIME
-------------------- ------- ---------------- ------------- ------------ ----------------
prim01.localdomain   orcldb  orcldb           PRIMARY       READ WRITE   27-OCT-22

SQL> col USERNAME for a10
```

```
SQL> select username,account_status from dba_users where
username='GSMUSER';

USERNAME    ACCOUNT_STATUS
---------- ----------------
GSMUSER     LOCKED

SQL> alter user gsmuser identified by welcome;

User altered.

SQL> alter user gsmuser account unlock;

User altered.

SQL> select username,account_status from dba_users where
username='GSMUSER';

USERNAME    ACCOUNT_STATUS
---------- ---------------
GSMUSER     OPEN
```

To add a database to the GDS configuration, we must connect to the catalog first and then add the database using the add database command, as shown here:

```
GDSCTL> connect gsmadm/welcome@prim01:1521/CATGDS;
Catalog connection is established
GDSCTL> add database -connect prim01:1521/orcldb -region east
-gdspool SALES
"gsmuser" password:
DB Unique Name: orcldb
The operation completed successfully
GDSCTL>
```

In this example, we are adding the primary database, orcldb, to the gdspool sales in the east region. As you can see, we can give the hostname since the primary database is a single-instance database. If it's a RAC database, we must give the scan name while adding the RAC database.

Now, if the databases are part of Data Guard broker configuration, then instead of adding the primary and standby databases individually to the catalog, we should add the Data Guard broker configuration so that all the databases that are part of the Data Guard broker configurations can be managed as one entity. To add the Data Guard broker configuration, we can use the GDSCTl command add brokerconfig.

The following is the syntax for adding a broker configuration to the GDS configuration:

```
GDSCTL> add brokerconfig -connect scan/ip:port:Primary_database_
sid  -region region_name -gdspool gdspool_name
```

As you can see from the previous command, if it's a single instance database, we can give the hostname. If the gdspool databases are RAC databases, we must give the scan name when we add the Data Guard broker configuration.

In our case, we do have a Data Guard setup configured with the primary database orcldb and with two physical standby databases, orcldbp and orcldbs. The following is the Data Guard broker configuration for this setup. From the primary database, connect to the Data Guard broker command-line interface, DGMGRL, and run the show configuration command, as shown here:

```
[oracle@prim01 ~]$ dgmgrl
DGMGRL for Linux: Release 19.0.0.0.0 - Production on Thu Oct 27
17:35:46 2022
Version 19.17.0.0.0

Copyright (c) 1982, 2019, Oracle and/or its affiliates.  All rights
reserved.

Welcome to DGMGRL, type "help" for information.
DGMGRL> connect sys/welcome;
Connected to "orcldb"
Connected as SYSDBA.
DGMGRL> show configuration;

Configuration - orcldbcfg

  Protection Mode: MaxPerformance
  Members:
  orcldb  - Primary database
```

```
    orcldbp - Physical standby database
    orcldbs - Physical standby database

Fast-Start Failover:  Disabled

Configuration Status:
SUCCESS    (status updated 59 seconds ago)

DGMGRL>
```

From the GDSCTL prompt, we can now add the broker configuration to GDS as shown here. Let's first remove the database that we added manually. To remove the database, we can use the command remove database, as shown here:

```
GDSCTL> connect gsmadm/welcome@prim01:1521/CATGDS;
Catalog connection is established
GDSCTL> remove database -gdspool SALES -database orcldb
The operation completed successfully
GDSCTL>
```

We can run the databases command from GDSCTL to see the current gdspool databases that are present in the GDS configuration.

```
GDSCTL: Version 19.0.0.0.0 - Production on Thu Oct 27 17:40:52 CDT 2022

Copyright (c) 2011, 2019, Oracle.  All rights reserved.

Welcome to GDSCTL, type "help" for information.

Current GSM is set to GSMEAST
GDSCTL> connect gsmadm/welcome@prim01:1521/CATGDS;
Catalog connection is established
GDSCTL> databases;

GDSCTL>
```

As we can see, there are no databases currently added to the GDS configuration. Let's add the broker configuration now.

```
GDSCTL> add brokerconfig -connect prim01:1521/orcldb -gdspool sales
-region east;
"gsmuser" password:
```

```
DB Unique Name: orcldb
The operation completed successfully
GDSCTL>
```

After successfully adding the broker configuration, we can run the `databases` command from GDSCTL to verify whether all the databases got added to the GDS configuration.

```
GDSCTL> databases;
Database: "orcldb" Registered: Y State: Ok ONS: N. Role: PRIMARY Instances:
1 Region: east
   Registered instances:
     sales%1
Database: "orcldbp" Registered: N State: Ok ONS: N. Role: N/A Instances: 0
Region: N/A
Database: "orcldbs" Registered: N State: Ok ONS: N. Role: N/A Instances: 0
Region: N/A

GDSCTL>
```

As you can see from the previous output, all the databases that are part of Data Guard broker configuration got added to the GDS configuration.

Also from the previous output, we can see that the properties of the primary database are showing OK, whereas both the standby database properties are not looking correct. We can see that the role is N/A and the region is also showing as N/A with the instances count showing as zero. Also, when we run the `config database` command, we can see that there are no regions associated with the standby databases.

```
GDSCTL> config database
```

Name	Pool	Status	State	Region	Availability
----	----	------	-----	------	------------
orcldb	sales	Ok	none	east	ONLINE
orcldbp	sales	Ok	none		-
orcldbs	sales	Ok	none		-

```
GDSCTL>
```

Let's update the configuration for each of the databases. We can update the configuration for any database in the GDS configuration by running the modify database command from GDSCTL. Please note that if we are not sure of any of the GDSCTL commands, we can always run the help command in GDSCTL to get the syntax of the specific command. The following example gives the output of the help modify database command:

```
GDSCTL> help modify database
Syntax
MODIFY DATABASE -database db_name_list [-gdspool pool] [-region region_name
][-pwd password ] [-connect connect_identifier ] [-scan scan_address] [-ons
onsport] [-savename] [-cpu_threshold cpu][-disk_threshold disk]

Purpose
Modify the configuration parameters of the databases. Multiple databases
are allowed if and only if region property is modified

Usage Notes

Keywords and Parameters
connect:        an Oracle Net connect descriptor or net service name
                that resolves to a connect descriptor for the database (
                or shard)
cpu_threshold:  CPU Utilization percentage threshold.
database:       a comma-delimited list of databases.
disk_threshold: average latency in milliseconds of a synchronous single-
                block read.
gdspool:        the GDS pool (If not specified and there is only one
                gdspool with access granted to user, it will be used by
                default)
ons:            CRS ONS port.
pwd:            "gsmuser" password ("gsmrootuser" for add cdb).
region:         GDS region database, catalog, shard, shardgroup or GSM
                belong to.
savename:       store net service name specified with -connect option,
                rather than connect descriptor from tnsnames.ora.
scan:           database SCAN address.
```

Examples
Change GDS region of databases DB1 and DB3 to EAST
GDSCTL> modify database -database db1,db3 -region east

We can modify the database configuration to add the region for the primary and both standby databases.

Here's how to update the configuration for the first physical standby database, orcldbp:

```
GDSCTL> modify database -database orcldbp -region north -gdspool sales
The operation completed successfully
```

Here's how to update the configuration for the second physical standby database, orcldbs:

```
GDSCTL> modify database -database orcldbs -region south -gdspool sales
The operation completed successfully
```

Now if we check the configuration again by running GDSCTL from the primary database server, we can see the updated configuration.

```
GDSCTL>   config database
Name           Pool           Status   State      Region   Availability
----           ----           ------   -----      ------   ------------
orcldb         sales          Ok       none       east     ONLINE
orcldbp        sales          Ok       none       north    READ ONLY
orcldbs        sales          Ok       none       south    READ ONLY

GDSCTL>
```

Awesome, the config database command output looks good. Let's run the command databases to see if the region and database role for the primary and physical standby databases got updated and shows as expected.

```
GDSCTL> databases
Database: "orcldb" Registered: Y State: Ok ONS: N. Role: PRIMARY Instances:
1 Region: east
```

```
Registered instances:
    sales%1
Database: "orcldbp" Registered: Y State: Ok ONS: N. Role: PH_STNDBY
Instances: 1 Region: north
    Registered instances:
      sales%11
Database: "orcldbs" Registered: Y State: Ok ONS: N. Role: PH_STNDBY
Instances: 1 Region: south
    Registered instances:
      sales%21

GDSCTL>
```

As we can see, both the region property and the role property for each of the databases in the configuration show the correct expected values.

Please note that if it's a RAC database, initially the previous command will show only one node for each of the databases. You must add all the nodes to the GDS configuration and then validate the catalog to cross-check information to ensure that all the instances of the databases get registered in the configuration. For that, you need to add the IP addresses of the nodes using the add invitednode command.

If you are not sure about the syntax, you can run the help add invitenode command from GDSCTL and it will give the correct syntax.

```
GDSCTL> help add invitednode
Syntax
ADD INVITEDNODE [-group name] [-catalog catalogdb [-user username/
password]]
vncr_id

Purpose
Adds VNCR to GDS catalog. Allows to add VNCR before first GSM is started
(by establishing "direct" connection to GDS catalog db).

Usage Notes

Keywords and Parameters
catalog: GDS catalog connection string ( TNS alias).
```

group: group alias which defines a group of VNCRs (i.e. the same alias can be used
           in multiple ADD calls)
user: credentials (name[/password]) of the user that has the GDS administrator
           privileges on the catalog database
vncr_id: host address (ip4, ip6, host name, netmask, e.t.c).

Examples
ADD INVITEDNODE 127.0.0.1
ADD INVITEDNODE -group easteast1.us.oracle.com
ADD INVITEDNODE -group east east2.us.oracle.com

GDSCTL>

Let's say the primary database or standby database is a two-node RAC database. You can add the second node to the configuration using its IP address, as shown here:

GDSCTL> add invitednode 192.120.20.4;

Once you add all the nodes of both primary and standby databases, you must validate the catalog, which cross-checks the GDS catalog and databases, and it will also report any inconsistencies and errors. For this, you use the command validate catalog from GDSCTL.

GDSCTL> validate catalog;
Validation results:

Known Issues

If you don't add the broker configuration to the GDS catalog and if you add the primary and standby databases individually to the catalog, you will get the following error when you try to create and start a service:

GDSCTL> add service -service sales_rpt_srvc -gdspool sales -preferred_all
-role PHYSICAL_STANDBY -failover_primary
GSM-45007: Add Service failed

```
ORA-44870: The "role" property is only supported for pools that contain a
Data Guard broker configuration.
ORA-06512: at "SYS.DBMS_SYS_ERROR", line 79
ORA-06512: at "GSMADMIN_INTERNAL.DBMS_GSM_POOLADMIN", line 14080
ORA-06512: at line 1
GDSCTL>
```

Instead of adding the databases by adding the Data Guard broker configuration, the primary and physical standby databases were added separately, as shown here:

```
Adding Primary database,ORCLDB .

GDSCTL> add database -connect prima01:1521/orcldb -region east
-gdspool SALES
"gsmuser" password:
DB Unique Name: orcldb
The operation completed successfully
GDSCTL>
```

```
Adding standby database,ORCLDBW.

GDSCTL> add database -connect stby01:1521/orcldbn -region north -gdspool HR
"gsmuser" password:
DB Unique Name: orcldbw
The operation completed successfully
GDSCTL>
```

To fix this, always add the primary and standby databases to the GDS configuration by adding the broker configuration itself. First remove the primary and standby databases that were added individually and then add the broker configuration, as shown here:

```
GDSCTL>  remove database -database orcldbn -gdspool sales
The operation completed successfully
GDSCTL> remove database -database orcldbw -gdspool hr
The operation completed successfully
```

```
GDSCTL> remove database -database orcldbs -gdspool hr
The operation completed successfully
GDSCTL> databases
```

Add broker config

```
GDSCTL> add brokerconfig -connect prim01:1521/orcldb -region northeastus
-gdspool SALES
"gsmuser" password:
DB Unique Name: orcldb
The operation completed successfully
```

You will now be able to create the GDS services without any issues.

```
GDSCTL> add service -service sales_rpt_srvc -gdspool sales -preferred_all
-role PHYSICAL_STANDBY -failover_primary
The operation completed successfully
```

Summary

In this chapter, you saw a GDS configuration and how to add a GSM to the GDS configuration. You also saw how to create the GDS catalog and how you can connect to it from the GDSCTL utility. You also learned how to add regions, gdspools, and databases to the GDS configuration. In the next chapter, we will explore and test a few scenarios in GDS.

## CHAPTER 6

Test Cases: Using Oracle GDS with Oracle ADG

In this chapter, you will mainly see how Global Data Services (GDS) can be used in a real-time environment. We will explore the GDS options and test a few scenarios that demonstrate the use cases for GDS. Specifically, we will cover the following topics:

- You will see the environment setup used for the demonstrations.

- You will learn how to create a global service and start it.

- You will learn how to create a role-based global service and how it behaves when the primary database becomes unavailable or when the primary database is converted to the physical standby database in the Active Data Guard (ADG) environment.

- You will learn how to create a transparent application failover (TAF)–enabled GDS in our environment.

- You will learn how to create a GDS service with the attribute locality, which routes the traffic to a database in the local region.

Setting Up the Environment

The setup includes a primary database and two physical standby databases. We have installed and configured Oracle 19c (19.3.0) on both the primary and physical standby database servers and applied the October 2022 patch set update (PSU) to the environment.

We have created two scripts that we can use to check the database configuration. We will be using these two scripts throughout the book.

© Y V Ravi Kumar, Mariami Kupatadze, Sambaiah Sammeta 2023
Y V Ravi Kumar et al., *Oracle Global Data Services for Mission-critical Systems*,
https://doi.org/10.1007/978-1-4842-9553-3_6

The first script will pull the current database details such as the mode and the role of the database.

```
[oracle@prim01] cat /home/oracle/database_info.sql
SQL> set lines 190
SQL> col DATABASE_HOST for a31;
SQL> col DATABASE_ROLE for a11;
SQL> col OPEN_MODE for a11;
SQL> col HOST_NAME for a15;
SQL> col STARTUP_TIME for a21;

SQL> SELECT in.HOST_NAME "DATABASE_HOST" ,db.name "DB_NAME",db.db_unique_
name "DB_UNIQUE_NAME" , db.DATABASE_ROLE " DATABASE_ROLE", db.OPEN_MODE "
OPEN_MODE ", STARTUP_TIME
from GV$DATABASE db, gv$instance in
where in.INST_ID=db.INST_ID;
```

The second script will check the current lag on the physical standby database and display the physical standby database role and mode info as well. Please note that this script has three different SQL queries, First SQL will give the physical standby database information Second script will check if the managed recovery process is running, and the third SQL query will check the lag in then standby database.

```
[oracle@prim01] cat /home/oracle/standby_lag.sql

SQL> set lines 190;
SQL> col DATABASE_HOST for a31;
SQL> col DATABASE_ROLE for a11;
SQL> col OPEN_MODE for a11;
SQL> col HOST_NAME for a15;
SQL> col STARTUP_TIME for a21;
SQL> SELECT in.HOST_NAME "DATABASE_HOST" ,db.name "DB_NAME",db.db_unique_
name "DB_UNIQUE_NAME" , db.DATABASE_ROLE " DATABASE_ROLE", db.OPEN_MODE "
OPEN_MODE ", STARTUP_TIME
from GV$DATABASE db, gv$instance in
where in.INST_ID=db.INST_ID;

SQL> select inst_id,process, status, thread#, sequence#, block#, blocks
from gv$managed_standby
```

```
where process='MRP0';

SQL> select ar.thread#, (select max (sequence#)
from v$archived_log
where archived='YES' and thread#=ar.thread#) archived,max(ar.sequence#)
applied,
(select max(sequence#)
 from v$archived_log
 where archived='YES' and thread#=ar.thread#)-max(ar.sequence#)gap
from v$archived_log ar
where ar.applied='YES'
group by ar.thread#
order by thread#;
```

Primary Database Version and the Patch Set

Here are the details:

```
Primary DB server    : prim01.localdomain
OS version           : Oracle Enterprise Linux 7.1 64 bit
Oracle Home          : /u01/app/oracle/product/19.3.0.0/dbhome_1
Database Version     : 19.3.0.0 with October 2022 Database Bundle Patch

[oracle@ prim01 ~]$ export ORACLE_HOME=/u01/app/oracle/product/19.3.0.0/
dbhome_1
[oracle@ prim01 ~]$ export PATH=$ORACLE_HOME/bin:$PATH

[oracle@prim01 ~]$ $ORACLE_HOME/OPatch/opatch lspatches
34419443;Database Release Update : 19.17.0.0.221018 (34419443)
29585399;OCW RELEASE UPDATE 19.3.0.0.0 (29585399)

OPatch succeeded
```

The primary database is orcldb, located in the east region. The following are the instance details:

```
SQL> @/home/oracle/database_info.sql

DATABASE_HOST         DB_NAME  DB_UNIQUE_NAME   DATABASE_ROLE  OPEN_MODE    STARTUP_TIME
--------------------  -------  ---------------  -------------  -----------  ----------------
prim01.localdomain    orcldb   orcldb           PRIMARY        READ WRITE   28-OCT-22
```

Physical Standby Database Server

We have two physical standby databases for this exercise.

The following are the details of the first physical standby database:

```
First Standby server : stbyh01.localdomain
OS version           : Oracle Enterprise Linux 7.1 64 bit
Oracle Home          : /u01/app/oracle/product/19.3.0.0/dbhome_1
Database Version      : 19.3.0.0 with October 2022 Database Bundle Patch

[oracle@stbyh01 ]$ export ORACLE_HOME=/u01/app/oracle/product/19.3.0.0/
dbhome_1
[oracle@stbyh01 ]$ export PATH=$ORACLE_HOME/bin:$PATH

[oracle@stbyh01 ~]$ $ORACLE_HOME/OPatch/opatch lspatches
34419443;Database Release Update : 19.17.0.0.221018 (34419443)
29585399;OCW RELEASE UPDATE 19.3.0.0.0 (29585399)

OPatch succeeded.
[oracle@stbyh01 ~]
```

The first physical standby database is orcldbp, and the region is south.

```
SQL> @/home/oracle/database_info.sql

DATABASE_HOST       DB_NAME DB_UNIQUE_NAME  DATABASE_ROLE    OPEN_MODE            STARTUP_TIME
------------------- ------- --------------- ---------------- -------------------- ------------
stbyh01.localdomain orcldb  orcldbp         PHYSICAL STANDBY READ ONLY WITH APPLY 26-OCT-22
```

Second Physical Standby Database Server

The following are the details of the second physical standby database used in this chapter:

```
Second Standby server : cstbyh01.localdomain
OS version            : Oracle Enterprise Linux 7.1 64 bit
Oracle Home           : /u01/app/oracle/product/19.3.0.0/dbhome_1
Database Version      : 19.3.0.0 with October 2022 Database Bundle Patch

[oracle@cstbyh01 ]$ export ORACLE_HOME=/u01/app/oracle/product/19.3.0.0/
dbhome_1
```

```
[oracle@cstbyh01 ]$ export PATH=$ORACLE_HOME/bin:$PATH
```

```
[oracle@stbyh01 ~]$ $ORACLE_HOME/OPatch/opatch lspatches
34419443;Database Release Update : 19.17.0.0.221018 (34419443)
29585399;OCW RELEASE UPDATE 19.3.0.0.0 (29585399)
```

```
OPatch succeeded.
[oracle@cstbyh01 ~]
```

The name of the second physical standby database is orcldbs, and the region is north.

```
SQL> @/home/oracle/database_info.sql
```

DATABASE_HOST	DB_NAME	DB_UNIQUE_NAME	DATABASE_ROLE	OPEN_MODE	STARTUP_TIME
cstbyh01.localdomain	orcldb	orcldbs	PHYSICAL STANDBY	READ ONLY WITH APPLY	26-OCT-22

Catalog Database Used in This Chapter

We have also created a catalog database named catgds on the same server, prim01, where we have our primary database running. The following is the catalog database information:

```
SQL> @/home/oracle/database_info.sql
```

DATABASE_HOST	DB_NAME	DB_UNIQUE_NAME	DATABASE_ROLE	OPEN_MODE	STARTUP_TIME
prim01.localdomain	catgds	catgds	PRIMARY	READ WRITE	28-OCT-22

To provide high availability for the catalog database, a physical standby database named catgdsdr has been set up. The following are the standby database details:

```
SQL> @/home/oracle/database_info.sql
```

DATABASE_HOST	DB_NAME	DB_UNIQUE_NAME	DATABASE_ROLE	OPEN_MODE	STARTUP_TIME
stbyh01.localdomain	catgds	catgdsdr	PHYSICAL STANDBY	READ ONLY WITH APPLY	28-OCT-22

Starting and Stopping GDS Components

In this section, you will see how to start a global service manager (GSM), how to connect to the catalog repository from the GSM, and also how to check the status of the services and the databases that are part of the GDS configuration.

Sourcing the GSM Environment

To start, stop, and manage the GDS components, you should use the GDSCTL utility, which is a command-line interface used for configuring and managing the GDS framework. To connect to the GDSCTL command-line interface, we must source the environment to point to the Oracle home directory of the GSM. We can do this by exporting the ORACLE_HOME and PATH variables and running GDSCTL at the operating system prompt, as shown here:

```
[oracle@prim01 ~]export ORACLE_HOME= /u01/app/oracle/product/19.3.0.0/
gsmhome_1
[oracle@prim01 ~]export ORACLE_BASE=/u01/app/oracle
[oracle@prim01 ~]export PATH=$ORACLE_HOME/bin:$PATH
[oracle@prim01 ~]$ gdsctl
GDSCTL: Version 19.0.0.0.0 - Production on Fri Oct 28 06:52:12 CDT 2022

Copyright (c) 2011, 2019, Oracle.  All rights reserved.

Welcome to GDSCTL, type "help" for information.

Current GSM is set to GSMEAST
GDSCTL>
```

We can also include the Oracle home directory of the GSM in the /etc/oratab directory, run the .oraenv command at the operating system prompt, and source the environment as we typically do for Oracle databases.

```
[oracle@prim01 ~]$ . oraenv
ORACLE_SID = [oracle] ? gsm
The Oracle base has been set to /u01/app/oracle
[oracle@prim01 ~]$ echo $ORACLE_HOME
/u01/app/oracle/product/19.3.0.0/gsm_1
[oracle@prim01 ~]$ gdsctl
```

```
GDSCTL: Version 19.0.0.0.0 - Production on Fri Oct 28 06:54:08 CDT 2022
Copyright (c) 2011, 2019, Oracle.  All rights reserved.

Welcome to GDSCTL, type "help" for information.

Current GSM is set to GSMEAST
GDSCTL>
```

Connecting to the Catalog

We can connect to the catalog repository from GDSCTL by using the command connect, as shown here:

```
GDSCTL> connect gsmcatuser/welcome@prim01:1521/CATGDS;
Catalog connection is established
GDSCTL>
```

Setting the Current GSM

Once we log in to the GDSCTL prompt, if we have to set the GSM to a specific GSM, we can do that using the set gsm -gsm gsmname command, as shown here:

```
GDSCTL> set gsm -gsm GSMEAST;
GDSCTL>
```

Starting the GSM

We can use the command start gsm -gsm gsmname to start the GSM. We must run this command from the server where the GSM is installed and from where we want the GSM to be started.

```
GDSCTL> start gsm -gsm GSMEAST;
GSM is started successfully
GDSCTL>
```

Checking the Status of GDS Components

We can check the status of any of the GDS components by using the status command. For example, to check the status of the GSM, we can use the status gsm -gsm gsmname command.

```
GDSCTL> status gsm -gsm GSMEAST
Alias                     gsmeast
Version                   19.0.0.0.0
Start Date                27-OCT-2022 19:05:08
Trace Level               off
Listener Log File         /u01/app/oracle/diag/gsm/prim01/gsmeast/
                          alert/log.xml
Listener Trace File       /u01/app/oracle/diag/gsm/prim01/gsmeast/trace/
                          ora_11036_139777818475584.trc
Endpoint summary          (ADDRESS=(HOST=prim01.localdomain)(PORT=1581)
                          (PROTOCOL=tcp))
GSMOCI Version            3.0.180702
Mastership                Y
Connected to GDS catalog  Y
Process Id                11039
Number of reconnections   0
Pending tasks.    Total   0
Tasks in  process. Total  0
Regional Mastership       TRUE
Total messages published  3
Time Zone                 -05:00
Orphaned Buddy Regions:
                          None
GDS region                east

GDSCTL>
```

Checking the GSM Configuration

We can use the `config gsm -gsm gsmname` command to get the configuration of the GSM.

```
GDSCTL> config gsm -gsm GSMEAST;
Name: gsmeast
Endpoint 1: (ADDRESS=(HOST=prim01.localdomain)(PORT=1581)(PROTOCOL=tcp))
Local ONS port: 6123
Remote ONS port: 6234
ORACLE_HOME path: /u01/app/oracle/product/19.3.0.0/gsmhome_1
GSM Host name: prim01.localdomain
Region: east

Buddy
-----------------------

GDSCTL>
```

As you can see, we don't have a buddy region set for this region. We will come to that part later in this chapter. We have one test case where we will explore this option.

To find and check the databases that are part of this GSM configuration, we can run the `databases` command from GDSCTL.

```
GDSCTL> databases;
Database: "orcldb" Registered: Y State: Ok ONS: N. Role: PRIMARY Instances:
1 Region: east
   Registered instances:
     sales%1
Database: "orcldbp" Registered: Y State: Ok ONS: N. Role: PH_STNDBY
Instances: 1 Region: north
   Registered instances:
     sales%11
Database: "orcldbs" Registered: Y State: Ok ONS: N. Role: PH_STNDBY
Instances: 1 Region: south
   Registered instances:
     sales%21
GDSCTL>
```

We have successfully started and validated the GSM in the east region, which is running on the primary database server. Let's move to the standby database servers where we have two GSMs that need to be started.

Starting the GSM Named gsmnorth

We will now start the gsmnorth GSM, which is configured on the first physical database server, stbyh01. Set the GSM environment to the first GSM home in the physical database server.

```
[oracle@stbyh01 ~]$ . oraenv
ORACLE_SID = [gsm] ?
The Oracle base remains unchanged with value /u01/app/oracle
[oracle@stbyh01 ~]$ echo $ORACLE_HOME
/u01/app/oracle/product/19.3.0.0/gsmhome_1
[oracle@stbyh01 ~]$ gdsctl
GDSCTL: Version 19.0.0.0.0 - Production on Fri Oct 28 06:56:51 CDT 2022

Copyright (c) 2011, 2019, Oracle.  All rights reserved.

Welcome to GDSCTL, type "help" for information.

Current GSM is set to GSMNORTH
GDSCTL>
```

Starting the GSM

Here's how to start the GSM:

```
GDSCTL>start gsm -gsm GSMNORTH
GSM is started successfully
GDSCTL>
```

Checking the Status of the GSM

Here's how to check the status of the GSM:

```
GDSCTL> status gsm -gsm GSMNORTH;
Alias                    gsmnorth
Version                  19.0.0.0.0
Start Date               27-OCT-2022 19:06:01
Trace Level              off
Listener Log File        /u01/app/oracle/diag/gsm/stbyh01/gsmnorth/
                         alert/log.xml
Listener Trace File      /u01/app/oracle/diag/gsm/stbyh01/gsmnorth/trace/
                         ora_22969_140311640628288.trc
Endpoint summary         (ADDRESS=(HOST=stbyh01.localdomain)(PORT=1582)
                         (PROTOCOL=tcp))
GSMOCI Version           3.0.180702
Mastership               N
Connected to GDS catalog Y
Process Id               22972
Number of reconnections  0
Pending tasks.    Total  0
Tasks in  process. Total 0
Regional Mastership      TRUE
Total messages published 3
Time Zone                -05:00
Orphaned Buddy Regions:
    None
GDS region               north
Network metrics:
  Region: east Network factor:0

GDSCTL>
```

Starting the GSM Named gsmsouth

We will now start the gsmsouth GSM, which is configured on the second physical standby database server, cstbyh01. Set the GSM environment to the second GSM home in the physical database server and connect to the GDSCTL command line.

```
[oracle@cstbyh01 ~]$ . oraenv
ORACLE_SID = [gsm] ? gsm
The Oracle base remains unchanged with value /u01/app/oracle
[oracle@cstbyh01 ~]$ gdsctl
GDSCTL: Version 19.0.0.0.0 - Production on Fri Oct 28 07:05:49 CDT 2022

Copyright © 2011, 2019, Oracle.  All rights reserved.

Welcome to GDSCTL, ty"e "h"lp" for information.

Current GSM is set to GSMSOUTH
GDSCTL>
```

Setting the Current GSM

Here's how to set the current GSM:

```
GDSCTL>set gsm -gsm GSMSOUTH
GDSCTL>
```

Starting the GSM

Here's how to start the GSM:

```
GDSCTL>start gsm -gsm GSMSOUTH
GSM is started successfully
GDSCTL>
```

Checking the Status of the GSM

Here's how to check the status of the GSM:

```
GDSCTL> status gsm -gsm GSMSOUTH
Alias                       gsmsouth
Version                     19.0.0.0.0
Start Date                  27-OCT-2022 19:06:48
Trace Level                 off
Listener Log File           /u01/app/oracle/diag/gsm/cstbyh01/gsmsouth/
                            alert/log.xml
Listener Trace File         /u01/app/oracle/diag/gsm/cstbyh01/gsmsouth/trace/
                            ora_22756_140376848170048.trc
Endpoint summary            (ADDRESS=(HOST=cstbyh01.localdomain)(PORT=1583)
                            (PROTOCOL=tcp))
GSMOCI Version              3.0.180702
Mastership                  N
Connected to GDS catalog    Y
Process Id                  22759
Number of reconnections     0
Pending tasks.     Total    0
Tasks in  process. Total    0
Regional Mastership         TRUE
Total messages published    3
Time Zone                   -05:00
Orphaned Buddy Regions:
    None
GDS region                  south
Network metrics:
   Region: north Network factor:0
   Region: east Network factor:0
GDSCTL>
```

We have successfully started and validated that all the GSMs are up and running.

GDSpool Databases

Before looking at different test scenarios, we must make sure that all the gdspool databases that are part of the GSM configuration are up. In this case, please make sure that the primary and both the physical standby databases are up and that the physical standby databases are in sync with the primary database. Also, make sure that the Data Guard broker configuration looks good without any issues.

Log in to the primary database, `orcldb`, as SYSDBA.

```
SQL> @/home/oracle/database_info.sql
```

DATABASE_HOST	DB_NAME	DB_UNIQUE_NAME	DATABASE_ROLE	OPEN_MODE	STARTUP_TIME
prim01.localdomain	orcldb	orcldb	PRIMARY	READ WRITE	27-OCT-22

```
SQL>
```

Log in to the first physical standby database, `orcldbp`, as SYSDBA.

```
SQL>@/home/oracle/database_info.sql;
```

DATABASE_HOST	DB_NAME	DB_UNIQUE_NAME	DATABASE_ROLE	OPEN_MODE	STARTUP_TIME
stbyh01.localdomain	orcldb	orcldbp	PHYSICAL STANDBY	READ ONLY WITH APPLY	27-OCT-22

Log in to the second physical standby database, `orcldbs`, as SYSDBA.

```
SQL> @/home/oracle/database_info.sql;
```

DATABASE_HOST	DB_NAME	DB_UNIQUE_NAME	DATABASE_ROLE	OPEN_MODE	STARTUP_TIME
cstbyh01.localdomain	orcldb	orcldbs	PHYSICAL STANDBY	READ ONLY WITH APPLY	27-OCT-22

```
SQL>
```

Make sure that the Data Guard broker configuration looks good, and validate each of the databases to ensure that they are in sync with the primary database.

```
[oracle@prim01 ~]$ dgmgrl

DGMGRL> connect sys/welcome
Connected to "orcldb"
Connected as SYSDBA.
DGMGRL> show configuration;
```

Configuration - orcldbcfg

  Protection Mode: MaxPerformance
  Members:
  orcldb - Primary database
    orcldbp - Physical standby database
    orcldbs - Physical standby database

Fast-Start Failover: Disabled

Configuration Status:
SUCCESS   (status updated 10 seconds ago)

DGMGRL>

    From the DGMGRL command line, run validate database for the primary database, orcldb.

DGMGRL> validate database orcldb

  Database Role: Primary database

  Ready for Switchover: Yes

  Flashback Database Status:
    orcldb: Off

  Managed by Clusterware:
    orcldb: NO
    Validating static connect identifier for the primary database orcldb...
    The static connect identifier allows for a connection to database
    "orcldb".

DGMGRL>

    From the DGMGRL command line, run validate database for the physical standby database, orcldbp.

DGMGRL> validate database orcldbp

  Database Role: Physical standby database
  Primary Database: orcldb

```
  Ready for Switchover:  Yes
  Ready for Failover:    Yes (Primary Running)

  Flashback Database Status:
    orcldb : Off
    orcldbp: Off

  Managed by Clusterware:
    orcldb : NO
    orcldbp: NO
    Validating static connect identifier for the primary database orcldb...
    The static connect identifier allows for a connection to database
    "orcldb".

DGMGRL>
```

From the DGMGRL command line, run validate database for the physical standby database, orcldbs.

```
DGMGRL> validate database orcldbs;

  Database Role:      Physical standby database
  Primary Database:   orcldb

  Ready for Switchover:  Yes
  Ready for Failover:    Yes (Primary Running)

  Flashback Database Status:
    orcldb : Off
    orcldbs: Off

  Managed by Clusterware:
    orcldb : NO
    orcldbs: NO
    Validating static connect identifier for the primary database orcldb...
    The static connect identifier allows for a connection to database
    "orcldb".

DGMGRL>
```

To do a physical standby database lag check, check to ensure that both the physical standby databases are in sync with the primary database.

Log in to the first physical standby database, orcldbp, as SYSDBA and check for the lag information.

```
[oracle@stbyh01 ~]$ sqlplus / as sysdba

SQL>@/home/oracle/standby_database_lag.sql;
```

DATABASE_HOST	DB_NAME	DB_UNIQUE_NAME	DATABASE_ROLE	OPEN_MODE	STARTUP_TIME
stbyh01.localdomain	orcldb	orcldbp	PHYSICAL STANDBY	READ ONLY WITH APPLY	28-OCT-22

INST_ID	PROCESS	STATUS	THREAD#	SEQUENCE#	BLOCK#	BLOCKS
1	MRP0	APPLYING_LOG	1	19	65372	409600

THREAD#	ARCHIVED	APPLIED	GAP
1	18	18	0

Log in to the second physical standby database. Do a lag check on the standby database, orcldbs, as SYSDBA.

```
[oracle@cstbyh01 ~]$ sqlplus / as sysdba

SQL> @/home/oracle/standby_database_lag.sql;
```

DATABASE_HOST	DB_NAME	DB_UNIQUE_NAME	DATABASE_ROLE	OPEN_MODE	STARTUP_TIME
cstbyh01.localdomain	orcldb	orcldbs	PHYSICAL STANDBY	READ ONLY WITH APPLY	28-OCT-22

INST_ID	PROCESS	STATUS	THREAD#	SEQUENCE#	BLOCK#	BLOCKS
1	MRP0	APPLYING_LOG	1	19	65586	409600

THREAD#	ARCHIVED	APPLIED	GAP
1	18	18	0

```
SQL>
```

Summary of This Section

In this section, we saw how to set up the GSM and start and check the status of GSMs. You also saw how to check the configured gdspool databases that are part of the GSM configuration. We also ensured that the Data Guard broker configuration looks good and that both the physical standby databases are in sync with the primary database. In the next section, we will demonstrate the first test case scenario.

Test Case: Global Service Failover

In mission-critical environments, all the reporting and batch jobs will generally be connected to the physical standby database through a database service instead of connecting to the primary database to reduce the workloads on the primary database. Now if the physical standby database goes down, the respective services will also go down, impacting the application connections. In the GDS framework, we can avoid this kind of scenario by creating the services globally by using the Oracle GDS framework.

In this test case, we will create a global service with the role `physical_standby` so that the service will run only on the available physical standby databases. If all the available physical standby databases become unavailable, then the service will automatically failover to the primary database. This is achieved by adding the option `failover_primary` while creating this service.

When all the physical standby databases are not available, then the service will failover to the primary database automatically. The following are the high-level steps performed as part of this test case demonstration.

High-Level Steps of This Test Case

Here are the steps (see Figure 6-1):

1. Connect to the catalog from the GSM running on the primary database server.

2. Set the GSM to `gsmeast` and check the status of the databases and services from `GSDCTL`.

3. Create a service named `sales_reporting_srvc` with the previously mentioned options.

4. Check the services from GDSCTL to see if the service was created as expected.

5. Define the TNS alias for this service, sales_reporting_srvc.

6. Connect to the database using the service sales_reporting_srvc and see to which standby database it's connecting.

7. Shut down the first standby database and see if we are still able to connect the service as it connects to the second standby database.

8. Shut down the second standby database.

9. Connect to the database using the service and see if the service failover to the primary database as both (all) the physical standby databases are not available.

10. Start both the physical standby databases.

11. Now check the services again; they should be running only on the physical standby databases.

12. Remove the service sales_reporting_srvc from the GDSCTL command prompt.

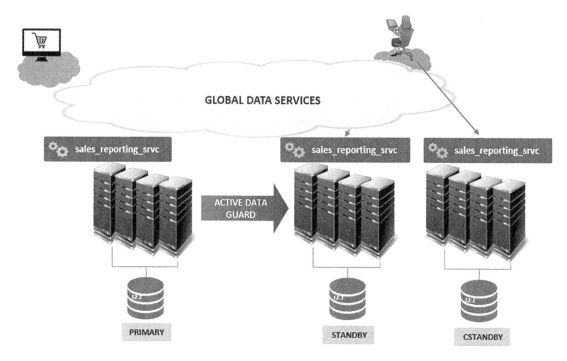

Figure 6-1. *Test case Global_dataservice_failover*

Prerequisites

Before starting this test case, we need to make sure that all the gdspool databases, GSMs, and the catalog database are up and running without any issues.

Logging In to the GDS Catalog

Log in to the primary database server and log in to the GDS catalog.

```
[oracle@prim01 ~]$ . oraenv
ORACLE_SID = [oracle] ? gsm
The Oracle base remains unchanged with value /u01/app/oracle
[oracle@prim01 ~]$ echo $ORACLE_HOME
/u01/app/oracle/product/19.3.0.0/gsm_1
[oracle@prim01 ~]$ gdsctl
GDSCTL: Version 19.0.0.0.0 - Production on Sat Aug 14 10:15:31 CDT 2021
```

Welcome to GDSCTL, type "help" for information.

Current GSM is set to GSMEAST
GDSCTL>

As we can see from the previous output, GSM is already set to GSMEAST, which is running on node 1.

Connecting to the GDS Catalog

Do the following:

```
GDSCTL> connect gsmcatuser/welcome@prim01:1521/CATGDS;
Catalog connection is established
GDSCTL>
```

Checking the Status of the GSM gsmeast

Do the following:

```
GDSCTL> status gsm -gsm GSMEAST
Alias                    GSMEAST
Version                  19.0.0.0.0
Start Date               28-OCT-2022 13:09:09
Trace Level              off
Listener Log File        /u01/app/oracle/diag/gsm/prim01/gsmeast/
                         alert/log.xml
Listener Trace File      /u01/app/oracle/diag/gsm/prim01/gsmeast/trace/
                         ora_8527_140702770981952.trc
Endpoint summary         (ADDRESS=(HOST=prim01.localdomain)(PORT=1581)
(PROTOCOL=tcp))
GSMOCI Version           3.0.180702
Mastership               Y
Connected to GDS catalog Y
Process Id               8530
Number of reconnections  0
```

```
Pending tasks.      Total  0
Tasks in  process. Total  0
Regional Mastership        TRUE
Total messages published  3
Time Zone                  -05:00
Orphaned Buddy Regions:
     None
GDS region                 east
Network metrics:
   Region: south Network factor:0
   Region: north Network factor:0

GDSCTL>
```

Checking the Status of the Databases

Do the following:

```
GDSCTL> databases;
Database: "orcldb" Registered: Y State: Ok ONS: N. Role: PRIMARY Instances:
1 Region: east
   Registered instances:
     sales%1
Database: "orcldbp" Registered: Y State: Ok ONS: N. Role: PH_STNDBY
Instances: 1 Region: north
   Registered instances:
     sales%11
Database: "orcldbs" Registered: Y State: Ok ONS: N. Role: PH_STNDBY
Instances: 1 Region: south
   Registered instances:
     sales%21
GDSCTL>
```

Checking the Current Configured Services

Do the following:

```
GDSCTL> services;
GDSCTL>
```

Checking the Current gdspool in the GSM Configuration

Do the following:

```
GDSCTL> config gdspool
Name                            Broker                  Sharded
----                            ------                  -------
dbpoolora                       No                      No
hr                              No                      No
sales                           Yes                     No

GDSCTL>
```

Checking the Configuration of the Regions

Do the following:

```
GDSCTL> config region;
Name                            Buddy
----                            -----
east
north
south

GDSCTL>
```

Creating a Role-Based Global Data Service

We will create a service called sales_reporting_srvc with the options -preferred_all and -failover_primary, which should always run on the physical standby database. In the event where all the physical standby databases are not available, then the service can automatically failover to the primary database.

```
GDSCTL> add service -service sales_reporting_srvc -gdspool sales
-preferred_all -role PHYSICAL_STANDBY -failover_primary
The operation completed successfully

GDSCTL>
```

Now if we run the commands config services and databases from the GDSCTL command prompt, we can see that the service has been created but not started yet.

```
GDSCTL> config service
```

Name	Network name	Pool	Started	Preferred all
sales_reportin g_srvc	sales_reporting_srvc.sales.or adbcloud	sales	No	Yes

```
GDSCTL> databases;        ⟸
Database: "orcldb" Registered: Y State: Ok ONS: N. Role:
PRIMARY Instances: 1 Region: east
   Service: "sales_reporting_srvc" Globally started: N Started: N
          Scan: Y Enabled: Y Preferred: Y
   Registered instances:
     sales%1
Database: "orcldbp" Registered: Y State: Ok ONS: N. Role: PH_STNDBY
Instances: 1 Region: north
   Service: "sales_reporting_srvc" Globally started: N Started: N
          Scan: Y Enabled: Y Preferred: Y
   Registered instances:
     sales%11
```

```
Database: "orcldbs" Registered: Y State: Ok ONS: N. Role: PH_STNDBY
Instances: 1 Region: south
    Service: "sales_reporting_srvc" Globally started: N Started: N
            Scan: Y Enabled: Y Preferred: Y
    Registered instances:
      sales%21

GDSCTL>
```

Starting the Service

We can start the service using the start service command.

```
GDSCTL> start service -service sales_reporting_srvc -gdspool sales;
The operation completed successfully
```

Execute the command services from the GDSCTL command prompt. We can see the status of the service including the databases on which the service is currently running and accepting the client connections.

```
GDSCTL> services
Service "sales_reporting_srvc.sales.oradbcloud" has 2 instance(s).
Affinity: ANYWHERE
    Instance "sales%11", name: "orcldbp", db: "orcldbp", region: "north",
    status: ready.
    Instance "sales%21", name: "orcldbs", db: "orcldbs", region: "south",
    status: ready.

GDSCTL>
```

Please note that if the gdspool databases are RAC databases, once we add the service, we must modify the service configuration and include all the instances of each gdspool databases as shown here:

```
GDSCTL> modify service -service sales_reporting_srvc -gdspool sales
-database dbname -modify_instances -preferred instance1,instance2;
The operation completed successfully
```

Checking the Status of the Database

Execute the command databases from the GDSCTL command prompt. We can see that the service is available and started in both the physical standby databases. The service is also available in the primary database, but it is not started there. In the following output, we can check for the Started entity to see where the service is started:

```
GDSCTL> databases
Database: "orcldb" Registered: Y State: Ok ONS: N. Role: PRIMARY Instances:
1 Region: east
   Service: "sales_reporting_srvc" Globally started: Y Started: N
           Scan: Y Enabled: Y Preferred: Y
   Registered instances:
     sales%1
Database: "orcldbp" Registered: Y State: Ok ONS: N. Role: PH_STNDBY
Instances: 1 Region: north
   Service: "sales_reporting_srvc" Globally started: Y Started: Y
           Scan: Y Enabled: Y Preferred: Y
   Registered instances:
     sales%11
Database: "orcldbs" Registered: Y State: Ok ONS: N. Role: PH_STNDBY
Instances: 1 Region: south
   Service: "sales_reporting_srvc" Globally started: Y Started: Y
           Scan: Y Enabled: Y Preferred: Y
   Registered instances:
     sales%21

GDSCTL>
```

Checking the Configuration of the Service

To get the configuration information of a given service, execute the config service command, as shown here:

```
GDSCTL> config service -service sales_reporting_srvc;
Name: sales_reporting_srvc
Network name: sales_reporting_srvc.sales.oradbcloud
Pool: sales
```

Started: Yes
Preferred all: Yes
Locality: ANYWHERE
Region Failover: No
Role: PHYSICAL_STANDBY
Primary Failover: Yes
Lag: ANY
Runtime Balance: SERVICE_TIME
Connection Balance: LONG
Notification: Yes
TAF Policy: NONE
Policy: AUTOMATIC
DTP: No
Failover Method: NONE
Failover Type: NONE
Failover Retries:
Failover Delay:
Edition:
PDB:
Commit Outcome:
Retention Timeout:
Replay Initiation Timeout:
Session State Consistency:
SQL Translation Profile:
Stop option: NONE
Drain timeout:
Table family:

Databases

Database	Preferred	Status
orcldb	Yes	Enabled
orcldbp	Yes	Enabled
orcldbs	Yes	Enabled

GDSCTL>

Execute the `config` command without any options; it will display the configuration information of all the components that are part of a given GDS configuration.

```
GDSCTL> config

Regions
-----------------------
east
north ·
south

GSMs
-----------------------
gsmeast
gsmnorth
gsmsouth

GDS pools
-----------------------
dbpoolora
hr
sales

Databases
-----------------------
orcldb
orcldbp
orcldbs

Services
-----------------------
sales_reporting_srvc

GDSCTL pending requests
-----------------------
Command                         Object                          Status
-------                         ------                          ------
```

```
Global properties
-----------------------
Name: oradbcloud
Master GSM: gsmsouth
DDL sequence #: 0

GDSCTL>
```

Checking the Active Services in the Database orcldb

Now that the global service has been created and started, we can query the database system views, dba_services and v$active_services, to learn more about the global services.

Check the service status in the primary database to see if the service shows up because our aim is to create a service that will failover to the primary database only when physical standby databases are not available, so initially the service status will show as down in the primary database. Execute the following dba_services view to check the status of the service in the primary database:

```
[oracle@prim01 ~]$ sqlplus / as sysdba

SQL*Plus: Release 19.0.0.0.0 - Production on Fri Oct 28 13:44:02 2022
Version 19.17.0.0.0

Copyright (c) 1982, 2022, Oracle.  All rights reserved.

Connected to:
Oracle Database 19c Enterprise Edition Release 19.0.0.0.0 - Production
Version 19.17.0.0.0

SQL> column name format a20
SQL> column network_name format a40
SQL> column global_service a19
SQL> set linesize 120
SQL> col global for a10
SQL> select name, network_name, global_service from dba_services;
```

```
NAME                      NETWORK_NAME                          GLOBAL_SERVICE
----------------------    ------------------------------------  --------------
SYS$BACKGROUND                                                  NO
SYS$USERS                                                       NO
orcldb_CFG                orcldb_CFG                            NO
sales_reporting_srvc      sales_reporting_srvc.sales.oradbcloud YES
orcldbXDB                 orcldbXDB                             NO
orcldb                    orcldb                                NO

6 rows selected.
```

From the previous output, we can see that, for sales_reporting_srvc, the value of the column GLOBAL_SERVICE is Yes, denoting that it is a global service.

Now if we query v$active_services in the primary database (orcldb), we can see that the global service, sales_reporting_srvc, is not listed, indicating that it is not started in the primary database.

```
SQL> select name, network_name, global from v$active_services;

NAME                      NETWORK_NAME                            GLOBAL
----------------------    ------------------------------------    -------
orcldb                    orcldb                                  NO
SYS$BACKGROUND                                                    NO
SYS$USERS                                                         NO
orcldb_CFG                orcldb_CFG                              NO
orcldbXDB                 orcldbXDB                               NO

SQL>
```

Now let's check the active services in the physical standby databases, orcldbp and orcldbs.

Log in to the first physical standby database, orcldbp, and check the status of the service.

```
[oracle@stbyh01 ~]$ . oraenv
ORACLE_SID = [orcldbp] ?
The Oracle base remains unchanged with value /u01/app/oracle
[oracle@stbyh01 ~]$ sqlplus / as sysdba

SQL*Plus: Release 19.0.0.0.0 - Production on Fri Oct 28 13:46:15 2022
Version 19.17.0.0.0
```

Connected to:
Oracle Database 19c Enterprise Edition Release 19.0.0.0.0 - Production
Version 19.17.0.0.0

```
SQL> column name format a20
SQL> column network_name format a40
SQL> column global_service a19
SQL> set linesize 120
SQL> col global for a10
SQL> select name, network_name, global_service from dba_services;

NAME                 NETWORK_NAME                             GLOBAL_SERVICE
-------------------- ---------------------------------------- ----------------
SYS$BACKGROUND                                                NO
SYS$USERS                                                     NO
orcldb_CFG           orcldb_CFG                               NO
sales_reporting_srvc sales_reporting_srvc.sales.oradbcloud    YES
orcldbXDB            orcldbXDB                                NO
orcldb               orcldb                                   NO

6 rows selected.

SQL>

SQL> select name, network_name, global from v$active_services;

NAME                 NETWORK_NAME                             GLOBAL
-------------------- ---------------------------------------- ---------
SYS$BACKGROUND                                                NO
sales_reporting_srvc sales_reporting_srvc.sales.oradbcloud    YES    <------
SYS$USERS                                                     NO
orcldb_CFG           orcldb_CFG                               NO
orcldbXDB            orcldbXDB                                NO

SQL>
```

As you can see from the previous output, the global data service sales_reporting_srvc is started and running in the physical standby database, orcldbp. Let's check the status of the service in another physical standby database, orcldbs.

```
[oracle@cstbyh01 ~]$ . oraenv
ORACLE_SID = [orcldbs] ?
The Oracle base remains unchanged with value /u01/app/oracle
[oracle@cstbyh01 ~]$ sqlplus / as sysdba

SQL*Plus: Release 19.0.0.0.0 - Production on Fri Oct 28 13:47:57 2022
Version 19.17.0.0.0

Copyright (c) 1982, 2022, Oracle.  All rights reserved.

Connected to:
Oracle Database 19c Enterprise Edition Release 19.0.0.0.0 - Production
Version 19.17.0.0.0

SQL> column name format a20
SQL> column network_name format a40
SQL> column global_service a19
SQL> set linesize 120
SQL> col global for a10
SQL> select name, network_name, global_service from dba_services;

NAME                 NETWORK_NAME                             GLOBAL_SERVICE
-------------------- ---------------------------------------- --------------
SYS$BACKGROUND                                                NO
SYS$USERS                                                     NO
orcldb_CFG           orcldb_CFG                               NO
sales_reporting_srvc sales_reporting_srvc.sales.oradbcloud    YES
orcldbXDB            orcldbXDB                                NO
orcldb               orcldb                                   NO

6 rows selected.

SQL>
SQL> select name, network_name, global from v$active_services;
```

NAME	NETWORK_NAME	GLOBAL
SYS$BACKGROUND		NO
sales_reporting_srvc	sales_reporting_srvc.sales.oradbcloud	YES
SYS$USERS		NO
orcldb_CFG	orcldb_CFG	NO
orcldbXDB	orcldbXDB	NO

```
SQL>
```

So, we can see that the service is running only on the databases that have the role PHYSICAL_STANDBY.

Testing the Database Connection Using the Service sales_reporting_srvc

Create a TNS entry for this service and test the database connection. The following is the TNS entry for the global service sales_reporting_srvc:

```
sales_reporting_srvc =
  (DESCRIPTION =
    (FAILOVER = ON)
    (ADDRESS_LIST =
      (LOAD_BALANCE = ON)
      (ADDRESS = (PROTOCOL = TCP)(HOST = prim01)(PORT = 1581)))
    (ADDRESS_LIST =
      (LOAD_BALANCE = ON)
      (ADDRESS = (PROTOCOL = TCP)(HOST = stbyh01)(PORT = 1582)))
    (ADDRESS_LIST =
      (LOAD_BALANCE = ON)
      (ADDRESS = (PROTOCOL = TCP)(HOST = cstbyh01)(PORT = 1583)))
    (CONNECT_DATA =
      (SERVICE_NAME = sales_reporting_srvc.sales.oradbcloud)
      (REGION = east)
    )
  )
```

In the previous TNS entry, SERVICE_NAME is the name of the global service, and REGION is the region from which the client connection is coming. The connection string also has the port information in which 1581 is the GSM listener port on prim01, 1582 is the GSM1 listener port on stbyh01, and 1583 is the port of the GSM2 listener on cstbyh01.

Note   The connect descriptor in tnsnames.ora in a GDS configuration will be using the GSM listener endpoints and not the local listeners or the RAC scan listeners.

We can test the database connection using the previous TNS alias, as shown here:

```
[oracle@cstbyh01 ~]$ sqlplus system/welcome@sales_reporting_srvc

SQL*Plus: Release 19.0.0.0.0 - Production on Sat Oct 29 20:22:49 2022
Version 19.17.0.0.0

Copyright (c) 1982, 2022, Oracle.  All rights reserved.

Last Successful login time: Sat Oct 29 2022 19:45:05 -05:00

Connected to:
Oracle Database 19c Enterprise Edition Release 19.0.0.0.0 - Production
Version 19.17.0.0.0

SQL> @/home/oracle/database_info.sql
```

DATABASE_HOST	DB_NAME	DB_UNIQUE_NAME	DATABASE_ROLE	OPEN_MODE	STARTUP_TIME
cstbyh01.localdomain	orcldb	orcldbs	PHYSICAL STANDBY	READ ONLY WITH APPLY	29-OCT-22

As you can see, the service is routed to one of the available physical standby databases; in this case, it is connected to the physical standby database orcldbs. Now if we stop this physical standby database, the connection will go to another physical standby database, orcldbp.

Shutting Down the Physical Standby Databases

Let's shut down both the physical standby databases, orcldbp and orcldbs.

First shut down the first physical standby database, orcldbp.

```
[oracle@stbyh01 admin]$ . oraenv
ORACLE_SID = [orcldbp] ?
The Oracle base remains unchanged with value /u01/app/oracle
[oracle@stbyh01 admin]$ sqlplus / as sysdba

SQL*Plus: Release 19.0.0.0.0 - Production on Sat Oct 29 09:03:04 2022
Version 19.17.0.0.0

Copyright (c) 1982, 2022, Oracle.  All rights reserved.

Connected to:
Oracle Database 19c Enterprise Edition Release 19.0.0.0.0 - Production
Version 19.17.0.0.0

SQL>shut immediate;
Database closed.
Database dismounted.
ORACLE instance shut down.
SQL>
```

We will now shut down the second physical standby database, orcldbs also.

```
[oracle@cstbyh01 admin]$ . oraenv
ORACLE_SID = [orcldbs] ?
The Oracle base remains unchanged with value /u01/app/oracle
[oracle@cstbyh01 admin]$ sqlplus / as sysdba

SQL*Plus: Release 19.0.0.0.0 - Production on Sat Oct 29 09:04:15 2022
Version 19.17.0.0.0

Copyright (c) 1982, 2022, Oracle.  All rights reserved.

Connected to:
Oracle Database 19c Enterprise Edition Release 19.0.0.0.0 - Production
Version 19.17.0.0.0
```

```
SQL>shutdown immediate;
Database closed.
Database dismounted.
ORACLE instance shut down.
SQL>
```

After shutting down both the physical standby databases, execute the services command, and we can see that the service had a failover to the primary database.

Below is the status of the services before and after stopping the physical standby databases.

Check the status of the service, sales_reporting_srvc, when both the physical standby databases are up and running.

```
GDSCTL> services
Service "sales_reporting_srvc.sales.oradbcloud" has 2 instance(s).
Affinity: ANYWHERE
    Instance "sales%11", name: "orcldbp", db: "orcldbp", region: "north",
    status: ready.
    Instance "sales%21", name: "orcldbs", db: "orcldbs", region: "south",
    status: ready.

GDSCTL>
```

Check the status of the service, sales_reporting_srvc, when both the physical standby databases are shut down.

```
GDSCTL> services
Service "sales_reporting_srvc.sales.oradbcloud" has 1 instance(s).
Affinity: ANYWHERE
    Instance "sales%1", name: "orcldb", db: "orcldb", region: "east",
    status: ready.

GDSCTL>
```

Now, if we connect using the same service, sales_reporting_srvc, it should connect to the primary database, orcldb, because both the physical standby databases are not available.

```
[oracle@cstbyh01 ~]$ sqlplus system/welcome@sales_reporting_srvc

SQL*Plus: Release 19.0.0.0.0 - Production on Sat Oct 29 09:05:46 2022
Version 19.17.0.0.0

Copyright (c) 1982, 2022, Oracle.  All rights reserved.

Last Successful login time: Sat Oct 29 2022 08:03:58 -05:00

Connected to:
Oracle Database 19c Enterprise Edition Release 19.0.0.0.0 - Production
Version 19.17.0.0.0

SQL> @/home/oracle/rac_database_info.sql
```

DATABASE_HOST	DB_NAME	DB_UNIQUE_NAME	DATABASE_ROLE	OPEN_MODE	STARTUP_TIME
prim01.localdomain	orcldb	orcldb	PRIMARY	READ WRITE	29-OCT-22

From the previous output, we can see that the service, sales_reporting_srvc, has automatically failed over to the primary database (orcldb).

Starting Both the Standby Databases

We can start both the physical standby databases and see if the service will come to the phyical standby databases.

Execute the following commands to start the first physical standby database, orcldbp:

```
[oracle@stbyh01 admin]$ sqlplus / as sysdba

SQL*Plus: Release 19.0.0.0.0 - Production on Sat Oct 29 09:06:38 2022
Version 19.17.0.0.0
```

Start Connected to an idle instance.

```
SQL> startup;
ORACLE instance started.

Total System Global Area 3053449816 bytes
Fixed Size                   8901208 bytes
Variable Size              620756992 bytes
Database Buffers          2415919104 bytes
Redo Buffers                 7872512 bytes
Database mounted.
Database opened.
SQL>
```

Execute the following commands to start the second physical standby database, orcldbs:

```
[oracle@cstbyh01 admin]$ sqlplus / as sysdba

SQL*Plus: Release 19.0.0.0.0 - Production on Sat Oct 29 09:06:50 2022
Version 19.17.0.0.0
```

```
Connected to an idle instance.

SQL> startup;
ORACLE instance started.

Total System Global Area 3053449816 bytes
Fixed Size                   8901208 bytes
Variable Size              620756992 bytes
Database Buffers          2415919104 bytes
Redo Buffers                 7872512 bytes
Database mounted.
Database opened.
SQL>
```

Now, check the status of the service again from the GDSCTL command prompt.

The following is the output of the GDSCTL command services when both the physical standby databases are down:

```
GDSCTL> services
Service "sales_reporting_srvc.sales.oradbcloud" has 1 instance(s).
Affinity: ANYWHERE
    Instance "sales%1", name: "orcldb", db: "orcldb", region: "east",
    status: ready.
GDSCTL>
```

The following is the output of the GDSCTL command services when both the physical standby databases are started. We can see that the service failed over from the primary database to the physical standby database automatically.

```
GDSCTL> services
Service "sales_reporting_srvc.sales.oradbcloud" has 2 instance(s).
Affinity: ANYWHERE
    Instance "sales%11", name: "orcldbp", db: "orcldbp", region: "north",
    status: ready.
    Instance "sales%21", name: "orcldbs", db: "orcldbs", region: "south",
    status: ready.
GDSCTL>
```

If we connect to the database using the service, it will connect to one of the available physical standby databases.

```
[oracle@stbyh01 ~]$ sqlplus system/welcome@sales_reporting_srvc

SQL*Plus: Release 19.0.0.0.0 - Production on Sat Oct 29 20:33:19 2022
Version 19.17.0.0.0

Copyright (c) 1982, 2022, Oracle.  All rights reserved.

Last Successful login time: Sat Oct 29 2022 19:45:05 -05:00

Connected to:
Oracle Database 19c Enterprise Edition Release 19.0.0.0.0 - Production
Version 19.17.0.0.0
```

```
SQL> @/home/oracle/database_info.sql

DATABASE_HOST        DB_NAME  DB_UNIQUE_NAME  DATABASE_ROLE     OPEN_MODE             STARTUP_TIME
-------------------  -------  --------------  ----------------  --------------------  ------------
stbyh01.localdomain  orcldb   orcldbp         PHYSICAL STANDBY  READ ONLY WITH APPLY  29-OCT-22
```

As we saw, the service failed over to the physical standby database as soon as they became available. This completes the demonstration of this test case. We can stop the service and remove the service created for this test case.

```
GDSCTL>stop service -service sales_reporting_srvc -gdspool sales
The operation completed successfully

GDSCTL>remove service -gdspool sales -service sales_reporting_srvc
The operation completed successfully
GDSCTL>
```

Summary of This Test Case

This test case illustrated the automatic global service failover capability of Oracle GDS. We saw that as soon as all the physical standby databases became unavailable, GDS failed over to the primary database and then failed back as soon as the physical standby databases were available. Let's check out one more test case of GDS.

Test Case: Role-Based Global Services

In this test case, you will see that when a Data Guard role transition is performed either manually using a Data Guard broker or via fast-start failover, the global data service will automatically relocate the global services based on the role of the databases. GDS does this without the Oracle clusterware. To demonstrate how the role-based GDS function works, we will create a GDS service named srvc_prim that is configured to run only on the primary database. We will then perform the Data Guard switchover operation, making one of the physical standby databases as a primary, and we will observe that upon the role change, the global service srvc_prim automatically gets relocated to the new primary database.

High-Level Steps of This Test Case

Here are the steps:

1. Make sure that all the GSMs in all the regions are up and running.

2. Check that all the databases are up and running and ensure that both the physical standby databases are in sync with the primary database.

3. Check the status of the Data Guard broker configuration and run the `validate database` commands for each of the databases in the broker configuration to make sure that the status of all the databases looks good.

4. Create and start a global data service named `srvc_prim` to run on the primary database.

5. Test the database connections using the service and see which database this service connects to.

6. Perform the Data Guard switchover operation.

7. Test the database connection again using the same service and see which database this service connects to.

8. Stop the service and remove the service.

Prerequisites

Before starting the test case, we need to make sure that all the databases, the GSMs, and the catalog database are up and running without any issues.

Log in to GDSCTL, start the GSM gsmeast, and check the status.

```
[oracle@prim01 admin]$ gdsctl
GDSCTL: Version 19.0.0.0.0 - Production on Sat Oct 29 09:20:27 CDT 2022

Copyright (c) 2011, 2019, Oracle.  All rights reserved.

Welcome to GDSCTL, type "help" for information.

Current GSM is set to GSMEAST
GDSCTL> status
```

```
Alias                     GSMEAST
Version                   19.0.0.0.0
Start Date                29-OCT-2022 08:24:29
Trace Level               off
Listener Log File         /u01/app/oracle/diag/gsm/prim01/gsmeast/
alert/log.xml
Listener Trace File       /u01/app/oracle/diag/gsm/prim01/gsmeast/trace/
ora_5851_140000528739392.trc
Endpoint summary          (ADDRESS=(HOST=prim01.localdomain)(PORT=1581)
(PROTOCOL=tcp))
GSMOCI Version            3.0.180702
Mastership                N
Connected to GDS catalog  Y
Process Id                5854
Number of reconnections   0
Pending tasks.     Total  0
Tasks in  process. Total  0
Regional Mastership       TRUE
Total messages published  72
Time Zone                 -05:00
Orphaned Buddy Regions:
     None
GDS region                east
Network metrics:
   Region: south Network factor:0
   Region: north Network factor:0

GDSCTL>
```

Log in to GDSCTL and check the status of the GSM gsmnorth.

```
[oracle@stbyh01 admin]$ gdsctl
GDSCTL: Version 19.0.0.0.0 - Production on Sat Oct 29 09:20:50 CDT 2022

Copyright (c) 2011, 2019, Oracle.  All rights reserved.

Welcome to GDSCTL, type "help" for information.
```

Current GSM is set to GSMNORTH
GDSCTL> connect gsmcatuser/welcome@prim01:1521/CATGDS;
Catalog connection is established
GDSCTL> status

Alias	GSMNORTH
Version	19.0.0.0.0
Start Date	29-OCT-2022 08:24:14
Trace Level	off
Listener Log File	/u01/app/oracle/diag/gsm/stbyh01/gsmnorth/ alert/log.xml
Listener Trace File	/u01/app/oracle/diag/gsm/stbyh01/gsmnorth/trace/ ora_5187_139757816208448.trc
Endpoint summary	(ADDRESS=(HOST=stbyh01.localdomain)(PORT=1582) (PROTOCOL=tcp))
GSMOCI Version	3.0.180702
Mastership	N
Connected to GDS catalog	Y
Process Id	5190
Number of reconnections	0
Pending tasks. Total	0
Tasks in process. Total	0
Regional Mastership	TRUE
Total messages published	74
Time Zone	-05:00
Orphaned Buddy Regions: None	
GDS region	north

Network metrics:
   Region: south Network factor:0
   Region: east Network factor:0

GDSCTL>

Log in to GDSCTL and check the status of the GSM gsmsouth.

[oracle@cstbyh01 admin]$ gdsctl
GDSCTL: Version 19.0.0.0.0 - Production on Sat Oct 29 09:21:06 CDT 2022

Welcome to GDSCTL, type "help" for information.

Current GSM is set to GSMSOUTH
GDSCTL> connect gsmcatuser/welcome@prim01:1521/CATGDS;
Catalog connection is established
GDSCTL> status
Alias   GSMSOUTH
Version   19.0.0.0.0
Start Date   29-OCT-2022 08:23:54
Trace Level   off
Listener Log File   /u01/app/oracle/diag/gsm/cstbyh01/gsmsouth/
alert/log.xml
Listener Trace File   /u01/app/oracle/diag/gsm/cstbyh01/gsmsouth/trace/
ora_5059_140348924025920.trc
Endpoint summary   (ADDRESS=(HOST=cstbyh01.localdomain)(PORT=1583)
(PROTOCOL=tcp))
GSMOCI Version   3.0.180702
Mastership   Y
Connected to GDS catalog Y
Process Id   5062
Number of reconnections 0
Pending tasks.   Total 0
Tasks in process. Total 0
Regional Mastership   TRUE
Total messages published 73
Time Zone   -05:00
Orphaned Buddy Regions:
    None
GDS region   south
Network metrics:
   Region: north Network factor:0
   Region: east Network factor:0
GDSCTL>

Check the status of the databases.

```
GDSCTL> databases;
Database: "orcldb" Registered: Y State: Ok ONS: N. Role: PRIMARY Instances:
1 Region: east
   Service: "sales_reporting_srvc" Globally started: Y Started: N
            Scan: Y Enabled: Y Preferred: Y
   Registered instances:
     sales%1
Database: "orcldbp" Registered: Y State: Ok ONS: N. Role: PH_STNDBY
Instances: 1 Region: north
   Service: "sales_reporting_srvc" Globally started: Y Started: N
            Scan: Y Enabled: Y Preferred: Y
   Registered instances:
     sales%11
Database: "orcldbs" Registered: Y State: Ok ONS: N. Role: PH_STNDBY
Instances: 1 Region: south
   Service: "sales_reporting_srvc" Globally started: Y Started: N
            Scan: Y Enabled: Y Preferred: Y
   Registered instances:
     sales%21

GDSCTL>
```

Check the status of configured services; since we have not created any services yet, it will not return any output.

```
GDSCTL> config service;

Catalog connection is established
Name            Network name    Pool        Started Preferred all
----            ------------    ----        ------- -------------

GDSCTL>
```

205

Creating a Role-Based Global Service Named srvc_prim

Create a role-based global service named srvc_prim with the -role option and set it to the primary, as shown here:

```
GDSCTL> add service -service srvc_prim -gdspool sales -preferred_all
-role PRIMARY
The operation completed successfully
```

Modify the service srvc_prim configuration and add both the physical standby databases, orcldbp and orcldbs, to it.

```
GDSCTL>  modify service -service prim -gdspool sales -database orcldb
-modify_instances -preferred orcldb1,orcldb2;

The operation completed successfully

GDSCTL> modify service -service prim -gdspool sales -gdspool sales
-database orcldbs -modify_instances -preferred orcldbs1,orcldbs2;

The operation completed successfully

GDSCTL>  modify service -service prim -gdspool sales -gdspool sales
-database orcldbp -modify_instances -preferred orcldbp1,orcldbp2;

The operation completed successfully

GDSCTL>
```

Start the service srvc_prim and check the status of the service.

```
GDSCTL> start service -service srvc_prim -gdspool sales;
The operation completed successfully

GDSCTL> services
Service "srvc_prim.sales.oradbcloud" has 1 instance(s). Affinity: ANYWHERE
   Instance "sales%1", name: "orcldb", db: "orcldb", region: "east",
   status: ready.

GDSCTL>
```

```
GDSCTL> databases
Database: "orcldb" Registered: Y State: Ok ONS: N. Role: PRIMARY Instances:
1 Region: east
   Service: "srvc_prim" Globally started: Y Started: Y
           Scan: Y Enabled: Y Preferred: Y
   Registered instances:
     sales%1
Database: "orcldbp" Registered: Y State: Ok ONS: N. Role: PH_STNDBY
Instances: 1 Region: north
   Service: "srvc_prim" Globally started: Y Started: N
           Scan: Y Enabled: Y Preferred: Y
   Registered instances:
     sales%11
Database: "orcldbs" Registered: Y State: Ok ONS: N. Role: PH_STNDBY
Instances: 1 Region: south
   Service: "srvc_prim" Globally started: Y Started: N
           Scan: Y Enabled: Y Preferred: Y
   Registered instances:
     sales%21

GDSCTL>
```

As you can see, the service srvc_prim is running on the database orcldb, which is now holding the primary database role.

Testing the Database Connection

Test the database connection using this service. For this, we can use the following TNS entry:

```
srvc_prim =
(DESCRIPTION =
    (FAILOVER = ON)
    (ADDRESS_LIST =
      (LOAD_BALANCE = ON)
      (ADDRESS = (PROTOCOL = TCP)(HOST = prim01)(PORT = 1581)))
```

```
  (ADDRESS_LIST =
    (LOAD_BALANCE = ON)
    (ADDRESS = (PROTOCOL = TCP)(HOST = stbyh01)(PORT = 1582)))
  (ADDRESS_LIST =
    (LOAD_BALANCE = ON)
    (ADDRESS = (PROTOCOL = TCP)(HOST = stbyh01)(PORT = 1583)))
  (CONNECT_DATA =
    (SERVICE_NAME = srvc_prim.sales.oradbcloud) (REGION = east)
 (FAILOVER_MODE=
 (TYPE=SELECT)
 (METHOD=basic)
 (RETRIES=20)
 (DELAY=15))
   )
 )
```

Once a TNS entry is configured, test the database connection using the service srvc_prim.

```
[oracle@cstbyh01 admin]$ sqlplus system/welcome@srvc_prim

SQL*Plus: Release 19.0.0.0.0 - Production on Sat Oct 29 09:25:43 2022
Version 19.17.0.0.0

Copyright (c) 1982, 2022, Oracle.  All rights reserved.

Last Successful login time: Sat Oct 29 2022 09:05:46 -05:00

Connected to:
Oracle Database 19c Enterprise Edition Release 19.0.0.0.0 - Production
Version 19.17.0.0.0

SQL> @/home/oracle/rac_database_info.sql
```

DATABASE_HOST	DB_NAME	DB_UNIQUE_NAME	DATABASE_ROLE	OPEN_MODE	STARTUP_TIME
prim01.localdomain	orcldb	orcldb	PRIMARY	READ WRITE	29-OCT-22

We can see from the previous output that the service prim is connected to the database orcldb, which is the primary database at this moment.

Performing the Switchover Operation

We can perform the database switchover operation using the Data Guard broker (DGMGRL) command-line utility and make the physical standby database orcldbs the new primary database. Check the current broker configuration, execute the switchover command from DGMGRL, and make orcldbs the primary database.

```
DGMGRL> show configuration;

Configuration -bentdbcfg

  Protection Mode: MaxPerformance
  Members:
  orcldb - Primary database
    orcldbs - Physical standby database
    orcldbp - Physical standby database

Fast-Start Failover:  Disabled

Configuration Status:
SUCCESS (status updated 59 seconds ago)

DGMGRL>
```

Executing Switchover command

```
DGMGRL> switchover to orcldbs;
Performing switchover NOW, please wait...
Operation requires a connection to database "orcldbs"
Connecting ...
Connected to "orcldbs"
Connected as SYSDBA.
New primary database "orcldbs" is opening...
Oracle Clusterware is restarting database "orcldb" ...
Connected to "orcldb"
Connected to "orcldb"
Switchover succeeded, new primary is "orcldbs"
DGMGRL>
```

Here's the new configuration:

```
DGMGRL> show configuration;            ⬅
```

```
Configuration - bentdbcfg

  Protection Mode: MaxPerformance
  Members:
  orcldbs - Primary database
    orcldb - Physical standby database
    orcldbp - Physical standby database

Fast-Start Failover:  Disabled

Configuration Status:
SUCCESS (status updated 26 seconds ago)

DGMGRL>
```

Now, `orcldbs` is the new primary database, and `orcldb` is the new physical standby database. Connect the database using the TNS entry; it will connect to the new primary database, `orcldbs`.

```
[oracle@cstbyh01 admin]$ sqlplus system/welcome@srvc_prim

SQL*Plus: Release 19.0.0.0.0 - Production on Sat Oct 29 09:33:43 2022
Version 19.17.0.0.0

Copyright (c) 1982, 2022, Oracle.  All rights reserved.

Last Successful login time: Sat Oct 29 2022 09:05:46 -05:00

Connected to:
Oracle Database 19c Enterprise Edition Release 19.0.0.0.0 - Production
Version 19.17.0.0.0

SQL> SQL> @/home/oracle/database_info.sql;
```

DATABASE_HOST	DB_NAME	DB_UNIQUE_NAME	DATABASE_ROLE	OPEN_MODE	STARTUP_TIME
cstbyh01.localdomain	orcldbs	orcldbs	PRIMARY	READ WRITE	29-OCT-22

```
SQL>
```

As you can see, it has now connected to the new primary database, `orcldbs`. Isn't that cool? If you perform another switchover and make the physical standby database `orcldbp` the primary database and retry the database connection using the same service, in fact it will connect to the `orcdpb` database as it becomes the new primary database.

This completes the demonstration of this test case. We can stop and remove the service created for this test case.

```
GDSCTL> stop service -service srvc_prim -gdspool sales
The operation completed successfully

GDSCTL> remove service -service srvc_prim -gdspool sales
The operation completed successfully

GDSCTL>
```

Summary of This Test Case

In this test case, we created a role-based global service to run only on the primary database, and we demonstrated how the service is automatically failing over to the primary database whenever the switchover operation happens, making one of the physical standby databases the primary database.

Test Case: Replication Lag-Based Routing

Let's assume that we have a specific scenario where the application team is allowed to connect the physical standby ADG database to reduce the load on the primary database, but the application team needs the most current data and cannot afford reading any data that is behind the primary database for a specific amount of time. How can we handle this kind of situation?

To handle this kind of situation, we do have an option to create a global data service with the attribute `-lag` set to a specific amount of time. Once the replication lag in one of the physical standby ADG databases exceeds this lag limit, the global service will automatically relocate to another available database where the lag is below the specified threshold value. We can also use the option `-failover_primary` while creating the service, and with this option, we can even relocate the service to the primary database if all the physical standby databases are lagging behind the primary database by more than the specified lag limit.

To understand this specific scenario, let's create a global service named sales_
lag20_srvc and set the -lag attribute to 20 seconds with the option -failover_
primary. Whenever the physical standby database lag exceeds the 20 seconds of the
specified threshold, the global service will relocate another physical standby database
(if available) where the lag is less than this threshold value. If all the physical standby
databases are lagging behind the primary database by more than 20 seconds, then the
global service will automatically failover to the primary database as the option
-failover_primary is used while creating the global service sales_lag20_srvc.

For this demonstration, we will create the lag in the physical standby database
by turning off the log apply process in the physical standby database and see what
happens when the lag exceeds 20 seconds in that physical standby database.

High-Level Steps of This Test Case

Here are the high-level steps:

1. Make sure that all the GSMs in all the regions are up and running.

2. Check that all the databases are up and running, and ensure that
   both the physical standby databases are in sync with the primary
   database.

3. Check the status Data Guard broker configuration and run the
   validate database commands for each of the databases in
   the broker configuration to make sure that the status of all the
   databases looks good.

4. Create a global data service named sales_lag20_srvc with the
   attribute -lag set to 15 seconds and with the attribute failover_
   primary.

5. Create a TNS entry for the new service.

6. Test the database connections using both the services and save
   the results.

7. Stop the MRP process in the physical standby database to which
   the service is connected.

8. Test the service connection after waiting more than the lag
   interval.

9. Stop the MRP process on the second standby database also and see if the global data service fails over to the primary database.

10. Start the MRP process in both the physical standby databases and check if the service fails back to the physical standby databases once the lag is cleared.

11. Stop the service and remove the service.

Prerequisites

Before creating the service, make sure all the GSMs and databases are up and running.

Connect to the GSM GSMEAST, and check the current services and databases from GDSCTL.

```
GDSCTL: Version 19.0.0.0.0 - Production on Sat Oct 29 20:35:43 CDT 2022

Copyright (c) 2011, 2019, Oracle.  All rights reserved.

Welcome to GDSCTL, type "help" for information.

Current GSM is set to GSMEAST

GDSCTL> connect gsmcatuser/welcome@prim01:1521/CATGDS;
Catalog connection is established

GDSCTL> databases
Database: "orcldb" Registered: Y State: Ok ONS: N. Role: PRIMARY Instances:
1 Region: east
   Registered instances:
     sales%1
Database: "orcldbp" Registered: Y State: Ok ONS: N. Role: PH_STNDBY
Instances: 1 Region: north
   Registered instances:
     sales%11
Database: "orcldbs" Registered: Y State: Ok ONS: N. Role: PH_STNDBY
Instances: 1 Region: south
   Registered instances:
     sales%21

GDSCTL> services
```

Physical Standby Database Lag Check

For this test case, we need to make sure that both the physical standby databases are in sync with the primary database and there is no lag in any of the physical standby databases. For this scenario, switch a couple of log files in the primary database and check if both the physical standby databases are receiving the log files and applying the log files.

Log in to the primary database, orcldb, and do a couple of log switches.

```
[oracle@prim01 admin]$ sqlplus / as sysdba

SQL*Plus: Release 19.0.0.0.0 - Production on Sat Oct 29 20:36:40 2022
Version 19.17.0.0.0
Copyright (c) 1982, 2022, Oracle.  All rights reserved.

Connected to:
Oracle Database 19c Enterprise Edition Release 19.0.0.0.0 - Production
Version 19.17.0.0.0

SQL> alter system switch logfile;
System altered.

SQL> alter system switch logfile;
System altered.

SQL> @/home/oracle/database_info.sql
```

DATABASE_HOST	DB_NAME	DB_UNIQUE_NAME	DATABASE_ROLE	OPEN_MODE	STARTUP_TIME
prim01.localdomain	orcldb	orcldb	PRIMARY	READ WRITE	29-OCT-22

```
SQL> archive log list;
Database log mode              Archive Mode
Automatic archival             Enabled
Archive destination            USE_DB_RECOVERY_FILE_DEST
Oldest online log sequence     24
Next log sequence to archive   25
Current log sequence           25
```

Log in to the physical standby database, orcldbp, and check the lag.

```
[oracle@stbyh01 admin]$ . oraenv
ORACLE_SID = [orcldbp] ?
The Oracle base remains unchanged with value /u01/app/oracle
[oracle@stbyh01 admin]$ sqlplus / as sysdba

SQL*Plus: Release 19.0.0.0.0 - Production on Sat Oct 29 20:37:54 2022
Version 19.17.0.0.0

Copyright (c) 1982, 2022, Oracle.  All rights reserved.

Connected to:
Oracle Database 19c Enterprise Edition Release 19.0.0.0.0 - Production
Version 19.17.0.0.0

SQL>@/home/oracle/database_info.sql;
```

DATABASE_HOST	DB_NAME	DB_UNIQUE_NAME	DATABASE_ROLE	OPEN_MODE	STARTUP_TIME
stbyh01.localdomain	orcldb	orcldbp	PHYSICAL STANDBY	READ ONLY WITH APPLY	29-OCT-22

INST_ID	PROCESS	STATUS	THREAD#	SEQUENCE#	BLOCK#	BLOCKS
1	MRP0	APPLYING_LOG	1	26	16	409600

THREAD#	ARCHIVED	APPLIED	GAP
1	25	25	0

```
SQL>
```

Log in to physical standby database, orcldbs, and check the lag.

```
[oracle@cstbyh01 admin]$ . oraenv
ORACLE_SID = [orcldbs] ?
The Oracle base remains unchanged with value /u01/app/oracle
[oracle@cstbyh01 admin]$ sqlplus / as sysdba

SQL*Plus: Release 19.0.0.0.0 - Production on Sat Oct 29 20:39:53 2022
Version 19.17.0.0.0
```

Connected to:
Oracle Database 19c Enterprise Edition Release 19.0.0.0.0 - Production
Version 19.17.0.0.0

SQL>@/home/oracle/database_info.sql;

DATABASE_HOST	DB_NAME	DB_UNIQUE_NAME	DATABASE_ROLE	OPEN_MODE	STARTUP_TIME
cstbyh01.localdomain	orcldb	orcldbs	PHYSICAL STANDBY	READ ONLY WITH APPLY	29-OCT-22

INST_ID	PROCESS	STATUS	THREAD#	SEQUENCE#	BLOCK#	BLOCKS
1	MRP0	APPLYING_LOG	1	26	113	409600

THREAD#	ARCHIVED	APPLIED	GAP
1	25	25	0

SQL>

We can see from the previous output that all the physical standby databases are in sync with the primary database.

Let's create a new global service named sales_lag20_srvc. We will create this service with the attribute -lag set to 20 seconds and the attribute -role set to physical_standby. We will also use the attribute -failover_primary.

```
GDSCTL> connect gsmcatuser/welcome@prim01:1521/CATGDS;
Catalog connection is established
GDSCTL>
```

```
GDSCTL>add service -service sales_lag20_srvc -gdspool sales -preferred_all
-role PHYSICAL_STANDBY -lag 20 -failover_primary
```

```
GDSCTL>
```

Check the configuration of the service using the following command:

```
GDSCTL> config service -service sales_lag20_srvc
Name: sales_lag20_srvc
Network name: sales_lag20_srvc.sales.oradbcloud
Pool: sales
```

Started: No
Preferred all: Yes
Locality: ANYWHERE
Region Failover: No
Role: PHYSICAL_STANDBY
Primary Failover: Yes
Lag: 20   ⬅
Runtime Balance: SERVICE_TIME
Connection Balance: LONG
Notification: Yes
TAF Policy: NONE
Policy: AUTOMATIC
DTP: No
Failover Method: NONE
Failover Type: NONE
Failover Retries:
Failover Delay:
Edition:
PDB:
Commit Outcome:
Retention Timeout:
Replay Initiation Timeout:
Session State Consistency:
SQL Translation Profile:
Stop option: NONE
Drain timeout:
Table family:

Databases

Database	Preferred	Status
orcldb	Yes	Enabled
orcldbp	Yes	Enabled
orcldbs	Yes	Enabled

GDSCTL>

Let's start the service sales_lag20_srvc and check its status.

```
GDSCTL> start service -service sales_lag20_srvc -gdspool sales
The operation completed successfully

GDSCTL> services
Service "sales_lag20_srvc.sales.oradbcloud" has 2 instance(s). Affinity:
ANYWHERE
    Instance "sales%11", name: "orcldbp", db: "orcldbp", region: "north",
    status: ready.
    Instance "sales%21", name: "orcldbs", db: "orcldbs", region: "south",
    status: ready.

GDSCTL>
```

When we execute the command databases from the GDSCTL prompt, we can see that the service sales_lag20_srvc is started on both the physical standby databases.

```
GDSCTL> databases
Database: "orcldb" Registered: Y State: Ok ONS: N. Role: PRIMARY Instances:
1 Region: east
    Service: "sales_lag20_srvc" Globally started: Y Started: N
            Scan: Y Enabled: Y Preferred: Y
    Registered instances:
      sales%1
Database: "orcldbp" Registered: Y State: Ok ONS: N. Role: PH_STNDBY
Instances: 1 Region: north
    Service: "sales_lag20_srvc" Globally started: Y Started: Y
            Scan: Y Enabled: Y Preferred: Y
    Registered instances:
      sales%11
Database: "orcldbs" Registered: Y State: Ok ONS: N. Role: PH_STNDBY
Instances: 1 Region: south
    Service: "sales_lag20_srvc" Globally started: Y Started: Y
            Scan: Y Enabled: Y Preferred: Y
    Registered instances:
      sales%21

GDSCTL>
```

Use the following TNS entry to test this service:

```
sales_lag20_srvc =
  (DESCRIPTION =
   (FAILOVER = ON)
   (ADDRESS_LIST =
     (LOAD_BALANCE = ON)
     (ADDRESS = (PROTOCOL = TCP)(HOST = prim01)(PORT = 1581)))
   (ADDRESS_LIST =
     (LOAD_BALANCE = ON)
     (ADDRESS = (PROTOCOL = TCP)(HOST = stbyh01)(PORT = 1582)))
   (ADDRESS_LIST =
     (LOAD_BALANCE = ON)
     (ADDRESS = (PROTOCOL = TCP)(HOST = cstbyh01)(PORT = 1583)))
   (CONNECT_DATA =
     (SERVICE_NAME = sales_lag20_srvc.sales.oradbcloud) (REGION = east)
   )
 )
```

Log in to DGMGRL and check the status for each of the physical standby databases.

```
[oracle@prim01 admin]$ dgmgrl
DGMGRL for Linux: Release 19.0.0.0.0 - Production on Sat Oct 29 20:44:54 2022
Version 19.17.0.0.0

Copyright (c) 1982, 2019, Oracle and/or its affiliates.  All rights reserved.

Welcome to DGMGRL, type "help" for information.
DGMGRL> connect sys/welcome;
Connected to "orcldb"
Connected as SYSDBA.

DGMGRL> show configuration;

Configuration - orcldbcfg

  Protection Mode: MaxPerformance
  Members:
  orcldb  - Primary database
```

```
    orcldbp - Physical standby database
    orcldbs - Physical standby database

Fast-Start Failover:  Disabled

Configuration Status:
SUCCESS    (status updated 59 seconds ago)

DGMGRL> show database orcldbs;

Database - orcldbs

  Role:               PHYSICAL STANDBY
  Intended State:     APPLY-ON
  Transport Lag:      0 seconds (computed 1 second ago)
  Apply Lag:          0 seconds (computed 1 second ago)  <=======
  Average Apply Rate: 0 Byte/s
  Real Time Query:    ON
  Instance(s):
    orcldbs

Database Status:
SUCCESS

DGMGRL> show database orcldbp;

Database - orcldbp

  Role:               PHYSICAL STANDBY
  Intended State:     APPLY-ON
  Transport Lag:      0 seconds (computed 1 second ago)
  Apply Lag:          0 seconds (computed 1 second ago)  <=======
  Average Apply Rate: 0 Byte/s
  Real Time Query:    ON
  Instance(s):
    orcldbp

Database Status:
SUCCESS

DGMGRL>
```

From the previous output, we can see that there is no lag in both the physical standby databases. Now try to connect the database using this service and see which physical standby database it's connecting to.

```
[oracle@cstbyh01 admin]$ sqlplus system/welcome@sales_lag20_srvc

SQL*Plus: Release 19.0.0.0.0 - Production on Sat Oct 29 21:00:14 2022
Version 19.17.0.0.0

Copyright (c) 1982, 2022, Oracle.  All rights reserved.

Last Successful login time: Sat Oct 29 2022 19:45:05 -05:00

Connected to:
Oracle Database 19c Enterprise Edition Release 19.0.0.0.0 - Production
Version 19.17.0.0.0
```

```
SQL> @/home/oracle/database_info.sql;

DATABASE_HOST        DB_NAME  DB_UNIQUE_NAME  DATABASE_ROLE     OPEN_MODE             STARTUP_TIME
-------------------- -------- --------------- ----------------- --------------------- ------------
cstbyh01.localdomain orcldb   orcldbs         PHYSICAL STANDBY  READ ONLY WITH APPLY  29-OCT-22

SQL>
```

We can see that it has connected to the physical standby database, orcldbs.

We can make sure the physical standby database falls behind the primary database by at least 20 seconds (we defined this option while creating the service) so that we can test the service whether it is failing over to other databases. We can do this by stopping the log apply process in the physical standby database. For this scenario, we will stop the log apply for the physical standby database, orcldbs.

Log in to DGMGRL, edit the database's orcldbs properties, and set state= 'apply-off'.

```
DGMGRL> edit database orcldbs set state='APPLY-OFF';
Succeeded.
```

Please wait for a minimum of 20 seconds and check the status of this database from the DGMGRL prompt.

```
DGMGRL> show database orcldbs;

Database - orcldbs

  Role:               PHYSICAL STANDBY
  Intended State:     APPLY-OFF
  Transport Lag:      0 seconds (computed 0 seconds ago)
  Apply Lag:          1 minute 05 seconds (computed 0 seconds ago)    <==
  Average Apply Rate: (unknown)
  Real Time Query:    OFF
  Instance(s):
    orcldbs

Database Status:
SUCCESS

DGMGRL>
```

From the previous output, we can see that there is a lag of more than 20 seconds in the physical standby database, orcldbs. Now, if we check the services, we will observe that the sales_lag20_srvc global service has failed over to the other available physical standby database in the configuration; in this case, the service has failed to the database orcdbp.

Check the status of the services before stopping the LAG apply for the physical standby database, orcldbs.

```
GDSCTL> services
Service "sales_lag20_srvc.sales.oradbcloud" has 2 instance(s). Affinity:
ANYWHERE
   Instance "sales%11", name: "orcldbp", db: "orcldbp", region: "north",
   status: ready.
   Instance "sales%21", name: "orcldbs", db: "orcldbs", region: "south",
   status: ready.

GDSCTL>
```

Check the status of the services before stopping the LAG apply for the physical standby database, orcldbs.

```
GDSCTL> services
Service "sales_lag20_srvc.sales.oradbcloud" has 1 instance(s). Affinity:
ANYWHERE
    Instance "sales%11", name: "orcldbp", db: "orcldbp", region: "north",
    status: ready.

GDSCTL>
```

If we try to connect the database using this service, now the service is connecting to the other available physical standby database, orcldbp.

```
[oracle@cstbyh01 admin]$ sqlplus system/welcome@sales_lag20_srvc

SQL*Plus: Release 19.0.0.0.0 - Production on Sat Oct 29 21:06:01 2022
Version 19.17.0.0.0

Copyright (c) 1982, 2022, Oracle.  All rights reserved.

Last Successful login time: Sat Oct 29 2022 19:45:05 -05:00

Connected to:
Oracle Database 19c Enterprise Edition Release 19.0.0.0.0 - Production
Version 19.17.0.0.0

SQL>@/home/oracle/rac_database_info.sql;
```

DATABASE_HOST	DB_NAME	DB_UNIQUE_NAME	DATABASE_ROLE	OPEN_MODE	STARTUP_TIME
stbyh01.localdomain	orcldb	orcldbp	PHYSICAL STANDBY	READ ONLY WITH APPLY	29-OCT-22

```
SQL>
```

Stop the log apply services and see if the service that is running in the physical standby database, orcldbp, will fail over to the primary database. Log in to DGMGRL, edit the database orcldbp, and set the state to apply-off.

```
DGMGRL> edit database orcldbp set state='APPLY-OFF';
Succeeded.
```

Please wait for 30 seconds and check the status of this database from DGMGRL. We can do a couple of log switches in the primary database and then check the status.

```
DGMGRL>  show database orcldbp

Database - orcldbp

  Role:               PHYSICAL STANDBY
  Intended State:     APPLY-OFF
  Transport Lag:      0 seconds (computed 0 seconds ago)
  Apply Lag:          1 minute 34 seconds (computed 0 seconds ago) ⬅
  Average Apply Rate: (unknown)
  Real Time Query:    OFF
  Instance(s):
    orcldbp

Database Status:
SUCCESS

DGMGRL>
```

Now, wait for 15 seconds and recheck the services. Observe that the sales_lag20_srvc global service has failed over to the primary database, orcldb.

```
GDSCTL> databases
Database: "orcldb" Registered: Y State: Ok ONS: N. Role: PRIMARY Instances:
1 Region: east
   Service: "sales_lag20_srvc" Globally started: Y Started: Y
           Scan: Y Enabled: Y Preferred: Y
   Registered instances:
     sales%1
Database: "orcldbp" Registered: Y State: Ok ONS: N. Role: PH_STNDBY
Instances: 1 Region: north
   Service: "sales_lag20_srvc" Globally started: Y Started: N
           Scan: Y Enabled: Y Preferred: Y
   Registered instances:
     sales%11
```

Database: "orcldbs" Registered: Y State: Ok ONS: N. Role: PH_STNDBY
Instances: 1 Region: south
    Service: "sales_lag20_srvc" Globally started: Y Started: N
                Scan: Y Enabled: Y Preferred: Y
    Registered instances:
      sales%21

GDSCTL> services

Now try to connect to the service; this time it will connect to the primary database.

[oracle@cstbyh01 admin]$ sqlplus system/welcome@sales_lag20_srvc

SQL*Plus: Release 19.0.0.0.0 - Production on Sat Oct 29 21:29:12 2022
Version 19.17.0.0.0

Copyright (c) 1982, 2022, Oracle. All rights reserved.

Oracle Database 19c Enterprise Edition Release 19.0.0.0.0 - Production
Version 19.17.0.0.0

SQL> @/home/oracle/database_info.sql

DATABASE_HOST	DB_NAME	DB_UNIQUE_NAME	DATABASE_ROLE	OPEN_MODE	STARTUP_TIME
prim01.localdomain	orcldb	orcldb	PRIMARY	READ WRITE	29-OCT-22

We can see that the service sales_lag20_srvc has failed to the primary database as both the physical standby databases are lagging behind the primary database for more than the specified threshold time.

We can start the lag apply for both the physical standby databases and see if the service will fail back to this database. Log in to DGMGRL and set the state to apply-on for both the physical standby databases.

DGMGRL> edit database orcldbp set state='APPLY-ON';
Succeeded.

DGMGRL> edit database orcldbs set state='APPLY-ON';
Succeeded.

DGMGRL> show configuration;

Configuration - bentdbcfg

  Protection Mode: MaxPerformance
  Members:
  orcldb - Primary database
    orcldbs - Physical standby database
    orcldbp - Physical standby database

Fast-Start Failover: Disabled

Configuration Status:
SUCCESS (status updated 50 seconds ago)

    Please wait for 20 seconds and recheck the services; we can see that the service sales_lag20_srvc will fail back to the physical standby databases.
    Check the status of the services from the GDSCTL prompt.

```
GDSCTL> services
Service "sales_lag20_srvc.sales.oradbcloud" has 2 instance(s). Affinity:
ANYWHERE
   Instance "sales%11", name: "orcldbp", db: "orcldbp", region: "north",
   status: ready.
   Instance "sales%21", name: "orcldbs", db: "orcldbs", region: "south",
   status: ready.
GDSCTL>

GDSCTL> databases
Database: "orcldb" Registered: Y State: Ok ONS: N. Role: PRIMARY Instances:
1 Region: east
   Service: "sales_lag20_srvc" Globally started: Y Started: N
           Scan: Y Enabled: Y Preferred: Y
   Registered instances:
     sales%1
Database: "orcldbp" Registered: Y State: Ok ONS: N. Role: PH_STNDBY
Instances: 1 Region: north
   Service: "sales_lag20_srvc" Globally started: Y Started: Y
           Scan: Y Enabled: Y Preferred: Y
   Registered instances:
     sales%11
```

```
Database: "orcldbs" Registered: Y State: Ok ONS: N. Role: PH_STNDBY
Instances: 1 Region: south
   Service: "sales_lag20_srvc" Globally started: Y Started: Y
            Scan: Y Enabled: Y Preferred: Y
   Registered instances:
     sales%21

GDSCTL>
```

From the previous output, we can see that the service has successfully failed back to the physical standby databases. This completes the demonstration of this test case. At this point, you can stop and remove the services that we have created for this test case.

```
GDSCTL>stop service -service sales_lag20_srvc -gdspool sales
The operation completed successfully

GDSCTL>remove service -gdspool sales -service sales_lag20_srvc
The operation completed successfully

GDSCTL>services
GDSCTL>
```

Summary of This Test Case

This test case illustrated replication lag tolerance-based routing for an ADG configuration, which allows applications to always access the most current data.

Test Case: TAF-Enabled Global Service in the GDS Environment

In this test case, we will see how we can create the TAF-enabled GDS in our environment, and it will allow application continuity when a switchover is in place from the primary database to the physical standby database and vice versa.

High-Level Steps of This Test Case

Here are the steps:

1. Make sure that all the GSMs in all the regions are up and running.

2. Check that all the databases are up and running and ensure that both the physical standby databases are in sync with the primary database.

3. Check the status of the Data Guard broker configuration and run the `validate database` commands for each of the databases in the broker configuration to make sure that the status of all the databases looks good.

4. Create a GDS named `sale_reader_lag15_srvc` with the attribute `-lag` set to 15 seconds and the attribute `failover_primary`.

5. Create a TNS entry for the new service.

6. Test the database connections using both the services and save the results.

7. Stop the MRP process in the physical standby database to which the service is connected.

8. Test the service connection after waiting more than the lag interval.

9. Stop the MRP process on the second physical standby database also and see if the global data service fails over to the primary database.

10. Start the MRP process in both the physical standby databases and check if the service fails back to the physical standby databases.

11. Stop the service and remove the service.

Prerequisites

Before creating any new services, make sure that all the GSMs and databases are up and running. Connect to the GSM GSMEAST and check the current services and databases from GDSCTL.

```
[oracle@prim01 ~]$ gdsctl
GDSCTL: Version 19.0.0.0.0 - Production on Wed Dec 14 11:53:31 CST 2022

Copyright (c) 2011, 2019, Oracle.  All rights reserved.

Welcome to GDSCTL, type "help" for information.

Current GSM is set to GSMEAST
GDSCTL> databases
Database: "orcldb" Registered: Y State: Ok ONS: N. Role: PRIMARY Instances:
1 Region: east
   Registered instances:
     sales%1
Database: "orcldbp" Registered: Y State: Ok ONS: N. Role: PH_STNDBY
Instances: 1 Region: north
   Registered instances:
     sales%11
Database: "orcldbs" Registered: Y State: Ok ONS: N. Role: PH_STNDBY
Instances: 1 Region: south
   Registered instances:
     sales%21

GDSCTL> services
```

Connecting to the GDS Catalog

Do the following:

```
GDSCTL> connect gsmcatuser/welcome@prim01:1521/CATGDS;
Catalog connection is established
GDSCTL>
```

Creating a Role-Based Global Service Named prim

Create a new global service named prim with role-based and TAF-related parameters, as shown here:

```
GDSCTL>add service -service prim -gdspool sales -preferred_all -role
PRIMARY -tafpolicy BASIC -failovertype SELECT -failovermethod BASIC
-failoverretry 20 -failoverdelay 15
The operation completed successfully
```

Please note that if the databases in the GSM configuration are Real Application Cluster (RAC) databases, we need to add all the instances of all the databases in the configuration to the service using the modify service command, as shown here:

```
GDSCTL> modify service -service prim -gdspool sales -database orcldb
-modify_instances -preferred orcldb1,orcldb2
The operation completed successfully

GDSCTL> modify service -service prim -gdspool sales -database orcldbs
-modify_instances -preferred orcldbs1,orcldbs2
The operation completed successfully

GDSCTL> modify service -service prim -gdspool sales -database orcldbp
-modify_instances -preferred orcldbp1,orcldbp2
The operation completed successfully

GDSCTL>
```

Starting the Service and Checking Its Status

Do the following:

```
GDSCTL> start service -service prim -gdspool sales
The operation completed successfully

GDSCTL> services
Service "prim.sales.oradbcloud" has 1 instance(s). Affinity: ANYWHERE
    Instance "sales%1", name: "orcldb", db: "orcldb", region: "east",
    status: ready.
```

```
GDSCTL> config service -service prim -gdspool sales
Name: prim
Network name: prim.sales.oradbcloud
Pool: sales
Started: Yes
Preferred all: Yes
Locality: ANYWHERE
Region Failover: No
Role: PRIMARY
Primary Failover: No
Lag: ANY
Runtime Balance: SERVICE_TIME
Connection Balance: LONG
Notification: Yes
TAF Policy: BASIC
Policy: AUTOMATIC
DTP: No
Failover Method: BASIC
Failover Type: SELECT
Failover Retries: 20
Failover Delay: 15
Edition:
PDB:
Commit Outcome:
Retention Timeout:
Replay Initiation Timeout:
Session State Consistency:
SQL Translation Profile:
Stop option: NONE
Drain timeout:
Table family:
```

```
Databases
------------------------
Database               Preferred Status
--------               --------- ------
orcldb                 Yes       Enabled
orcldbp                Yes       Enabled
orcldbs                Yes       Enabled

GDSCTL>
```

Checking the Status of the Running Services and the Databases

Do the following:

```
GDSCTL> status service -service prim
Service "prim.sales.oradbcloud" has 1 instance(s). Affinity: ANYWHERE
    Instance "sales%1", name: "orcldb", db: "orcldb", region: "east",
    status: ready.

GDSCTL> databases
Database: "orcldb" Registered: Y State: Ok ONS: N. Role: PRIMARY Instances:
1 Region: east
    Service: "prim" Globally started: Y Started: Y
            Scan: N Enabled: Y Preferred: Y
    Registered instances:
      sales%1
Database: "orcldbp" Registered: Y State: Ok ONS: N. Role: PH_STNDBY
Instances: 1 Region: north
    Service: "prim" Globally started: Y Started: N
            Scan: N Enabled: Y Preferred: Y
    Registered instances:
      sales%11
```

```
Database: "orcldbs" Registered: Y State: Ok ONS: N. Role: PH_STNDBY
Instances: 1 Region: south
   Service: "prim" Globally started: Y Started: N
            Scan: N Enabled: Y Preferred: Y
   Registered instances:
     sales%21
GDSCTL>
```

Preparing the TNS Entry

We can use the following TNS entry to test this service:

```
PRIM =
(DESCRIPTION =
    (FAILOVER = ON)
    (ADDRESS_LIST =
      (LOAD_BALANCE = ON)
      (ADDRESS = (PROTOCOL = TCP)(HOST = prim01)(PORT = 1581)))
    (ADDRESS_LIST =
      (LOAD_BALANCE = ON)
      (ADDRESS = (PROTOCOL = TCP)(HOST = stbyh01)(PORT = 1582)))
    (ADDRESS_LIST =
      (LOAD_BALANCE = ON)
      (ADDRESS = (PROTOCOL = TCP)(HOST = stbyh01)(PORT = 1583)))
    (CONNECT_DATA =
      (SERVICE_NAME = prim.sales.oradbcloud) (REGION = east)
  (FAILOVER_MODE=
   (TYPE=SELECT)
   (METHOD=basic)
   (RETRIES=20)
   (DELAY=15))
    )
  )
)
```

Add the previous TNS entry to the primary database server's tnsnames.ora file.

Testing the Database Connection

Connect to the database using this service and see which database this service connects to.

```
[oracle@cstbyh01 ~]$ sqlplus system/welcome@prim

SQL*Plus: Release 19.0.0.0.0 - Production on Thu Dec 15 14:27:50 2022
Version 19.17.0.0.0

Copyright © 1982, 2022, Oracle.  All rights reserved.

Last Successful login time: Thu Dec 15 2022 14:27:44 -06:00

Connected to:
Oracle Database 19c Enterprise Edition Release 19.0.0.0.0 - Production
Version 19.17.0.0.0

SQL>@/home/oracle/rac_database_info.sql
```

DATABASE_HOST	DB_NAME	DB_UNIQUE_NAME	DATABASE_ROLE	OPEN_MODE	STARTUP_TIME
prim01.localdomain	orcldb	orcldb	PRIMARY	READ WRITE	14-DEC-22

```
SQL>
```

As you can see, this service has connected to the primary database, orcldb.

Running the SELECT Statement

Run the following SQL statement: select * from the dba_objects. This statement takes some time to get all the data. The following is the SELECT statement and the truncated output of the SELECT statement:

```
SQL>@/home/oracle/rac_database_info.sql
```

DATABASE_HOST	DB_NAME	DB_UNIQUE_NAME	DATABASE_ROLE	OPEN_MODE	STARTUP_TIME
prim01.localdomain	orcldb1	orcldb	PRIMARY	READ WRITE	15-AUG-21
19cracp2.localdomain	orcldb2	orcldb	PRIMARY	READ WRITE	15-AUG-21

```
SQL> select * from dba_objects;     ⟸

OWNER
```

```
--------------------------------------------------------------------------
OBJECT_NAME
--------------------------------------------------------------------------
SUBOBJECT_NAME
--------------------------------------------------------------------------
 OBJECT_ID DATA_OBJECT_ID OBJECT_TYPE              CREATED    LAST_DDL_
---------- -------------- ---------------------- ---------- ----------
TIMESTAMP              STATUS  T G S  NAMESPACE
----------------- ------- - - - ----------
EDITION_NAME
--------------------------------------------------------------------------
SHARING            E O A
----------------- - - -
DEFAULT_COLLATION
--------------------------------------------------------------------------
D S CREATED_APPID CREATED_VSNID MODIFIED_APPID MODIFIED_VSNID
- - ------------- ------------- -------------- --------------
N N
OWNER
--------------------------------------------------------------------------
```

Performing a Switchover Operation to Make orcldbs the Primary Database

While the previous SQL is still running, open a new session and perform the switchover to the physical standby database orcldbs using DGMGRL. Before doing the switchover, we should always check to make sure that the Data Guard broker configuration status looks good.

```
[oracle@prim01 ~]$ dgmgrl
DGMGRL for Linux: Release 19.0.0.0.0 - Production on Thu Dec 15
14:29:24 2022
Version 19.17.0.0.0
```

Welcome to DGMGRL, type "help" for information.
DGMGRL> connect sys/welcome;
Connected to "orcldb"
Connected as SYSDBA.
DGMGRL> show configuration;

Configuration - orcldbcfg

  Protection Mode: MaxPerformance
  Members:
  orcldb - Primary database
    orcldbp - Physical standby database
    orcldbs - Physical standby database

Fast-Start Failover: Disabled

Configuration Status:
SUCCESS (status update d 50 seconds ago)

DGMGRL> switchover to orcldbs   ⬅
Performing switchover NOW, please wait...
Operation requires a connection to database "orcldbs"
Connecting ...
Connected to "orcldbs"
Connected as SYSDBA.
New primary database "orcldbs" is opening...
Operation requires start up of instance "orcldb" on database "orcldb"
Starting instance "orcldb"...
Connected to an idle instance.
ORACLE instance started.
Connected to "orcldb"
Database mounted.
Database opened.
Switchover succeeded, new primary is "orcldbs"
DGMGRL> show configuration;

```
Configuration - orcldbcfg

  Protection Mode: MaxPerformance
  Members:
  orcldbs - Primary database
    orcldb  - Physical standby database
    orcldbp - Physical standby database

Fast-Start Failover:  Disabled


Configuration Status:
SUCCESS    (status updated 31 seconds ago)

DGMGRL>
```

Monitoring the SELECT Statement

Now, check the session where select * from dba_objects is running. You can see
that the session freezes for a few seconds while the current primary database is being
switched over to the physical standby database. Once the switchover completes,
this session resumes (as it internally connects to the new primary database without
disconnecting/killing the current session) and continues the SELECT statement. Once the
SELECT statement completes, we can see that it has now connected to orcldbs (the new
primary database). This is brilliant, right?

```
OWNER
--------------------------------------------------------------------------------
OBJECT_NAME
--------------------------------------------------------------------------------
SUBOBJECT_NAME
--------------------------------------------------------------------------------
 OBJECT_ID DATA_OBJECT_ID OBJECT_TYPE             CREATED   LAST_DDL_
---------- -------------- ----------------------- --------- ----------
TIMESTAMP             STATUS  T G S  NAMESPACE
-------------------- ------- - - - ----------
EDITION_NAME
--------------------------------------------------------------------------------
```

```
SHARING          E O
------------- - -

73060 rows selected.
```

```
SQL> @/home/oracle/rac_database_info.sql;

DATABASE_HOST          DB_NAME DB_UNIQUE_NAME  DATABASE_ROLE OPEN_MODE    STARTUP_TIME
--------------------   ------- --------------  ------------- ----------   -------------
-cstbyh01.localdomain  orcldbs orcldbs         PRIMARY       READ WRITE   14-DEC-22

SQL>
```

We can switch back to the original primary database and stop and remove the services.

```
DGMGRL> switchover to orcldb;
Performing switchover NOW, please wait...
Operation requires a connection to database "orcldb"
Connecting ...
Connected to "orcldb"
Connected as SYSDBA.
New primary database "orcldb" is opening...
Oracle Clusterware is restarting database "orcldbs" ...
Connected to "orcldbs"
Connected to "orcldbs"
Switchover succeeded, new primary is "orcldb"
DGMGRL> show configuration;

Configuration - bentdbcfg

  Protection Mode: MaxPerformance
  Members:
  orcldb - Primary database
    orcldbs - Physical standby database
    orcldbp - Physical standby database

Fast-Start Failover:  Disabled

Configuration Status:
SUCCESS   (status updated 62 seconds ago)

DGMGRL>
```

We can now stop the service prim and remove it.

```
GDSCTL>stop service -service prim -gdspool sales
GDSCTL>

GDSCTL>remove service -service prim -gdspool sales
GDSCTL>

GDSCTL>services

GDSCTL> databases;
Database: "orcldbs" Registered: Y State: Ok ONS: Y. Role: PH_STNDBY
Instances: 2 Region: north
   Registered instances:
     sales%11
     sales%12
Database: "orcldb" Registered: Y State: Ok ONS: Y. Role: PRIMARY Instances:
2 Region: east
   Registered instances:
     sales%1
     sales%2
Database: "orcldbp" Registered: Y State: Ok ONS: Y. Role: PH_STNDBY
Instances: 2 Region: south
   Registered instances:
     sales%21
     sales%22

GDSCTL>
```

Summary of This Test Case

In this test case, we incorporated the TAF feature in GDS and demonstrated the use case with an example.

Test Case: Local-Based Routing

Local-based routing in GDS allows us to maximize an application's performance by providing the customers with the ability to configure the GDS service in such a way that all the client connections are routed to the replicated databases in the local region. In this way, the application can avoid all the latency overhead issues that can be caused if the application is accessing the databases in the remote region.

To demonstrate this capability, we will create a couple of global services with the attribute -`locality` set to different available options. The `locality` attribute specifies the service region locality, and depending upon the option set, the service connection will be routed to the database accordingly. Two options can be set to the `locality` attribute: `anywhere` and `local_only`. When we create the service with the `locality` option set to `anywhere`, the client connections are routed to any of the regions and provide the load balancing. When we use the option `local_only`, regardless of the load, all the connections will be routed to the local region. If we do not specify this option, then GDSCTL uses the default value, `ANYWHERE`, for the service. We can also use the -`region_failover` option along with the `local_only` option. When we create a service with these two options, all the client connections first route to the databases in the local region, and when all the databases in the local regions are not available, the connections are routed to other regions.

We will now see how we can use the attribute -`locality` with an example.

High-Level Steps of This Test Case

Here are the steps:

1. Make sure that all the GSMs in all the regions are up and running.

2. Check that all the databases are up and running and ensure that both the physical standby databases are in sync with the primary database.

3. Check the status of the Data Guard broker configuration and run the `validate database` commands for each of the database in the broker configuration to make sure that status of all the databases looks good.

4. Create a global data service named `srvc_read_anywhere` with the attribute `-locality` set to ANYWHERE and test the connection to understand how this option works.

5. Stop and remove the service `srvc_read_anywhere`.

6. Create a global data service named `srvc_read_local_only` with the attribute `-locality` set to LOCAL_ONLY and test the connection to understand how this option works.

7. Stop and remove the service `srvc_read_local_only`.

8. Create a GDS named `srvc_read_local_only_region_failover` with the attribute `-locality` set to LOCAL_ONLY and with the attribute `-region_failover` set to YES and test the connection to understand how this option works.

9. Stop and remove the service `srvc_read_local_only_region_failover`.

Prerequisites

Before starting this test case, we need to make sure that all the databases, GSMs, and catalog database are up and running without any issues.

Checking the Status of the GSMs

Check the status of all the GSMs using the following command:

```
GDSCTL> status gsm -gsm GSMEAST
Alias                 GSMEAST
Version               19.0.0.0.0
Start Date            29-OCT-2022 08:24:29
Trace Level           off
Listener Log File     /u01/app/oracle/diag/gsm/prim01/gsmeast/alert/log.xml
Listener Trace File   /u01/app/oracle/diag/gsm/prim01/gsmeast/trace/
                      ora_5851_140000528739392.trc
Endpoint summary      (ADDRESS=(HOST=prim01.localdomain)(PORT=1581)
                      (PROTOCOL=tcp))
```

```
GSMOCI Version          3.0.180702
Mastership              N
Connected to GDS catalog Y
Process Id              5854
Number of reconnections 0
Pending tasks.    Total 0
Tasks in  process. Total 0
Regional Mastership     TRUE
Total messages published 1535
Time Zone               -05:00
Orphaned Buddy Regions:
    None
GDS region                    east
Network metrics:
   Region: south Network factor:0
   Region: north Network factor:0

GDSCTL>
```

Checking the Status of the Databases

Do the following:

```
GDSCTL> databases
Database: "orcldb" Registered: Y State: Ok ONS: N. Role: PRIMARY Instances:
1 Region: east
   Registered instances:
     sales%1
Database: "orcldbp" Registered: Y State: Ok ONS: N. Role: PH_STNDBY
Instances: 1 Region: north
   Registered instances:
     sales%11
Database: "orcldbs" Registered: Y State: Ok ONS: N. Role: PH_STNDBY
Instances: 1 Region: south
   Registered instances:
     sales%21

GDSCTL>
```

Checking the Current Configured Services

Do the following:

```
GDSCTL> services;
GDSCTL>
```

Checking the Current gdspools in the GSM Configuration

Do the following:

```
GDSCTL> config gdspool
Name                              Broker                    Sharded
----                              ------                    -------
dbpoolora                         No                        No
hr                                No                        No
sales                             Yes                       No

GDSCTL>
```

Checking the Configuration of the Regions

Do the following:

```
GDSCTL> config region
Name                              Buddy
----                              -----
east
north
south

GDSCTL>
```

Testing the Global Service with Attribute locality Set to anywhere

In this test case, we will create a global service named srvc_read_anywhere with the attribute -locality option set to the value ANYWHERE, which is also the default value for the attribute.

```
GDSCTL> add service -service srvc_read_anywhere -gdspool sales -preferred_
all -locality ANYWHERE
The operation completed successfully
GDSCTL>
```

Starting the Service

We can start the service using the GDSCTL command start service.

```
GDSCTL>  start service -service srvc_read_anywhere -gdspool sales
The operation completed successfully
GDSCTL>
```

Checking the Status of the Service

If we check the status of this service by running the services command from GDSCTL, we can see the affinity of this service as ANYWHERE.

```
GDSCTL> services
Service "srvc_read_anywhere.sales.oradbcloud" has 3 instance(s). Affinity:
ANYWHERE
   Instance "sales%1", name: "orcldb", db: "orcldb", region: "east",
   status: ready.
   Instance "sales%11", name: "orcldbp", db: "orcldbp", region: "north",
   status: ready.
   Instance "sales%21", name: "orcldbs", db: "orcldbs", region: "south",
   status: ready.

GDSCTL>
```

Checking the Configuration of the Service

We can check the configuration of the service using the config service command from GDSCTL.

```
GDSCTL> config service -service srvc_read_anywhere
Name: srvc_read_anywhere
Network name: srvc_read_anywhere.sales.oradbcloud
Pool: sales
Started: Yes
Preferred all: Yes
Locality: ANYWHERE
```

```
Region Failover: No
Role: NONE
Primary Failover: No
Lag: ANY
Runtime Balance: SERVICE_TIME
Connection Balance: LONG
Notification: Yes
TAF Policy: NONE
Policy: AUTOMATIC
DTP: No
Failover Method: NONE
Failover Type: NONE
Failover Retries:
Failover Delay:
Edition:
PDB:
Commit Outcome:
Retention Timeout:
Replay Initiation Timeout:
Session State Consistency:
SQL Translation Profile:
Stop option: NONE
Drain timeout:
Table family:
```

Databases

```
Database                        Preferred Status
--------                        --------- ------
orcldb                          Yes       Enabled
orcldbp                         Yes       Enabled
orcldbs                         Yes       Enabled
```

GDSCTL>

In the previous output, we can see that the locality is set to ANYWHERE.

Checking the Status of the Databases

Do the following:

```
GDSCTL> databases
Database: "orcldb" Registered: Y State: Ok ONS: N. Role: PRIMARY Instances:
1 Region: east
    Service: "srvc_read_anywhere" Globally started: Y Started: Y
            Scan: Y Enabled: Y Preferred: Y
    Registered instances:
      sales%1
Database: "orcldbp" Registered: Y State: Ok ONS: N. Role: PH_STNDBY
Instances: 1 Region: north
    Service: "srvc_read_anywhere" Globally started: Y Started: Y
            Scan: Y Enabled: Y Preferred: Y
    Registered instances:
      sales%11
Database: "orcldbs" Registered: Y State: Ok ONS: N. Role: PH_STNDBY
Instances: 1 Region: south
    Service: "srvc_read_anywhere" Globally started: Y Started: Y
            Scan: Y Enabled: Y Preferred: Y
    Registered instances:
      sales%21

GDSCTL>
```

From the previous output, we can see that the service is started in all the databases that are running in different regions.

TNS Entry for the Service

The following is the TNS entry that we can add to the tnsnames.ora configuration file to test the database connection:

```
srvc_read_anywhere =
  (DESCRIPTION =
   (FAILOVER = ON)
   (ADDRESS_LIST =
     (LOAD_BALANCE = ON)
     (ADDRESS = (PROTOCOL = TCP)(HOST = prim01)(PORT = 1581)))
   (ADDRESS_LIST =
     (LOAD_BALANCE = ON)
     (ADDRESS = (PROTOCOL = TCP)(HOST = stbyh01)(PORT = 1582)))
   (ADDRESS_LIST =
     (LOAD_BALANCE = ON)
     (ADDRESS = (PROTOCOL = TCP)(HOST = stbyh01)(PORT = 1583)))
   (CONNECT_DATA =
     (SERVICE_NAME = srvc_read_anywhere.sales.oradbcloud)
     (REGION = north)                                        ⬅
   )
)
```

Note that in the previous TNS entry we are specifying the parameter region = north. Even though we set the region parameter to north in the TNS entry, the service need not necessarily be routed to the database running in this region. The connection can be routed to any of the available regions where the database supporting this service is up and running. This is because we set the -locality attribute to ANYWHERE while creating the service.

Testing the Database Connection Using This Service

Do the following:

```
[oracle@cstbyh01 admin]$ sqlplus system/welcome@srvc_read_anywhere

SQL*Plus: Release 19.0.0.0.0 - Production on Sat Oct 29 22:19:50 2022
Version 19.17.0.0.0

Copyright (c) 1982, 2022, Oracle.  All rights reserved.

Last Successful login time: Sat Oct 29 2022 19:45:05 -05:00

Connected to:
Oracle Database 19c Enterprise Edition Release 19.0.0.0.0 - Production
Version 19.17.0.0.0

SQL> @/home/oracle/database_info.sql;

DATABASE_HOST        DB_NAME  DB_UNIQUE_NAME  DATABASE_ROLE    OPEN_MODE            STARTUP_TIME
-------------------- -------  --------------- -------------    ------------ ------- ---------------
cstbyh01.localdomain orcldb   orcldbs         PHYSICAL STANDBY READ ONLY WITH APPLY 29-OCT-22

SQL>
```

As you can see from the previous output, the service is connected to the database orcldbs, which is running in the region south.

If we try the connection multiple times without changing anything, each time the connection will be routed to different regions. Let's try the connection again.

```
[oracle@cstbyh01 admin]$ sqlplus system/welcome@srvc_read_anywhere

SQL*Plus: Release 19.0.0.0.0 - Production on Sat Oct 29 22:22:25 2022
Version 19.17.0.0.0

Copyright (c) 1982, 2022, Oracle.  All rights reserved.

Last Successful login time: Sat Oct 29 2022 19:45:05 -05:00

Connected to:
Oracle Database 19c Enterprise Edition Release 19.0.0.0.0 - Production
Version 19.17.0.0.0

SQL> @/home/oracle/database_info.sql;
```

DATABASE_HOST	DB_NAME	DB_UNIQUE_NAME	DATABASE_ROLE	OPEN_MODE	STARTUP_TIME
prim01.localdomain	orcldb	orcldb	PRIMARY	READ WRITE	29-OCT-22

As you can see from the previous output, this time the service is connected to the database orcldb, which is running in the region east. This shows that even though we set the parameter region to a specific region in the TNS entry, the service will still be routed to any of the available regions where the service is running, and this is because the service was created with the attribute locality set to anywhere.

Stopping the Service and Removing the Service

Do the following:

```
GDSCTL> stop service -service srvc_read_anywhere -gdspool sales
The operation completed successfully

GDSCTL> remove  service -service  srvc_read_anywhere -gdspool sales
The operation completed successfully
```

Testing the Global Service with the Attribute locality Set to local_only

In this test case, we will create a service called srvc_read_local_only with the attribute locality set to the value local_only and see how the service will be routed based on the parameter region set in the TNS entry in tnsnames.ora.

```
GDSCTL> add service -service srvc_read_local_only -gdspool sales
-preferred_all -locality LOCAL_ONLY
The operation completed successfully
GDSCTL>
```

Starting the Service

We can start the service using the start service command.

```
GDSCTL> start service -service srvc_read_local_only -gdspool sales
The operation completed successfully
```

Checking the Status of This Service

Check the status of the service by running the services command from GDSCTL; we can see the affinity of this service as LOCALONLY.

```
GDSCTL> services
Service "srvc_read_local_only.sales.oradbcloud" has 3 instance(s).
Affinity: LOCALONLY          <---
    Instance "sales%1", name: "orcldb", db: "orcldb",
    region: "east", status: ready.
    Instance "sales%11", name: "orcldbp", db: "orcldbp", region: "north",
    status: ready.
    Instance "sales%21", name: "orcldbs", db: "orcldbs", region: "south",
    status: ready.

GDSCTL>
```

Checking the Configuration of the Service

We can check the configuration of the service using the config service command from GDSCTL.

```
GDSCTL> config service -service srvc_read_local_only  -gdspool sales
Name: srvc_read_local_only
Network name: srvc_read_local_only.sales.oradbcloud
Pool: sales
Started: Yes
Preferred all: Yes
Locality: LOCAL_ONLY          <---
Region Failover: No
Role: NONE
Primary Failover: No
Lag: ANY
Runtime Balance: SERVICE_TIME
Connection Balance: LONG
Notification: Yes
TAF Policy: NONE
```

```
Policy: AUTOMATIC
DTP: No
Failover Method: NONE
Failover Type: NONE
Failover Retries:
Failover Delay:
Edition:
PDB:
Commit Outcome:
Retention Timeout:
Replay Initiation Timeout:
Session State Consistency:
SQL Translation Profile:
Stop option: NONE
Drain timeout:
Table family:

Databases
------------------------

Database                   Preferred Status
--------                   --------- ------
orcldb                     Yes       Enabled
orcldbp                    Yes       Enabled
orcldbs                    Yes       Enabled

GDSCTL>
```

In the previous output, we can see that the locality is set to LOCAL_ONLY.

Checking the Status of the Databases

Do the following:

```
GDSCTL> databases
Database: "orcldb" Registered: Y State: Ok ONS: N. Role: PRIMARY Instances:
1 Region: east
   Service: "srvc_read_local_only" Globally started: Y Started: Y
           Scan: Y Enabled: Y Preferred: Y
```

```
Registered instances:
   sales%1
Database: "orcldbp" Registered: Y State: Ok ONS: N. Role: PH_STNDBY
Instances: 1 Region: north
  Service: "srvc_read_local_only" Globally started: Y Started: Y
          Scan: Y Enabled: Y Preferred: Y
  Registered instances:
     sales%11
Database: "orcldbs" Registered: Y State: Ok ONS: N. Role: PH_STNDBY
Instances: 1 Region: south
  Service: "srvc_read_local_only" Globally started: Y Started: Y
          Scan: Y Enabled: Y Preferred: Y
  Registered instances:
     sales%21

GDSCTL>
```

From the previous output, we can see that the service is started in all the databases that are running in different regions.

Let's prepare a TNS entry with a region parameter set to east and test the database connection using the service. The following is the TNS entry that we can add to the tnsnames.ora file and test the database connection:

```
srvc_read_local_only =
   (DESCRIPTION =
    (FAILOVER = ON)
    (ADDRESS_LIST =
      (LOAD_BALANCE = ON)
      (ADDRESS = (PROTOCOL = TCP)(HOST = prim01)(PORT = 1581)))
    (ADDRESS_LIST =
      (LOAD_BALANCE = ON)
      (ADDRESS = (PROTOCOL = TCP)(HOST = stbyh01)(PORT = 1582)))
    (ADDRESS_LIST =
      (LOAD_BALANCE = ON)
      (ADDRESS = (PROTOCOL = TCP)(HOST = stbyh01)(PORT = 1583)))
```

```
(CONNECT_DATA =
  (SERVICE_NAME = srvc_read_local_only.sales.oradbcloud)     ⬅
  (REGION = east)
)
)
```

We included the parameter region=east in the TNS entry. Now if we connect to the service using the service, it should connect only to the database that is running in the region east. In our case, it should connect to the database orcldb.

```
[oracle@cstbyh01 admin]$ sqlplus system/welcome@srvc_read_local_only

SQL*Plus: Release 19.0.0.0.0 - Production on Sat Oct 29 22:26:34 2022
Version 19.17.0.0.0

Copyright (c) 1982, 2022, Oracle.  All rights reserved.

Last Successful login time: Sat Oct 29 2022 22:22:25 -05:00

Connected to:
Oracle Database 19c Enterprise Edition Release 19.0.0.0.0 - Production
Version 19.17.0.0.0

SQL>@/home/oracle/database_info.sql;
```

DATABASE_HOST	DB_NAME	DB_UNIQUE_NAME	DATABASE_ROLE	OPEN_MODE	STARTUP_TIME
prim01.localdomain	orcldb	orcldb	PRIMARY	READ WRITE	29-OCT-22

```
SQL>
```

As you can see, based on the region property defined in the tnsnames.ora file, the service is routed to the database running in that specific region. This was possible because we used the option locality=local_only while creating the service.

If you change the region property to north and retry the database connection, this time the service will be routed to the database orcldb that is running in the region north. Let's update the region property to north for the TNS entry in the tnsnames.ora file.

```
srvc_read_local_only =
  (DESCRIPTION =
  (FAILOVER = ON)
```

```
    (ADDRESS_LIST =
      (LOAD_BALANCE = ON)
      (ADDRESS = (PROTOCOL· = TCP)(HOST = prim01)(PORT = 1581)))
    (ADDRESS_LIST =
      (LOAD_BALANCE = ON)
      (ADDRESS = (PROTOCOL = TCP)(HOST = stbyh01)(PORT = 1582)))
    (ADDRESS_LIST =
      (LOAD_BALANCE = ON)
      (ADDRESS = (PROTOCOL = TCP)(HOST = stbyh01)(PORT = 1583)))
    (CONNECT_DATA =
      (SERVICE_NAME = srvc_read_local_only.sales.oradbcloud)
      (REGION = north)
    )
)
```

Now if we connect to the database orcldbp using the service srvc_read_local_only, which is running in the region north, we get this:

```
[oracle@cstbyh01 admin]$ sqlplus system/welcome@srvc_read_local_only

SQL*Plus: Release 19.0.0.0.0 - Production on Sat Oct 29 22:27:59 2022
Version 19.17.0.0.0

Copyright (c) 1982, 2022, Oracle.  All rights reserved.

Last Successful login time: Sat Oct 29 2022 22:27:32 -05:00


Connected to:
Oracle Database 19c Enterprise Edition Release 19.0.0.0.0 - Production
Version 19.17.0.0.0

SQL>@/home/oracle/database_info.sql;
```

DATABASE_HOST	DB_NAME	DB_UNIQUE_NAME	DATABASE_ROLE	OPEN_MODE	STARTUP_TIME
stbyh01.localdomain	orcldb	orcldbp	PHYSICAL STANDBY	READ ONLY WITH APPLY	29-OCT-22

This shows that depending on the global service attribute and the property region in the TNS entry, the service will be routed to the database.

What will happen if the database running in that specific region is down and unavailable? In this case, if the database orcldbp that is running in the region north is not available for some reason, will the connection fail over to other databases running in other regions? Let's find out: shut down the database orcldbp that is running in the region north.

```
[oracle@stbyh01 admin]$ . oraenv
ORACLE_SID = [orcldbp] ?
The Oracle base remains unchanged with value /u01/app/oracle
[oracle@stbyh01 admin]$ sqlplus / as sysdba

SQL*Plus: Release 19.0.0.0.0 - Production on Sat Oct 29 22:29:14 2022
Version 19.17.0.0.0

Copyright (c) 1982, 2022, Oracle.  All rights reserved.

Connected to:
Oracle Database 19c Enterprise Edition Release 19.0.0.0.0 - Production
Version 19.17.0.0.0

SQL> shutdown immediate;
Database closed.
Database dismounted.
ORACLE instance shut down.
SQL>
```

Now if we connect to the database using the same TNS entry (with region = north), the connection will fail as the database in that region is not available.

```
[oracle@cstbyh01 admin]$ sqlplus system/welcome@srvc_read_local_only

SQL*Plus: Release 19.0.0.0.0 - Production on Sat Oct 29 22:30:11 2022
Version 19.17.0.0.0

Copyright (c) 1982, 2022, Oracle.  All rights reserved.

ERROR:
ORA-12541: TNS:no listener

Enter user-name:
```

So, if the database is running in the region defined in the TNS entry is not available, the database connection fails. Can we avoid this situation, and can we make the service work even if the database running in the specified regions is down? The answer is yes. When we create the service with the attribute locality = local_only, we can specify another option called region_failover. When we create the service with these two attributes, if the database running in the region (mentioned in the TNS entry) is not available, the service will automatically connect to the databases that are running in the other regions as the service is already up and running in the other regions. Let's test this scenario.

We will create a new service with the name srvc_read_local_only_region_faliver as shown here:

```
GDSCTL> add service -service srvc_read_local_only_region_faliver -gdspool
sales -preferred_all -locality LOCAL_ONLY -region_failover
The operation completed successfully
```

Please note that, as mentioned earlier, if the databases in the GSM configuration are RAC databases, we need to add all the instances of all the databases in the configuration to the service using the modify service command.

```
GDSCTL> modify service -service srvc_read_local_only_region_faliver
-gdspool sales -database orcldb -modify_instances -preferred
orcldb1,orcldb2;
```

Starting the Service

Do the following:

```
GDSCTL> start service -service srvc_read_local_only -gdspool sales
The operation completed successfully
```

Checking the Status of This Service

If we check the status of this service by running the services command from GDSCTL, we can see the affinity of this service as LOCALPREF, which means the local region is preferred for a new connection.

```
GDSCTL> services
Service "srvc_read_local_only_region_faliver.sales.oradbcloud" has 3
instance(s). Affinity: LOCALPREF
Instance "sales%1", name: "orcldb", db: "orcldb", region: "east",
status: ready.
Instance "sales%11", name: "orcldbp", db: "orcldbp", region: "north",
status: ready.
Instance "sales%21", name: "orcldbs", db: "orcldbs", region: "south",
status: ready.

GDSCTL>
```

Checking the Configuration of the Services

We can check the configuration of the service using the config service command from GDSCTL.

```
GDSCTL> config service -service srvc_read_local_only_region_faliver;
Name: srvc_read_local_only_region_faliver
Network name: srvc_read_local_only_region_faliver.sales.oradbcloud
Pool: sales
Started: Yes
Preferred all: Yes
Locality: LOCAL_ONLY
Region Failover: Yes
Role: NONE
Primary Failover: No
Lag: ANY
Runtime Balance: SERVICE_TIME
Connection Balance: LONG
Notification: Yes
TAF Policy: NONE
Policy: AUTOMATIC
DTP: No
Failover Method: NONE
Failover Type: NONE
```

Failover Retries:
Failover Delay:
Edition:
PDB:
Commit Outcome:
Retention Timeout:
Replay Initiation Timeout:
Session State Consistency:
SQL Translation Profile:
Stop option: NONE
Drain timeout:
Table family:

Databases

Database	Preferred	Status
orcldb	Yes	Enabled
orcldbp	Yes	Enabled
orcldbs	Yes	Enabled

GDSCTL>

In the previous output, we can see that the locality is set to LOCAL_ONLY and region_
failover is set to YES. With this combination, the service will first be routed to the region
defined in the parameter region in the TNS entry in the tnsnames.ora file. If, for some
reason, the database in that region is not available, the service will automatically failover
to the databases running in other regions.

Checking the Status of the Databases

Do the following:

```
GDSCTL> databases;
Database: "orcldb" Registered: Y State: Ok ONS: N. Role: PRIMARY Instances:
1 Region: east
   Service: "srvc_read_local_only_region_faliver" Globally started: Y Started: Y
           Scan: Y Enabled: Y Preferred: Y
```

```
Registered instances:
  sales%1
Database: "orcldbp" Registered: Y State: Ok ONS: N. Role: PH_STNDBY
Instances: 1 Region: north
  Service: "srvc_read_local_only_region_faliver" Globally started: Y
  Started: Y
          Scan: Y Enabled: Y Preferred: Y
  Registered instances:
    sales%11
Database: "orcldbs" Registered: Y State: Ok ONS: N. Role: PH_STNDBY
Instances: 1 Region: south
  Service: "srvc_read_local_only_region_faliver" Globally started: Y
  Started: Y
          Scan: Y Enabled: Y Preferred: Y
  Registered instances:
    sales%21

GDSCTL>
```

From this output, we can see that the service is started in all the databases that are running in different regions.

The following is the TNS entry that we can add to the tnsnames.ora file:

```
srvc_read_local_only_region_faliver =
  (DESCRIPTION =
   (FAILOVER = ON)
   (ADDRESS_LIST =
     (LOAD_BALANCE = ON)
     (ADDRESS = (PROTOCOL = TCP)(HOST = prim01)(PORT = 1581)))
   (ADDRESS_LIST =
     (LOAD_BALANCE = ON)
     (ADDRESS = (PROTOCOL = TCP)(HOST = stbyh01)(PORT = 1582)))
   (ADDRESS_LIST =
     (LOAD_BALANCE = ON)
     (ADDRESS = (PROTOCOL = TCP)(HOST = cstbyh01)(PORT = 1583)))
```

```
(CONNECT_DATA =
  (SERVICE_NAME = srvc_read_local_only_region_faliver.sales.oradbcloud)
  (REGION = north)
)
)
```

Note that in the previous TNS entry, we are specifying the region as north. And, when we launch a SQL*Plus session and try to connect the database using this service, it will always be routed to a database in the GDS region north.

Testing the Database Connection Using This Service

Do the following:

```
SQL*Plus: Release 19.0.0.0.0 - Production on Sat Oct 29 22:39:36 2022
Version 19.17.0.0.0

Copyright (c) 1982, 2022, Oracle.  All rights reserved.

Last Successful login time: Sat Oct 29 2022 22:27:32 -05:00

Connected to:
Oracle Database 19c Enterprise Edition Release 19.0.0.0.0 - Production
Version 19.17.0.0.0

SQL>@/home/oracle/database_info.sql;
```

DATABASE_HOST	DB_NAME	DB_UNIQUE_NAME	DATABASE_ROLE	OPEN_MODE	STARTUP_TIME
stbyh01.localdomain	orcldb	orcldbp	PHYSICAL STANDBY	READ ONLY WITH APPLY	29-OCT-22

```
SQL>
```

As you can see from the output, the service connected to the database orcldbp is running in the region north.

Now, let's shut down the database orcldbp that is running in the region north.

```
[[oracle@stbyh01 admin]$ sqlplus / as sysdba

SQL*Plus: Release 19.0.0.0.0 - Production on Sat Oct 29 22:40:29 2022
Version 19.17.0.0.0
```

Copyright (c) 1982, 2022, Oracle. All rights reserved.

Connected to:
Oracle Database 19c Enterprise Edition Release 19.0.0.0.0 - Production
Version 19.17.0.0.0

```
SQL> shutdown immediate;
Database closed.
Database dismounted.
ORACLE instance shut down.
```

Retry the database connection using the same service and same TNS entry and see if the connection will failover or if the connection fails like it did in our previous scenario where we created the service just with the locality attribute and not with the attribute region_failover.

[oracle@cstbyh01 admin]$ sqlplus system/welcome@srvc_read_local_only_region_faliver

SQL*Plus: Release 19.0.0.0.0 - Production on Sat Oct 29 22:41:30 2022
Version 19.17.0.0.0
Copyright (c) 1982, 2022, Oracle. All rights reserved.

Last Successful login time: Sat Oct 29 2022 22:27:32 -05:00

Connected to:
Oracle Database 19c Enterprise Edition Release 19.0.0.0.0 - Production
Version 19.17.0.0.0

SQL>@/home/oracle/database_info.sql;

DATABASE_HOST	DB_NAME	DB_UNIQUE_NAME	DATABASE_ROLE	OPEN_MODE	STARTUP_TIME
prim01.localdomain	orcldb	orcldb	PRIMARY	READ WRITE	29-OCT-22

SQL>

As you can see, even though the database orcldbs running from the region north is down, the connection didn't fail, and the service was failed over to another database, orcldb, which is up and running in another region, east. Isn't that cool? GDS provides different types of high availability for its services.

This completes the demonstration for the test case of local-based routing. We can start the database orcldbs and stop and remove the service that was created for this test case.

```
[oracle@stbyh01 admin]$ sqlplus / as sysdba

SQL*Plus: Release 19.0.0.0.0 - Production on Sat Oct 29 22:42:43 2022
Version 19.17.0.0.0

Copyright (c) 1982, 2022, Oracle.  All rights reserved.

Connected to an idle instance.

SQL> startup;
ORACLE instance started.

Total System Global Area 3053449816 bytes
Fixed Size                   8901208 bytes
Variable Size              620756992 bytes
Database Buffers          2415919104 bytes
Redo Buffers                 7872512 bytes
Database mounted.
Database opened.
SQL>
```

Log in to GDSCTL and stop and remove the service srvc_read_local_only_region_failover.

```
GDSCTL> stop service -service srvc_read_local_only_region_faliver
-gdspool sales;
The operation completed successfully

GDSCTL> remove service -service srvc_read_local_only_region_faliver
-gdspool sales;
The operation completed successfully
GDSCTL>
```

Summary of This Test Case

In this test case, we saw that based on the service attributes and the TNS entry property, the service will be routed to the database that is up and running in the specific region, and the service can also failover to the databases running in other regions if the database running in the region defined in the TNS entry becomes unavailable.

Summary

In this chapter, you learned how to create, start, and use GDS. You also saw the benefits of the database service when it was created as a global service when compared to the local database service. You saw how the global service automatically fails over to the physical standby database when the primary database becomes unavailable.

Known Issues

When we try to stop the global data service running on only a few RAC databases in the GSM configuration, it will display the following error message:

```
GDSCTL> stop service -service srvc_read_local_only_region_faliver
-gdspool sales;
GSM Warnings:
GSM-40138: Service management cannot be performed on a database.
orcldb:ORA-45540: Call to SRVCTL failed with status 2, errors: PRCD-1316
: failed to stop services srvc_read_local_only_region_faliver for
database orcldb
PRCR-1207 : There are no running resources to stop.
.
ORA-06512: at "GSMADMIN_INTERNAL.DBMS_GSM_DBADMIN", line 2834
ORA-06512: at "SYS.DBMS_SYS_ERROR", line 95
ORA-06512: at "GSMADMIN_INTERNAL.DBMS_GSM_DBADMIN", line 2782
ORA-06512: at line 1 (ngsmoci_execute)
orcldbp:ORA-45540: Call to SRVCTL failed with status 2, errors: PRCD-1316
: failed to stop services srvc_read_local_only_region_faliver for
database orcldbp
```

PRCR-1207 : There are no running resources to stop.
.
ORA-06512: at "GSMADMIN_INTERNAL.DBMS_GSM_DBADMIN", line 2834
ORA-06512: at "SYS.DBMS_SYS_ERROR", line 95
ORA-06512: at "GSMADMIN_INTERNAL.DBMS_GSM_DBADMIN", line 2782
ORA-06512: at line 1 (ngsmoci_execute)

GDSCTL>

When trying to stop a service that is not running in all the databases in the GSM configuration, we should use the -database option, as shown here:

GDSCTL> stop service -service srvc_read_local_only_region_faliver -gdspool sales -database orcldb;
The operation completed successfully

When a global service with the attribute locality set to LOCAL_ONLY is created, the affinity should show LOCAL_ONLY, and the service should always be routed to the database running in the region that is specified in the TNS entry. But this is not happening in some versions of Oracle databases.

Let's say, for example, we create a global service with the attribute -locality set to LOCAL_ONLY, as shown here:

GDSCTL> add service -service reg_local_only -gdspool sales -locality LOCAL_ONLY
The operation completed successfully

Now, when we run the service command from the GDSCTL prompt, we get this:

GDSCTL> services;
Service "srvc_read_local_only.sales.oradbcloud" has 6 ⬅——————
instance(s). Affinity: ANYWHERE
  Instance "sales%1", name: "orcldb1", db: "orcldb",
  region: "east", status: ready.
    Instance "sales%11", name: "orcldbs1", db: "orcldbs", region: "north",
    status: ready.
    Instance "sales%12", name: "orcldbs2", db: "orcldbs", region: "north",
    status: ready.

```
Instance "sales%2", name: "orcldb2", db: "orcldb", region: "east",
status: ready.
Instance "sales%21", name: "orcldbp1", db: "orcldbp", region: "south",
status: ready.
Instance "sales%22", name: "orcldbp2", db: "orcldbp", region: "south",
status: ready.

GDSCTL>
```

As you can see, the affinity is still showing the default value, which is ANYWHERE, whereas it should show LOCAL_ONLY.

We were having this issue in Oracle 19c (19.11.0), and Oracle has included a fix for this issue in the July 2021 PSU. Once you apply the patch, this issue is fixed.

CHAPTER 7

Test Cases: Using Oracle GDS with Oracle GG

In this chapter, you will learn how Global Data Services (GDS) can be used in an environment configured with Oracle GoldenGate (GG) replication. You will also explore the GSM options and test one scenario that demonstrates the use cases for GDS when you have Oracle GG configured in one of the GDS pool databases. We will cover the following topics:

- The environment setup used for the demonstrations

- The global service failover test case with examples using Oracle GoldenGate

Setting Up the Environment

Our setup includes a single-instance primary database and a single-instance target database that is being synced with the primary database using Oracle GoldenGate. We have installed Oracle 19c (19.3.0) and applied the October 2022 patch set update (PSU) for both environments.

Primary Database Version and the Patch Set

Here are the details:

```
Primary DB server   : prim01.localdomain
OS version          : Oracle Enterprise Linux 7.1 64 bit
Oracle Home         : /u01/app/oracle/product/19.3.0.0/dbhome_1
Database Version    : 19.3.0.0 with October 2022 Database Bundle Patch
```

© Y V Ravi Kumar, Mariami Kupatadze, Sambaiah Sammeta 2023
Y V Ravi Kumar et al., *Oracle Global Data Services for Mission-critical Systems*,
https://doi.org/10.1007/978-1-4842-9553-3_7

```
[oracle@ prim01 ~]$ export ORACLE_HOME=/u01/app/oracle/product/19.3.0.0/dbhome_1
[oracle@ prim01 ~]$ export PATH=$ORACLE_HOME/bin:$PATH

[oracle@prim01 ~]$ $ORACLE_HOME/OPatch/opatch lspatches
34419443;Database Release Update : 19.17.0.0.221018 (34419443)
29585399;OCW RELEASE UPDATE 19.3.0.0.0 (29585399)

OPatch succeeded
```

The primary database name is orcldb, and it's located in the east region. The following are the instance details:

```
SQL> @/home/oracle/database_info.sql
```

DATABASE_HOST	DB_NAME	DB_UNIQUE_NAME	DATABASE_ROLE	OPEN_MODE	STARTUP_TIME
prim01.localdomain	orcldb	orcldb	PRIMARY	READ WRITE	13-NOV-22

Oracle GoldenGate Replicated Database

The target replicated database environment is the same version as our primary database, i.e., Oracle 19c (19.3.0) database binaries patched with the Oct 2022 PSU.

```
First Standby server  : ggdbh01.localdomain
OS version            : Oracle Enterprise Linux 7.1 64 bit
Oracle Home           : /u01/app/oracle/product/19.3.0.0/dbhome_1
Database Version      : 19.3.0.0 with October 2022 Database Bundle Patch

[oracle@stbyh01]$ export ORACLE_HOME=/u01/app/oracle/product/19.3.0.0/
dbhome_1
[oracle@stbyh01]$ export PATH=$ORACLE_HOME/bin:$PATH

[oracle@stbyh01 ~]$ $ORACLE_HOME/OPatch/opatch lspatches
34419443;Database Release Update : 19.17.0.0.221018 (34419443)
29585399;OCW RELEASE UPDATE 19.3.0.0.0 (29585399)

Opatch succeeded.
[oracle@stbyh01 ~]
```

The target database name is ggoradb, and this database is in the west region.

```
SQL> @/home/oracle/database_info.sql
```

DATABASE_HOST	DB_NAME	DB_UNIQUE_NAME	DATABASE_ROLE	OPEN_MODE	STARTUP_TIME
ggdbh01.localdomain	ggoradb	ggoradb	PRIMARY NDBY	READ WRITE	13-NOV-22

Information About the GDS Catalog Database

We have also created a catalog database named catgds on the same server, prim01, where we have our primary database running. The following is the catalog database information:

```
SQL> @/home/oracle/database_info.sql
```

DATABASE_HOST	DB_NAME	DB_UNIQUE_NAME	DATABASE_ROLE	OPEN_MODE	STARTUP_TIME
prim01.localdomain	catgds	catgds	PRIMARY	READ WRITE	28-OCT-22

To provide high availability for the catalog database, a physical standby database named catgdsdr has been set up. The following are its physical standby database details:

```
SQL> @/home/oracle/database_info.sql
```

DATABASE_HOST	DB_NAME	DB_UNIQUE_NAME	DATABASE_ROLE	OPEN_MODE	STARTUP_TIME
stbyh01.localdomain	catgds	catgdsdr	PHYSICAL STANDBY	READ ONLY WITH APPLY	28-OCT-22

Database SQL Scripts

We have created two scripts that we can use to check the database and the lag in the physical standby database. We will be using these two scripts throughout this chapter.

The first script will pull the current database details such as the instance name, database mode, and role of the database.

[oracle@gdshol-p1] cat /home/oracle/databases_info.sql

SQL> SELECT in.HOST_NAME "DATABASE_HOST" ,in.INSTANCE_NAME "INST_NAME",db.
db_unique_name "DB_UNIQUE_NAME" , db.DATABASE_ROLE " DATABASE_ROLE",
db.OPEN_MODE " OPEN_MODE ", STARTUP_TIME
from GV$DATABASE db, gv$instance in
where n.INST_ID=d.INST_ID;

The second script will give the physical standby database information and lag in the physical standby database.

```
[oracle@gdshol-p1] cat /home/oracle/standby_db_lag.sql

SQL> SELECT in.HOST_NAME "DATABASE_HOST" ,in.INSTANCE_NAME "INST_NAME",db.
db_unique_name "DB_UNIQUE_NAME" , db.DATABASE_ROLE " DATABASE_ROLE",
db.OPEN_MODE " OPEN_MODE ", STARTUP_TIME
from GV$DATABASE db, gv$instance in
where n.INST_ID=d.INST_ID;

SQL> select inst_id,process, status, thread#, sequence#, block#, blocks
from gv$managed_standby
where process='MRP0';

SQL> select ar.thread#, (select max (sequence#)
from v$archived_log
where archived='YES' and thread#=ar.thread#) archived,max(ar.sequence#)
applied,
(select max(sequence#)
 from v$archived_log
 where archived='YES' and thread#=ar.thread#)-max(ar.sequence#)gap
from v$archived_log ar
 where ar.applied='YES'
group by ar.thread#
order by thread#;
```

Configuration of Oracle GoldenGate

In this chapter, we are going to look at how Oracle GDS can be used in the database environment where data is being replicated between the source Oracle database and the target Oracle database by using Oracle GoldenGate. For this demonstration, we have installed the Oracle 19c GG software in both the source and target database servers. The following is the location of the Oracle GoldenGate home:

```
[oracle@prim01 gghome_1]$ echo $ORACLE_HOME
/u01/app/oracle/product/19.3.0.0/gghome_1
[oracle@prim01 gghome_1]$
```

In the source database, orcldb, we have created one schema named appschema and have created a sample table under this schema named test_tab_1. We have set up unidirectional replication for this schema from the source database, orcldb, and the target database, ggordb.

The following are the details of the extract process (ext2) and pump process (extp2) configured in the source database, orcldb:

```
[oracle@prim01 gsmhome_1]$ cd /u01/app/oracle/product/19.3.0.0/gghome_1
[oracle@prim01 gghome_1]$ ./ggsci

Oracle GoldenGate Command Interpreter for Oracle
Version 19.1.0.0.4 OGGCORE_19.1.0.0.0_PLATFORMS_191017.1054_FBO
Linux, x64, 64bit (optimized), Oracle 19c on Oct 17 2019 21:16:29
Operating system character set identified as UTF-8.

Copyright (C) 1995, 2019, Oracle and/or its affiliates. All rights reserved.

GGSCI (prim01.localdomain) 1> info all

Program     Status     Group     Lag at Chkpt  Time Since Chkpt

MANAGER     RUNNING
EXTRACT     RUNNING    EXT2      00:00:00      00:00:00
EXTRACT     RUNNING    EXTP2     00:00:00      00:00:04

GGSCI (prim01.localdomain) 2> view param EXT2

EXTRACT ext2
USERID gguser@orcldb, PASSWORD welcome
EXTTRAIL /u01/app/oracle/product/19.3.0.0/gghome_1/dirdat/e2
DDL INCLUDE ALL
TABLE appschema.*;

GGSCI (prim01.localdomain) 3> view param EXTP2

EXTRACT extp2
USERID gguser@orcldb, PASSWORD welcome
RMTHOST ggdbh01, MGRPORT 7810
RMTTRAIL /u01/app/oracle/product/19.3.0.0/gghome_1/dirdat/e2
table appschema.*;

GGSCI (prim01.localdomain) 4>
```

The following are the details of the replicate process, rep2, in the target database, ggordb:

```
[oracle@ggdbh01 gghome_1]$ ./ggsci

Oracle GoldenGate Command Interpreter for Oracle
Version 19.1.0.0.4 OGGCORE_19.1.0.0.0_PLATFORMS_191017.1054_FBO
Linux, x64, 64bit (optimized), Oracle 19c on Oct 17 2019 21:16:29
Operating system character set identified as UTF-8.

Copyright (C) 1995, 2019, Oracle and/or its affiliates. All rights reserved.

GGSCI (ggdbh01.localdomain) 1> info all

Program     Status      Group       Lag at Chkpt  Time Since Chkpt

MANAGER     RUNNING
REPLICAT    RUNNING     REP2        00:00:00      00:00:00

GGSCI (ggdbh01.localdomain) 2> view params REP2

REPLICAT rep2
HANDLECOLLISIONS
ASSUMETARGETDEFS
USERID gguser@ggoradb, PASSWORD welcome
MAP appschema.*, TARGET appschema.*;

GGSCI (ggdbh01.localdomain) 3>
```

Currently there is no lag in the target database. The following is the row count of the table test_tab_1 from both the source and target databases.

Check the row count in the source database, orcldb.

```
[oracle@prim01 gghome_1]$ sqlplus / as sysdba

SQL*Plus: Release 19.0.0.0.0 - Production on Tue Nov 15 10:02:33 2022
Version 19.17.0.0.0

Copyright (c) 1982, 2022, Oracle.  All rights reserved.

Connected to:
Oracle Database 19c Enterprise Edition Release 19.0.0.0.0 - Production
Version 19.17.0.0.0
```

```
SQL> select * from appschema.test_tab_1;

NAME
-------------------------------------------------------------------------
FIRST_row

SQL>
```

Check the row count in the target database, ggordb.

```
[oracle@ggdbh01 gghome_1]$ sqlplus / as sysdba

SQL*Plus: Release 19.0.0.0.0 - Production on Tue Nov 15 10:03:13 2022
Version 19.17.0.0.0

Copyright (c) 1982, 2022, Oracle.  All rights reserved.

Connected to:
Oracle Database 19c Enterprise Edition Release 19.0.0.0.0 - Production
Version 19.17.0.0.0

SQL> select * from appschema.test_tab_1;

NAME
-------------------------------------------------------------------------
FIRST_row

SQL>
```

As you can see from these outputs, the table test_tab_1 in the schema appschema has one row at the moment, and it is getting synced using Oracle GoldenGate.

Global Data Service Components Configured for This Demonstration

The GSM is started with the name GSMEAST in the primary database environment, and it's started with the name GSMWEST in the replicated database environment. The primary database orcldb is configured to be in the east region, and the replicated database ggordb is configured to be in the west region. The following is the status of both GSMs and their GDS components.

273

Status of the GSM Running in the Primary Database Server

Here are the details:

```
[oracle@prim01 gghome_1]$ gdsctl
GDSCTL: Version 19.0.0.0.0 - Production on Tue Nov 15 09:06:56 CST 2022

Copyright (c) 2011, 2019, Oracle.  All rights reserved.

Welcome to GDSCTL, type "help" for information.

Current GSM is set to GSMEAST
GDSCTL> status
Alias                     GSMEAST
Version                   19.0.0.0.0
Start Date                13-NOV-2022 09:16:40
Trace Level               off
Listener Log File         /u01/app/oracle/diag/gsm/prim01/gsmeast/
                          alert/log.xml
Listener Trace File       /u01/app/oracle/diag/gsm/prim01/gsmeast/trace/
                          ora_4116_139628251016256.trc
Endpoint summary          (ADDRESS=(HOST=prim01.localdomain)(PORT=1581)
                          (PROTOCOL=tcp))
GSMOCI Version            3.0.180702
Mastership                Y
Connected to GDS catalog  Y
Process Id                4119
Number of reconnections   0
Pending tasks.    Total   0
Tasks in  process. Total  0
Regional Mastership       TRUE
Total messages published  5
Time Zone                 -06:00
Orphaned Buddy Regions:
    None
GDS region                east
```

Network metrics:
    Region: north Network factor:0
    Region: south Network factor:0
    Region: west Network factor:0

GDSCTL>

Status of the GSM Running in the Replicated Database Server

Here are the details:

```
[oracle@ggdbh01 ~]$ . oraenv
ORACLE_SID = [gsm] ? gsm
The Oracle base remains unchanged with value /u01/app/oracle
[oracle@ggdbh01 ~]$ gdsctl
GDSCTL: Version 19.0.0.0.0 - Production on Tue Nov 15 09:10:44 CST 2022

Copyright (c) 2011, 2019, Oracle.  All rights reserved.

Welcome to GDSCTL, type "help" for information.

Current GSM is set to GSMWEST
GDSCTL> status
Alias                       GSMWEST
Version                     19.0.0.0.0
Start Date                  13-NOV-2022 09:58:27
Trace Level                 off
Listener Log File           /u01/app/oracle/diag/gsm/ggdbh01/gsmwest/
                            alert/log.xml
Listener Trace File         /u01/app/oracle/diag/gsm/ggdbh01/gsmwest/trace/
                            ora_6529_140247902645312.trc
Endpoint summary            (ADDRESS=(HOST=ggdbh01.localdomain)(PORT=1584)
                            (PROTOCOL=tcp))
GSMOCI Version              3.0.180702
Mastership                  N
Connected to GDS catalog    Y
Process Id                  6532
Number of reconnections     0
```

```
Pending tasks.       Total  0
Tasks in   process. Total  0
Regional Mastership        TRUE
Total messages published  5
Time Zone                  -06:00
Orphaned Buddy Regions:
     None
GDS region                 west
Network metrics:
   Region: east Network factor:0
   Region: north Network factor:0
   Region: south Network factor:0
GDSCTL>
```

Let's create a new gdspool named datarep.

```
GDSCTL> add gdspool -gdspool datarep
The operation completed successfully

GDSCTL> config gdspool
Name                        Broker                Sharded
----                        ------                -------
datarep                     No                    No

GDSCTL>
```

Currently we have four regions added to the GDS configuration. These are the details:

```
GDSCTL> config region
Name                        Buddy
----                        -----
east                        north
north                       south
south                       west
west                        east
GDSCTL>
```

GDS Pool Databases

Let's check the present database in the GDS configuration.

```
GDSCTL> databases;
GDSCTL>
```

As you can see from the output, we currently don't have any databases in the GDS configuration. Let's add both the databases, orcldb and ggordb, to the gdspool datarep in the GDS configuration by using the add database command. Log in to one of the GSMs and add both databases from the GDSCTL command-line utility.

```
GDSCTL> add database -connect 192.168.2.28:1521:ggoradb -gdspool datarep
-region west
"gsmuser" password:
DB Unique Name: ggoradb
The operation completed successfully

GDSCTL> add database -connect 192.168.2.25:1521:orcldb -gdspool datarep
-region east
"gsmuser" password:
DB Unique Name: orcldb
The operation completed successfully

GDSCTL> databases;
Database: "ggoradb" Registered: Y State: Ok ONS: N. Role: PRIMARY
Instances: 1 Region: west
   Registered instances:
     datarep%11
Database: "orcldb" Registered: Y State: Ok ONS: N. Role: PRIMARY Instances:
1 Region: east
   Registered instances:
     datarep%1
GDSCTL>
```

We have successfully added both databases to the global data service configuration. We can check the configuration of each of the added databases by using the config database command from the GDSCTL utility.

```
GDSCTL> config database -database orcldb
Name: orcldb
Pool: datarep
Status: Ok
State: none
Region: east
Connection string: (DESCRIPTION=(ADDRESS=(HOST=192.168.2.25)(PORT=1521)
(PROTOCOL=tcp))(CONNECT_DATA=(SID=orcldb)))
SCAN address:
ONS remote port: 0
Disk Threshold, ms: 20
CPU Threshold, %: 75
Availability: ONLINE

Supported services
------------------------
Name                                                  Preferred Status
----                                                  ---------- ------

GDSCTL> config database -database ggoradb
Name: ggoradb
Pool: datarep
Status: Ok
State: none
Region: west
Connection string: (DESCRIPTION=(ADDRESS=(HOST=192.168.2.28)(PORT=1521)
(PROTOCOL=tcp))(CONNECT_DATA=(SID=ggoradb)))
SCAN address:
ONS remote port: 0
Disk Threshold, ms: 20
CPU Threshold, %: 75
Availability: ONLINE
```

```
Supported services
-----------------------
Name                                            Preferred Status
----                                            --------- ------

GDSCTL>
```

Please note that if we see that the role of the newly added databases is showing as N/A, we can run the `validate catalog` command from GDSCTL to update the role information.

Test Case: Global Service Failover

In this test case, we will create a service with the preferred database as `orcldb` and the available database as `ggoradb` so that when the service is started, it will start only on the preferred database. In this case, it should start on the database `orcldb`. When the preferred database is not available, the service should failover to the database `ggoradb` automatically. The following are the high-level steps performed as part of this test case demonstration.

High-Level Steps of This Test Case

Here are the steps:

1. Connect to the catalog from the GSM running on the primary database server.

2. Set the GSM to `gsmeast` and create a service named `gg_rep_srvc` with the previously mentioned options.

3. Check the services from GDSCTL to see if the service is created as expected.

4. Define the TNS alias for this service, `gg_rep_srvc`.

5. Connect to the database using the service `gg_rep_srvc` and see to which database it's connecting.

6. Insert some data into the `appschema.gg_test_1` table from the database `orcldb`, and check if the data is being replicated to the database, `ggoradb`.

7. Shut down the database orcldb and check if you are still able to connect the service, as it should connect to the available database, ggoradb.

8. Start the database orcldb.

9. Now check the services again; they should failover to run on the preferred database, orcldb.

10. Remove the service gg_rep_srvc from GDSCTL.

Create a new service as shown here:

```
GDSCTL> add service -service gg_rep_srvc -gdspool datarep -preferred orcldb
-available ggoradb
The operation completed successfully
GDSCTL>
```

Start the service gg_rep_srvc and check the status of the service and the database.

```
GDSCTL> start service -service gg_rep_srvc -gdspool datarep
The operation completed successfully

GDSCTL> services
Service "gg_rep_srvc.datarep.oradbcloud" has 1 instance(s). Affinity: ANYWHERE
   Instance "datarep%1", name: "orcldb", db: "orcldb", region: "east",
   status: ready.
GDSCTL>

GDSCTL> config service -service gg_rep_srvc
Name: gg_rep_srvc
Network name: gg_rep_srvc.datarep.oradbcloud
Pool: datarep
Started: Yes
Preferred all: No
Locality: ANYWHERE
Region Failover: No
Role: NONE
Primary Failover: No
Lag: ANY
```

```
Runtime Balance: SERVICE_TIME
Connection Balance: LONG
Notification: Yes
TAF Policy: NONE
Policy: AUTOMATIC
DTP: No
Failover Method: NONE
Failover Type: NONE
Failover Retries:
Failover Delay:
Edition:
PDB:
Commit Outcome:
Retention Timeout:
Replay Initiation Timeout:
Session State Consistency:
SQL Translation Profile:
Stop option: NONE
Drain timeout:
Table family:

Databases
------------------------

Database                   Preferred Status
--------                   --------- ------
ggoradb                    No        Enabled
orcldb                     Yes       Enabled
GDSCTL>
```

Check the status of the service and the databases from the GDSCTL command prompt. We can see that the service is started only on the database orcldb.

```
GDSCTL> services
Service "gg_rep_srvc.datarep.oradbcloud" has 1 instance(s). Affinity:
ANYWHERE
   Instance "datarep%1", name: "orcldb", db: "orcldb", region: "east",
   status: ready.
```

```
GDSCTL> databases
Database: "ggoradb" Registered: Y State: Ok ONS: N. Role: PRIMARY
Instances: 1 Region: west
   Service: "gg_rep_srvc" Globally started: Y Started: N
           Scan: Y Enabled: Y Preferred: N
   Service: "srvc_prim" Globally started: N Started: N
           Scan: Y Enabled: Y Preferred: Y
   Registered instances:
     datarep%11
Database: "orcldb" Registered: Y State: Ok ONS: N. Role: PRIMARY Instances:
1 Region: east
   Service: "gg_rep_srvc" Globally started: Y Started: Y
           Scan: Y Enabled: Y Preferred: Y
   Service: "srvc_prim" Globally started: N Started: N
           Scan: Y Enabled: Y Preferred: Y
   Registered instances:
     datarep%1

GDSCTL>
```

Checking the Active Services in the Database orcldb

The global service has been created and started; we can query DBA_SERVICES and
V$ACTIVE_SERVICES to learn more about the global services. So, let's connect to the
physical standby database where the global service is currently running.

Check the primary database to see if the service shows up. Connect to the primary
database (orcldb) and query the dba_services view.

```
[oracle@prim01 ~]$ sqlplus / as sysdba

SQL*Plus: Release 19.0.0.0.0 - Production on Fri Oct 28 13:44:02 2022
Version 19.17.0.0.0

Copyright (c) 1982, 2022, Oracle.  All rights reserved.

Connected to:
Oracle Database 19c Enterprise Edition Release 19.0.0.0.0 - Production
Version 19.17.0.0.0
```

```
SQL> column name format a20
SQL> column network_name format a40
SQL> column global_service a19
SQL> set linesize 120
SQL> col global for a10
SQL> select name, network_name, global_service from dba_services;

NAME                 NETWORK_NAME                      GLOBAL_SERVICE
-------------------- --------------------------------- -------------------
SYS$BACKGROUND                                         NO
SYS$USERS                                              NO
orcldb_CFG           orcldb_CFG                        NO
gg_rep_srvc          gg_rep_srvc.datarep.oradbcloud    YES  <=========
orcldbXDB            orcldbXDB                         NO
orcldb               orcldb                            NO
orcldbs              orcldbs                           NO
orcldbp              orcldbp                           NO

8 rows selected.
```

From the previous output, we can see that, for gg_rep_srvc, the value of the column GLOBAL_SERVICE is Yes, denoting that it is a global service.

Now if we query v$active_services in the primary database (orcldb), we can see that the global service gg_rep_srv is started in this database.

```
SQL> select name, network_name, global from v$active_services;

NAME                 NETWORK_NAME                      GLOBAL
-------------------- --------------------------------- ---------
gg_rep_srvc          gg_rep_srvc.datarep.oradbcloud    YES
orcldb               orcldb                            NO
SYS$BACKGROUND                                         NO
SYS$USERS                                              NO
orcldb_CFG           orcldb_CFG                        NO
orcldbXDB            orcldbXDB                         NO

6 rows selected.
SQL>
```

Checking the Active Services in the Database ggoradb

Log in to the first physical standby database, ggoradb, and check the services.

```
[oracle@stbyh01 ~]$ . oraenv
ORACLE_SID = [orcldbp] ?
The Oracle base remains unchanged with value /u01/app/oracle
[oracle@stbyh01 ~]$ sqlplus / as sysdba

SQL*Plus: Release 19.0.0.0.0 - Production on Tue Nov 15 12:16:12 2022
Version 19.17.0.0.0

Copyright (c) 1982, 2022, Oracle.  All rights reserved.

Connected to:
Oracle Database 19c Enterprise Edition Release 19.0.0.0.0 - Production
Version 19.17.0.0.0

SQL> column name format a20
SQL> column network_name format a40
SQL> column global_service for a19
SQL> set linesize 120
SQL> col global for a10
SQL> select name, network_name, global_service from dba_services;
```

NAME	NETWORK_NAME	GLOBAL_SERVICE
SYS$BACKGROUND		NO
SYS$USERS		NO
gg_rep_srvc	gg_rep_srvc.datarep.oradbcloud	YES
ggoradbXDB	ggoradbXDB	NO
ggoradb	ggoradb	NO

```
SQL>

SQL> select name, network_name, global from v$active_services;
```

NAME	NETWORK_NAME	GLOBAL
SYS$BACKGROUND		NO
SYS$USERS		NO
ggoradb	ggoradb	NO
ggoradbXDB	ggoradbXDB	NO

SQL>

As you can see from the output, the global data service gg_rep_srvc has not started in the GG replicated database ggoradb. Since the service was created with the preferred and available options, it is running only on the preferred database at this time. If the preferred database goes down, the service will failover to the available database, ggoradb.

Let's create a TNS alias for the service gg_rep_srvc and try to connect the database using this service. The TNS alias for the service is gg_rep_srvc.

```
gg_rep_srvc =
  (DESCRIPTION =
    (FAILOVER = ON)
    (ADDRESS_LIST =
      (LOAD_BALANCE = ON)
      (ADDRESS = (PROTOCOL = TCP)(HOST = prim01)(PORT = 1581)))
    (ADDRESS_LIST =
      (LOAD_BALANCE = ON)
      (ADDRESS = (PROTOCOL = TCP)(HOST = ggdbh01)(PORT = 1584)))
     (CONNECT_DATA =
      (SERVICE_NAME = gg_rep_srvc.datarep.oradbcloud) (REGION = east)
    )
  )
)
```

Testing the Database Connection

We can test the database connection using the TNS alias, as shown here:

```
[oracle@ggdbh01 ~]$ sqlplus system/welcome@gg_rep_srvc

SQL*Plus: Release 19.0.0.0.0 - Production on Wed Dec 14 10:36:10 2022
```

```
Version 19.17.0.0.0

Copyright (c) 1982, 2022, Oracle.  All rights reserved.

Last Successful login time: Sun Oct 30 2022 06:58:37 -06:00

Connected to:
Oracle Database 19c Enterprise Edition Release 19.0.0.0.0 - Production
Version 19.17.0.0.0
```
```
SQL> @/home/oracle/database_info.sql
```
```
DATABASE_HOST       DB_NAME  DB_UNIQUE_NAME  DATABASE_ROLE  OPEN_MODE    STARTUP_TIME
------------------  -------  --------------  -------------  -----------  ------------
prim01.localdomain  orcldb   orcldb          PRIMARY        READ WRITE   14-DEC-22
```

As expected, the service connection connected to the database orcdb, which is our preferred database in this scenario.

Now let's shut down the database orcldb and see if the connection gets failed over automatically to another database, ggoradb.

```
[oracle@prim01 ~]$ . oraenv
ORACLE_SID = [orcldb] ?
The Oracle base remains unchanged with value /u01/app/oracle
[oracle@prim01 ~]$ sqlplus / as sysdba

SQL*Plus: Release 19.0.0.0.0 - Production on Wed Dec 14 10:50:34 2022
Version 19.17.0.0.0

Copyright (c) 1982, 2022, Oracle.  All rights reserved.

Connected to:
Oracle Database 19c Enterprise Edition Release 19.0.0.0.0 - Production
Version 19.17.0.0.0

SQL> shutdown immediate;
Database closed.
Database dismounted.
ORACLE instance shut down.
SQL>
```

If we run the `services` and `databases` commands from the GDSCTL command prompt, we will see that the service has started and is running on database ggoradb.

```
[oracle@prim01 ~]$ gdsctl
GDSCTL: Version 19.0.0.0.0 - Production on Wed Dec 14 10:55:36 CST 2022

Copyright (c) 2011, 2019, Oracle.  All rights reserved.

Welcome to GDSCTL, type "help" for information.

Current GSM is set to GSMEAST

GDSCTL> services
Service "gg_rep_srvc.datarep.oradbcloud" has 1 instance(s). Affinity:
ANYWHERE
    Instance "datarep%11", name: "ggoradb", db: "ggoradb", region: "west",
status: ready.

GDSCTL> databases
Database: "ggoradb" Registered: Y State: Ok ONS: N. Role: PRIMARY
Instances: 1 Region: west
    Service: "gg_rep_srvc" Globally started: Y Started: Y
            Scan: N Enabled: Y Preferred: N
    Service: "srvc_prim" Globally started: N Started: N
            Scan: Y Enabled: Y Preferred: Y
    Registered instances:
      datarep%11
Database: "orcldb" Registered: N State: Ok ONS: N. Role: N/A Instances: 0
Region: east
    Service: "gg_rep_srvc" Globally started: Y Started: N
            Scan: N Enabled: Y Preferred: Y
    Service: "srvc_prim" Globally started: N Started: N
            Scan: Y Enabled: Y Preferred: Y

GDSCTL>
```

If we try to connect the database using the service gg_rep_srvc, it will connect to the database ggoradb where this service is currently running.

```
[oracle@ggdbh01 ~]$ sqlplus system/welcome@gg_rep_srvc
```

SQL*Plus: Release 19.0.0.0.0 - Production on Wed Dec 14 10:57:03 2022
Version 19.17.0.0.0

Copyright (c) 1982, 2022, Oracle. All rights reserved.

Last Successful login time: Sat Nov 12 2022 13:51:00 -06:00

Connected to:
Oracle Database 19c Enterprise Edition Release 19.0.0.0.0 - Production
Version 19.17.0.0.0

```
SQL> @/home/oracle/database_info.sql
```

DATABASE_HOST	DB_NAME	DB_UNIQUE_NAME	DATABASE_ROLE	OPEN_MODE	STARTUP_TIME
ggdbh01.localdomain	ggoradb	ggoradb	PRIMARY	READ WRITE	14-DEC-22

Relocating the Service in the GDS Environment

We can relocate the service in GDS using the relocate service command. Let's start the database orcldb and try to relocate the service gg_rep_srvc to this database.

```
[oracle@prim01 ~]$ . oraenv
ORACLE_SID = [orcldb] ?
The Oracle base remains unchanged with value /u01/app/oracle
[oracle@prim01 ~]$ sqlplus / as sysdba
```

SQL*Plus: Release 19.0.0.0.0 - Production on Wed Dec 14 11:16:24 2022
Version 19.17.0.0.0

Copyright (c) 1982, 2022, Oracle. All rights reserved.

Connected to an idle instance.

```
SQL> startup;
ORACLE instance started.
```

Total System Global Area 3053449816 bytes
Fixed Size   8901208 bytes
Variable Size   637534208 bytes

```
Database Buffers              2399141888 bytes
Redo Buffers                     7872512 bytes
Database mounted.
Database opened.
```

Since the database orcldb is now started, let's relocate the service using the relocate service command from GDSCTL, as shown here:

```
GDSCTL> services
Service "gg_rep_srvc.datarep.oradbcloud" has 1 instance(s). Affinity:
ANYWHERE
   Instance "datarep%11", name: "ggoradb", db: "ggoradb", region: "west",
   status: ready.

GDSCTL> relocate service -service gg_rep_srvc -gdspool datarep -old_db
ggoradb -new_db orcldb
The operation completed successfully

GDSCTL> services
Service "gg_rep_srvc.datarep.oradbcloud" has 1 instance(s). Affinity:
ANYWHERE
   Instance "datarep%1", name: "orcldb", db: "orcldb", region: "east",
   status: ready.

GDSCTL>
```

Summary

In this chapter, you learned how to create a global data service in an Oracle database environment, which has one source database and one target database and data replicated using Oracle GoldenGate. We also tested the scenario using GDS. We also worked on how to relocate an Oracle global service using the GDSCTL command relocate service.

CHAPTER 8

Test Cases: Using Oracle GDS with Oracle RAC

In this chapter, we will focus mainly on how Global Data Services (GDS) can be used in a Real Application Cluster (RAC) environment. We will test a few scenarios that demonstrate the use cases for GDS in RAC databases. Specifically, we will cover the following topics:

- The environment setup used for the demonstrations

- A few global database service test cases

- A test case with examples

Setting Up the Environment

For this chapter, we are going to use a two-node RAC setup for the primary database and for the two physical standby databases. We have installed Oracle 19c (19.3) for the database binaries on both the primary and physical standby database servers and have applied the October 2022 patch set update (PSU). The Grid Infrastructure (GI) version is Oracle 19c (19.17) in both the primary database and the physical standby database servers. All these servers have the operating system version Oracle Enterprise Linux 7.1.

Primary Database Version and the Patch Set

Here are the details:

```
Cluster nodes      : gdshol-p1
                     gdshol-p2
OS version         : Oracle Enterprise Linux 7.1 64 bit
```

```
Oracle Home            : /u01/app/oracle/product/19.3.0.0/dbhome_1
Database Version       : 19.3.0.0 with October 2022 Database Bundle Patch
Grid Version           : 19.17.0
```

```
[oracle@gdshol-p1 ]$ export ORACLE_HOME=/u01/app/oracle/product/19.3.0.0/
dbhome_1
[oracle@gdshol-p1 ]$ export PATH=$ORACLE_HOME/bin:$PATH

[oracle@gdshol-p1 ~]$ $ORACLE_HOME/OPatch/opatch lspatches
34419443;Database Release Update : 19.17.0.0.221018 (34419443)
29585399;OCW RELEASE UPDATE 19.3.0.0.0 (29585399)

OPatch succeeded.
```

The primary database name is oragdspr, and it's located in the east region. The following are its RAC instances:

```
SQL> @/home/oracle/databases_info.sql

DATABASE_HOST         INSTANCE_NAME  DB_UNIQUE_NAME  DATABASE_ROLE  OPEN_MODE   STARTUP_TIME
--------------------  -------------  --------------  -------------  ----------  ------------
gdshol-p1.localdomain oragdspr1      oragdspr        PRIMARY        READ WRITE  03-NOV-22
gdshol-p2.localdomain oragdspr2      oragdspr        PRIMARY        READ WRITE  03-NOV-22
```

Physical Standby Database Version and the Patch Set

The physical standby database environment is the same version as the primary database environment, i.e., Oracle 19c (19.17) database binaries patched with the Oct 2022 PSU.

```
Cluster nodes          : gdshol-ps1
                         gdshol-ps2
OS version             : Oracle Enterprise Linux 7.1 64 bit
Oracle Home            : /u01/app/oracle/product/19.3.0.0/dbhome_1
Database Version       : 19.3.0.0 with October 2020 Database Bundle Patch
Grid Version           : 19.9.0
```

```
[oracle@gdshol-p1 ]$ export ORACLE_HOME=/u01/app/oracle/product/19.3.0.0/
dbhome_1
[oracle@gdshol-p1 ]$ export PATH=$ORACLE_HOME/bin:$PATH

[oracle@gdshol-p1 ~]$ $ORACLE_HOME/OPatch/opatch lspatches
```

31772784;OCW RELEASE UPDATE 19.9.0.0.0 (31772784)
31771877;Database Release Update : 19.9.0.0.201020 (31771877)

OPatch succeeded.

We have two physical standby databases configured in two different regions. The following are the two standby physical databases and their RAC instances.

The first physical standby database is oragdsdr, and it is in the south region.

```
SQL> @/home/oracle/databases_info.sql
```

DATABASE_HOST	INST_NAME	DB_UNIQUE_NAME	DATABASE_ROLE	OPEN_MODE	STARTUP_TIME
gdshol-s1.localdomain	oragdsdr1	oragdsdr	PHYSICAL STANDBY	READ ONLY WITH APPLY	03-NOV-22
gdshol-s2.localdomain	oragdsdr2	oragdsdr	PHYSICAL STANDBY	READ ONLY WITH APPLY	03-NOV-22

The second physical standby database is oragdstr, and it is in the north region.

```
SQL> @/home/oracle/databases_info.sql
```

DATABASE_HOST	INST_NAME	DB_UNIQUE_NAME	DATABASE_ROLE	OPEN_MODE	STARTUP_TIME
gdshol-s1.localdomain	oragdstr1	oragdstr	PHYSICAL STANDBY	READ ONLY WITH APPLY	03-NOV-22
gdshol-s2.localdomain	oragdstr2	oragdstr	PHYSICAL STANDBY	READ ONLY WITH APPLY	03-NOV-22

We have created two scripts that we can use to check the database and the lag in the standby database. We will be using these two scripts throughout this chapter.

The following script will pull the current database details such as the instance name, database mode, and role of the database:

```
[oracle@gdshol-p1] cat /home/oracle/databases_info.sql

SQL> SELECT in.HOST_NAME "DATABASE_HOST" ,in.INSTANCE_NAME "INST_NAME",db.
db_unique_name "DB_UNIQUE_NAME", db.DATABASE_ROLE " DATABASE_ROLE",
db.OPEN_MODE " OPEN_MODE ", STARTUP_TIME
from GV$DATABASE db, gv$instance in
where n.INST_ID=d.INST_ID;
```

The following script will give the physical standby database information and lag in the physical standby database:

```
[oracle@gdshol-p1] cat /home/oracle/standby_db_lag.sql

SQL> SELECT in.HOST_NAME "DATABASE_HOST" ,in.INSTANCE_NAME "INST_NAME",db.
db_unique_name "DB_UNIQUE_NAME" , db.DATABASE_ROLE " DATABASE_ROLE",
db.OPEN_MODE " OPEN_MODE ", STARTUP_TIME
```

```
from GV$DATABASE db, gv$instance in
where n.INST_ID=d.INST_ID;

SQL> select inst_id,process, status, thread#, sequence#, block#, blocks
from gv$managed_standby
where process='MRPO';

SQL>select ar.thread#, (select max (sequence#)
from v$archived_log
where archived='YES' and thread#=ar.thread#) archived,max(ar.sequence#)
applied,
(select max(sequence#) from v$archived_log where archived='YES' and
thread#=ar.thread#)-max(ar.sequence#)gap
 from v$archived_log ar where ar.applied='YES' group by ar.thread# order by
thread#;
```

GSMGSMs, Regions, gdspools, and Databases

Let's go through a few details about what GSMs are configured and what regions and gdspools are created that will be used for the test cases demonstrated in this chapter.

Global Service Manager

In the RAC environment, we have more than one node in the cluster. It is recommended to install a GSM in all the nodes so that each GSM can provide high availability and avoid a single point of failure. As of today, Oracle doesn't support installing GSMs in multiple hosts; we will have to install them separately.

In our case, we have installed a GSM in both nodes of the primary and physical standby database servers. For this demonstration, we have created three GSMs. The first one runs from the primary database server, and the other two GSMs are running from two different homes on the first node of the physical standby database servers. We have also registered all three GSMs in the catalog database. The following are the details of all the three GSMs.

The first GSM is configured with the name gsmeast, and it is running from the first node of the primary database server.

```
gsm name         : gsmeast
Host running on : gdshol-p1
GSM home : /u01/app/oracle/product/19.3.0.0/gsmhome_1

GDSCTL> status gsm -gsm gsmeast
Alias                    GSMEAST
Version                  19.0.0.0.0
Start Date               03-NOV-2022 12:10:53
Trace Level              off
Listener Log File        /u01/app/oracle/diag/gsm/gdshol-p1/gsmeast/
                         alert/log.xml
Listener Trace File      /u01/app/oracle/diag/gsm/gdshol-p1/gsmeast/trace/
                         ora_20810_140021393914944.trc
Endpoint summary         (ADDRESS=(HOST=gdshol-p1.localdomain)(PORT=1581)
                         (PROTOCOL=tcp))
GSMOCI Version           3.0.180702
Mastership               N
Connected to GDS catalog Y
Process Id               20813
Number of reconnections  0
Pending tasks.     Total 0
Tasks in  process. Total 0
Regional Mastership      FALSE
Total messages published 0
Time Zone                -05:00
Orphaned Buddy Regions:
    None
GDS region               regionora

GDSCTL>
```

Since we have two physical standby databases on the same servers, we have configured two GSMs in two different homes on both nodes of the physical standby database servers. The following are the details of the two installed GSMs. We also added an entry for both GSMs in oratab so that we can source the environment when we want to use it.

The first GSM on the standby database server is configured with the name gsmnorth, and it's running from the Oracle home, gshome_1.

```
GSM home          : /u01/app/oracle/product/19.3.0.0/gsmhome_1
gsm name          : gsmnorth
Host running on : gdshol-s1
GDSCTL> status gsm -gsm gsmnorth
Alias                     GSMNORTH
Version                   19.0.0.0.0
Start Date                03-NOV-2022 12:10:40
Trace Level               off
Listener Log File         /u01/app/oracle/diag/gsm/gdshol-s1/gsmnorth/
                          alert/log.xml
Listener Trace File       /u01/app/oracle/diag/gsm/gdshol-s1/gsmnorth/
                          trace/ora_15484_140711147297856.trc
Endpoint summary          (ADDRESS=(HOST=gdshol-s1.localdomain)(PORT=1582)
                          (PROTOCOL=tcp))
GSMOCI Version            3.0.180702
Mastership                Y
Connected to GDS catalog  Y
Process Id                15490
Number of reconnections   0
Pending tasks.     Total  0
Tasks in  process. Total  0
Alert: GSM listener rejected database registration.
Regional Mastership       TRUE
Total messages published  0
Time Zone                 -05:00
Orphaned Buddy Regions:
     None
GDS region                regionora

GDSCTL>
```

The second GSM on the physical standby database server is configured with the name gsmsouth, and it's running from the Oracle home, gsmhome_2.

```
GSM home          : /u01/app/oracle/product/19.3.0.0/gsmhome_2
gsm name          : gsmsouth
Host running on : gdshol-s1

GDSCTL> status gsm -gsm gsmsouth
Alias                      GSMSOUTH
Version                    19.0.0.0.0
Start Date                 03-NOV-2022 12:10:49
Trace Level                off
Listener Log File          /u01/app/oracle/diag/gsm/gdshol-s1/gsmsouth/
                           alert/log.xml
Listener Trace File        /u01/app/oracle/diag/gsm/gdshol-s1/gsmsouth/
                           trace/ora_15622_139633660685376.trc
Endpoint summary           (ADDRESS=(HOST=gdshol-s1.localdomain)(PORT=1583)
                           (PROTOCOL=tcp))
GSMOCI Version             3.0.180702
Mastership                 N
Connected to GDS catalog   Y
Process Id                 15652
Number of reconnections    0
Pending tasks.     Total   0
Tasks in  process. Total   0
Alert: GSM listener rejected database registration.
Regional Mastership        FALSE
Total messages published   0
Time Zone                  -05:00
Orphaned Buddy Regions:
     None
GDS region                 regionora

GDSCTL>
```

gdspool Created for This Exercise

We have created a gdspool named `salespro`. The following is the gdspool information:

```
GDSCTL> config gdspool
Name                             Broker                Sharded
----                             ------                -------
dbpoolora                        No                    No
salespro                         No                    No
```

Regions Created for This Exercise

We have created three regions as part of this exercise. The first region is named `east`, and it's been assigned to the primary database, `oragdspr`. The second region is named `north`, and it's been assigned to the physical standby database, `oragdsdr`. The third region is named `south` and is assigned to the physical standby database, `oragdstr`. The following is the region information:

```
GDSCTL> config region
Name                             Buddy
----                             -----
east
north
regionora
south

GDSCTL>
```

GDS Catalog Repository and Database Information

We have created the catalog repository in the catalog database, `catgdspr`, which is a two-node 19c RAC database created on the same servers where we have our primary database running. The following is the catalog database information:

```
SQL> @/home/oracle/databases_info.sql
```

DATABASE_HOST	DB_NAME	DB_UNIQUE_NAME	DATABASE_ROLE	OPEN_MODE	STARTUP_TIME
gdshol-p1.localdomain	catgdspr1	catgdspr	PRIMARY	READ WRITE	03-NOV-22
gdshol-p2.localdomain	catgdspr2	catgdspr	PRIMARY	READ WRITE	03-NOV-22

The following is the TNS entry for the catalog database in our environment. Since this is a RAC database, we can use the scan name in the connect string while trying to connect the catalog database.

```
CATGDSPR =
  (DESCRIPTION =
    (ADDRESS = (PROTOCOL = TCP)(HOST = gdshol-p-scan)(PORT = 1521))
    (CONNECT_DATA =
      (SERVER = DEDICATED)
      (SERVICE_NAME = catgdspr)
    )
  )
```

As mentioned in one of the earlier chapters, Oracle recommends that the GDS administrator must use the GDSCTL utility to manage GDS and not to directly connect and use the catalog database to manage the GDS configuration.

We must make sure that we are able to use tnsping and connect to the catalog database from all the servers where the gdspool databases are running.

```
[oracle@gdshol-s1 admin]$ tnsping catgdspr

TNS Ping Utility for Linux: Version 19.0.0.0.0 - Production on 03-NOV-2022
11:09:45
Copyright (c) 1997, 2022, Oracle.  All rights reserved.
Used parameter files:

Used TNSNAMES adapter to resolve the alias
Attempting to contact (DESCRIPTION = (ADDRESS = (PROTOCOL = TCP)(HOST =
gdshol-p-scan)(PORT = 1521)) (CONNECT_DATA = (SERVER = DEDICATED) (SERVICE_
NAME = catgdspr)))
OK (0 msec)
[oracle@gdshol-s1 admin]$

[oracle@gdshol-s2 admin]$ sqlplus gsmadm/welcome@catgdspr

SQL*Plus: Release 19.0.0.0.0 - Production on Thu Nov 3 11:11:37 2022
Version 19.17.0.0.0
Copyright (c) 1982, 2022, Oracle.  All rights reserved.
```

```
Connected to:
Oracle Database 19c Enterprise Edition Release 19.0.0.0.0 - Production
Version 19.17.0.0.0
SQL>
```

Adding gdspool Databases to the GDS Configuration

We have created a GSM, region, and gdspool, and all are active. We can now add our databases to the GDS configuration. To create and start any global data services, we first need to add the database to the GDS configuration. As explained earlier, the database that is being added to the GDS pool must use the server parameter file (spfile), and it should also have scan set up if the database is a RAC database. In this case, all the primary and physical standby databases that will be added to GDS are RAC databases and are using spfiles.

Adding a RAC Database to the Global Data Service Configuration

If you want to add a RAC database to the global data service configuration, we must give the scan name in the add database command, as shown in the following example:

```
GDSCTL> add database -connect scan-19cracp:1521/orcldb -region east
-gdspool SALES
"gsmuser" password:
DB Unique Name: orcldb
The operation completed successfully
GDSCTL>
```

In the previous example, we are adding a RAC database called orcldb to the gdspool sales in the region east. As you can see, the add database command did ask for the password for the GDS administrator user account, gsmuser, and once we gave it the command, the execution was successful. As we can see, we gave the scan name while adding the RAC database.

In our scenario, since all the databases are part of the Data Guard broker configuration, we will add the Data Guard broker configuration directly to the catalog using the add brokerconfig command. When we add the Data Guard broker configuration into a GDS configuration, the broker configuration is managed as one entity. Also, we cannot add or delete individual databases that are part of the Data Guard broker configuration; we can only add or remove an entire broker configuration to or from a GDS pool. Also, a single broker configuration can belong to only one GDS pool, and it cannot span multiple pools.

The following is the command syntax for adding a broker configuration to the GDS:

```
GDSCTL> add brokerconfig -connect scan/ip:port:Primary_database_
sid  -region region_name -gdspool gdspool_name
```

From the GDSCTL prompt, connect to the catalog. Let's add our databases by adding the broker configuration to the global data service, as shown here:

```
[oracle@gdshol-p1 admin]$ gdsctl
GDSCTL: Version 19.0.0.0.0 - Production on Thu Nov 03 12:36:17 CDT 2022

Copyright (c) 2011, 2019, Oracle.  All rights reserved.

Welcome to GDSCTL, type "help" for information.

Current GSM is set to GSMEAST
GDSCTL> connect gsmadm/welcome@gdshol-p-scan:1521/CATGDSPR;
Catalog connection is established
GDSCTL> add brokerconfig -connect gdshol-p-scan:1521/oragdspr -gdspool
salespro -region east;
"gsmuser" password:
DB Unique Name: oragdspr
The operation completed successfully
GDSCTL>
```

After successfully adding the broker configuration, we can run the databases command from GDSCTL to verify if all the databases were added to the GDS configuration.

```
GDSCTL> databases;
Database: "oragdsdr" Registered: N State: Ok ONS: Y. Role: N/A Instances: 0
Region: N/A
Database: "oragdspr" Registered: Y State: Ok ONS: Y. Role: PRIMARY
Instances: 2 Region: east
```

```
    Registered instances:
      salespro%1
      salespro%2
Database: "oragdstr" Registered: N State: Ok ONS: Y. Role: N/A Instances: 0
Region: N/A

GDSCTL>
```

As you can see from the previous output, all the databases that are part of the Data Guard broker configuration were added to the GDS configuration.

Also, from the previous output, we can see that the status of the primary database and physical standby databases is showing ok. The Role is showing correctly for the primary database with its assigned region info, but the Role for the physical standby databases is showing as status N/A; the physical standby database region is also showing as status N/A with the physical standby database instances count showing as zero.

Also, when we run the config database command, we can see that there are no regions associated with the physical standby databases.

```
GDSCTL> config database
Name            Pool            Status      State       Region      Availability
----            ----            ------      -----       ------      ------------
oragdsdr        salespro        ok          none
oragdspr        salespro        Ok          none        east        ONLINE
oragdstr        salespro        ok          none

GDSCTL>
```

Let's update the configuration for each of the databases. We can update the configuration for any database in the GDS configuration by running the modify database command from GDSCTL. As discussed earlier, we can always run help commands in GDSCTL to get the syntax of the specific command. The following example gives the output of the help modify database command:

```
GDSCTL> help modify database
Syntax
MODIFY DATABASE -database db_name_list [-gdspool pool] [-region region_name
][-pwd password ] [-connect connect_identifier ] [-scan scan_address] [-ons
onsport] [-savename] [-cpu_threshold cpu][-disk_threshold disk]
```

Purpose
Modify the configuration parameters of the databases. Multiple
databases are
allowed if and only if region property is modified

Usage Notes

Keywords and Parameters
connect: an Oracle Net connect descriptor or net service name that
resolves

                to a connect descriptor for the database (or shard)
cpu_threshold: CPU Utilization percentage threshold.
database: a comma-delimited list of databases.
disk_threshold: average latency in milliseconds of a synchronous single-
block read.
gdspool: the GDS pool (If not specified and there is only one
gdspool with

                access granted to user, it will be used by default)
ons: CRS ONS port.
pwd: "gsmuser" password ("gsmrootuser" for add cdb).
region: GDS region database, catalog, shard, shardgroup or GSM
belong to.
savename: store net service name specified with -connect option,
rather than

                connect descriptor from tnsnames.ora.
scan: database SCAN address.

Examples
Change GDS region of databases DB1 and DB3 to EAST
GDSCTL> modify database -database db1,db3 -region east

Let's first modify the database configuration to add the region for both the physical
standby databases.

Update the configuration for the first physical standby database, oragdsdr.

GDSCTL> modify database -database oragdsdr -region north -gdspool
salespro;
The operation completed successfully

Update the configuration for the second physical standby database, oragdstr.

```
GDSCTL> modify database -database oragdstr  -region south -gdspool
salespro;
The operation completed successfully
```

Let's run the config database and databases commands and see if the region was reflected.

```
GDSCTL> config database
Name             Pool             Status    State     Region    Availability
----             ----             ------    -----     ------    ------------
oragdsdr         salespro         Ok        none      north     READ ONLY
oragdspr         salespro         Ok        none      east      ONLINE
oragdstr         salespro         Ok        none      south     READ ONLY

GDSCTL>

GDSCTL> databases;
Database: "oragdsdr" Registered: N State: Ok ONS: Y. Role: N/A Instances:
0 Region: north Database: "oragdspr" Registered: Y State: Ok ONS: Y. Role:
PRIMARY Instances: 2 Region: east
   Registered instances:
     salespro%1
     salespro%2
Database: "oragdstr" Registered: N State: Ok ONS: Y. Role: N/A Instances: 0
Region: south

GDSCTL>
```

Since this is a RAC database, we must add the second node of both the primary database and the physical standby databases to the GDS configuration; only then will the database instances running on other nodes be registered with the GSM. Once we add the nodes, we must validate the catalog to cross-check the catalog information. Once we do this, all the instances of both the primary and physical standby databases will be registered with the GSM. For this, we can use the command add invitenode to add the other nodes of the RAC databases.

If you are not sure about the syntax, you can run the help add invitenode command from GDSCTL, and it will give the correct syntax, as shown here:

```
GDSCTL> help add invitednode
Syntax
ADD INVITEDNODE [-group name] [-catalog catalogdb [-user username/
password]]
vncr_id
```

Purpose
Adds VNCR to GDS catalog. Allows to add VNCR before first GSM is started(by establishing "direct" connection to GDS catalog db).

Usage Notes

Keywords and Parameters
catalog: GDS catalog connection string (TNS alias).
group: group alias which defines a group of VNCRs (i.e. the same alias can be used
         in multiple ADD calls)
user: credentials (name[/password]) of the user that has the GDS administrator
         privileges on the catalog database
vncr_id: host address (ip4, ip6, host name, netmask, e.t.c).

Examples
```
ADD INVITEDNODE 127.0.0.1
ADD INVITEDNODE -group easteast1.us.oracle.com
ADD INVITEDNODE -group east east2.us.oracle.com
```

```
GDSCTL>
```

Using the IP address of the second node of the primary database, let's add it to the configuration.

```
GDSCTL> add invitednode 192.168.2.11;
```

Let's do the same to add the second node of the standby database server.

```
GDSCTL> add invitednode 192.168.2.13;
```

Now since both the physical standby databases are on the same nodes, running the previous command will update the configuration for both the databases.

We now must run the validate catalog command, which cross-checks the GDS catalog and databases, and it will also report any inconsistencies and errors.

```
GDSCTL>  validate catalog;
Validation results:

[Warning] VLD2: Region "regionora" does not have buddy region
[Warning] VLD2: Region "east" does not have buddy region
[Warning] VLD2: Region "north" does not have buddy region
[Warning] VLD2: Region "south" does not have buddy region
[Warning] VLD8: Database "oragdspr" has no global services defined for it
[Warning] VLD8: Database "oragdsdr" has no global services defined for it
[Warning] VLD8: Database "oragdstr" has no global services defined for it
[Warning] VLD9: Region "regionora" does not contain any databases
[Warning] VLD10: Region "north" does not contain any GSMs
[Warning] VLD10: Region "south" does not contain any GSMs
[Warning] VLD10: Region "east" does not contain any GSMs
[Warning] VLD11: GDS pool "dbpoolora" does not contain any databases
[Warning] VLD12: GDS pool "dbpoolora" does not contain any global services
[Warning] VLD12: GDS pool "salespro" does not contain any global services
[Warning] VLD24: GSM "GSMEAST" is not connected to any GSM from GDS
region "north"
[Warning] VLD24: GSM "GSMEAST" is not connected to any GSM from GDS
region "south"
[Warning] VLD24: GSM "GSMEAST" is not connected to any GSM from GDS
region "east"

 Total errors: 0. Total warnings:17
GDSCTL>
```

If we now run the databases command again, we can see that the configuration of all the databases is showing as correct. Sometimes it might take some time for the catalog to reflect the changes. So, please wait and run the databases command a few times, and you can see the changes.

```
GDSCTL> databases;
Database: "oragdsdr" Registered: Y State: Ok ONS: Y. Role: PH_STNDBY
Instances: 2 Region: north
   Registered instances:
     salespro%11
     salespro%12
Database: "oragdspr" Registered: Y State: Ok ONS: Y. Role: PRIMARY
Instances: 2 Region: east
   Registered instances:
     salespro%1
     salespro%2
Database: "oragdstr" Registered: Y State: Ok ONS: Y. Role: PH_STNDBY
Instances: 2 Region: south
   Registered instances:
     salespro%21
     salespro%22

GDSCTL>Database: "oragdstr" Registered: Y State: Ok ONS: Y. Role: PH_STNDBY
Instances: 2 Region: south
   Registered instances:
     salespro%21
     salespro%22

GDSCTL>

GDSCTL> config database
Name              Pool              Status    State
Region    Availability
----              ----              ------    -----       ------    ---
---------
oragdsdr          salespro          Ok        none        north     READ ONLY
oragdspr          salespro          Ok        none        east      ONLINE
oragdstr          salespro          Ok        none        south     READ ONLY

GDSCTL>
```

We can see the configuration is now looking good for all the databases, so let's proceed to the next section where we can test one scenario with the GDS service in the RAC environment.

Test Case: Global Service Failover in RAC

Let's test the same scenario we used for the single-instance databases in the RAC environment. We know from our previous chapter that if we create a service with the role Physical_standby, this service will run only on the available physical standby databases, and if all the available physical standby databases become unavailable, then the service will automatically failover to the primary database. This is achieved by adding the option failover_primary while creating the service. When all the physical standby databases are not available, the service should failover to the primary database.

High-Level Steps of This Test Case

The following are the high-level steps performed as part of this test case demonstration:

1. Connect to the catalog from the GSM running on the primary database server.

2. Set the GSM to gsmeast and check the status of the databases and services from GDSCTL.

3. Create a service named sales_reporting_rac_srvc with the previously mentioned options.

4. Check the services from GDSCTL to see if the service is created as expected.

5. Define the TNS alias for this service, sales_reporting_rac_srvc.

6. Connect to the database using the service sales_reporting_rac_srvc and see which physical standby database it's connecting to.

7. Shut down the first physical standby database and check if you are still able to connect the service as it connects to the second physical standby database.

8. Shut down the second physical standby database.

9. Connect to the database using the service and see if the service fails over to the primary database as both the physical standby databases are not available.

10. Start both the physical standby databases.

11. Now check the services again; they should be running on only the physical standby databases.

12. Remove the service sales_reporting_rac_srvc from GDSCTL.

Prerequisites

Before starting this test case, we need to make sure that all the databases, GSMs, and catalog database are up and running without any issues.

From node 1 of the primary database server, log in to the GDS catalog and check the status of the GSM gsmeast.

```
[oracle@gdshol-p1 admin]$ . oraenv
ORACLE_SID = [gsm] ?
The Oracle base remains unchanged with value /u01/app/oracle
[oracle@gdshol-p1 admin]$ gdsctl
GDSCTL: Version 19.0.0.0.0 - Production on Thu Nov 03 15:08:40 CDT 2022

Copyright (c) 2011, 2019, Oracle.  All rights reserved.

Welcome to GDSCTL, type "help" for information.

Current GSM is set to GSMEAST
GDSCTL>
```

Connecting to the GDS Catalog

Here are the details:

```
GDSCTL>  connect gsmcatuser/welcome@gdshol-p-scan:1521/CATGDSPR;
Catalog connection is established
GDSCTL>
```

Checking the Status of the GSM gsmeast

Here are the details:

```
GDSCTL> status gsm -gsm GSMEAST
Alias                     GSMEAST
Version                   19.0.0.0.0
Start Date                03-NOV-2022 12:10:53
Trace Level               off
Listener Log File         /u01/app/oracle/diag/gsm/gdshol-p1/gsmeast/
                          alert/log.xml
Listener Trace File       /u01/app/oracle/diag/gsm/gdshol-p1/gsmeast/trace/
                          ora_20810_140021393914944.trc
Endpoint summary          (ADDRESS=(HOST=gdshol-p1.localdomain)(PORT=1581)
                          (PROTOCOL=tcp))
GSMOCI Version            3.0.180702
Mastership                N
Connected to GDS catalog  Y
Process Id                20813
Number of reconnections   0
Pending tasks.    Total   0
Tasks in  process. Total  0
Regional Mastership       FALSE
Total messages published  0
Time Zone                 -05:00
Orphaned Buddy Regions:
     None
GDS region                regionora

GDSCTL>
```

Checking the Status of the Databases

Here are the details:

```
GDSCTL> databases;
Database: "oragdsdr" Registered: Y State: Ok ONS: Y. Role: PH_STNDBY
Instances: 2 Region: north
```

```
    Registered instances:
       salespro%11
       salespro%12
Database: "oragdspr" Registered: Y State: Ok ONS: Y. Role: PRIMARY
Instances: 2 Region: east
    Registered instances:
       salespro%1
       salespro%2
Database: "oragdstr" Registered: Y State: Ok ONS: Y. Role: PH_STNDBY
Instances: 2 Region: south
    Registered instances:
       salespro%21
       salespro%22

GDSCTL>
```

Checking the Currently Configured Services

Here are the details:

```
GDSCTL> services
GDSCTL>
```

Checking the Current gdspool in the GSM Configuration

Here are the details:

```
GDSCTL> config gdspool
Name                          Broker              Sharded
----                          ------              -------
dbpoolora                     No                  No
salespro                      Yes                 No

GDSCTL>
```

Checking the Configuration of the Regions

Here are the details:

```
GDSCTL> config region;
Name                          Buddy
----                          -----
east
north
regionora
south

GDSCTL>
```

So, all the databases, the GSMs, and the regions are looking good. Let's create a role-based global data service and test it.

For this, we will create a service called sales_reporting_rac_srvc, which must always run on the physical standby database. If the physical standby database is not available, then the service can run on the primary database.

```
GDSCTL> add service -service sales_reporting_rac_srvc -gdspool salespro
-preferred_all -role PHYSICAL_STANDBY -failover_primary;
The operation completed successfully
GDSCTL>
```

Now if we run the config services and databases commands from the GDSCTL prompt, we can see that the service is created but not started, yet we did not start the service.

```
GDSCTL> config service

Name            Network name                    Pool       Started  Preferred all
----            ------------                    ----       -------  -------------
sales_reportin  sales_reporting_rac_srvc.sale   salespro   No       Yes
g_rac_srvc      spro.oradbcloud

GDSCTL> databases;
Database: "oragdsdr" Registered: Y State: Ok ONS: Y. Role: PH_STNDBY
Instances: 2 Region: north
   Service: "sales_reporting_rac_srvc" Globally started: N Started: N
           Scan: Y Enabled: Y Preferred: Y
```

```
    Registered instances:
      salespro%11
      salespro%12
Database: "oragdspr" Registered: Y State: Ok ONS: Y. Role: PRIMARY
Instances: 2 Region: east
    Service: "sales_reporting_rac_srvc" Globally started: N Started: N
            Scan: Y Enabled: Y Preferred: Y
    Registered instances:
      salespro%1
      salespro%2
Database: "oragdstr" Registered: Y State: Ok ONS: Y. Role: PH_STNDBY
Instances: 2 Region: south
    Service: "sales_reporting_rac_srvc" Globally started: N Started: N
            Scan: Y Enabled: Y Preferred: Y
    Registered instances:
      salespro%21
      salespro%22

GDSCTL>
```

Starting the Service

If we try to start the service now, using the command start service, we get this:

```
GDSCTL> start service -service sales_reporting_rac_srvc -gdspool salespro;
GSM-45052: Service management error
ORA-44894: Service "sales_reporting_rac_srvc" was not found in the catalog.
ORA-06512: at "GSMADMIN_INTERNAL.DBMS_GSM_POOLADMIN", line 16285
ORA-06512: at "SYS.DBMS_SYS_ERROR", line 86
ORA-06512: at "GSMADMIN_INTERNAL.DBMS_GSM_POOLADMIN", line 16065
ORA-06512: at line 1

The operation completed successfully
GDSCTL>
```

What happened here? When we tried to start the service, we got the error ORA-45553: Service sales_reporting_rac_srvc does not have any instances defined for. This is because, for the RAC-enabled gdspool databases, once the service is added, the service is not aware of other instances of the databases. We must use the GDSCTL utility's modify service command with the preferred option to add all the instances of both the primary and physical standby databases. We will then be able to start the service without any issues.

Modify the service to add the second instance for the primary database, oragdspr.

```
GDSCTL> modify service -service sales_reporting_rac_srvc -gdspool salespro
-database oragdspr -modify_instances -preferred oragdspr1,oragdspr2;
The operation completed successfully
```

Modify the service configuration, and add the second instance of the physical standby database, oragdstr.

```
GDSCTL> modify service -service sales_reporting_rac_srvc -gdspool salespro
-database oragdstr -modify_instances -preferred oragdstr1,oragdstr2;
The operation completed successfully
```

Modify the service configuration and add the second instance of the physical standby database, oragdsdr.

```
GDSCTL> modify service -service sales_reporting_rac_srvc -gdspool salespro
-database oragdsdr -modify_instances -preferred oragdsdr1,oragdsdr2;
The operation completed successfully
GDSCTL>
```

If we start the service now, it should start without any issues.

```
GDSCTL> start service -service sales_reporting_rac_srvc -gdspool salespro;
The operation completed successfully
GDSCTL>
```

Checking the Status of the Service

Run the services command to see the status of the up-and-running services.

```
GDSCTL> services
Service "sales_reporting_rac_srvc.salespro.oradbcloud" has 4 instance(s).
Affinity: ANYWHERE
```

Instance "salespro%11", name: "oragdsdr1", db: "oragdsdr", region: "north", status: ready.
Instance "salespro%12", name: "oragdsdr2", db: "oragdsdr", region: "north", status: ready.
Instance "salespro%21", name: "oragdstr1", db: "oragdstr", region: "south", status: ready.
Instance "salespro%22", name: "oragdstr2", db: "oragdstr", region: "south", status: ready.

GDSCTL>

Checking the Status of the Database

If we now run the databases command, we can see that the service is available even in the primary database, but it's not started there, as shown here:

```
GDSCTL> databases;
Database: "oragdsdr" Registered: Y State: Ok ONS: Y. Role: PH_STNDBY Instances: 2
Region: north
   Service: "sales_reporting_rac_srvc" Globally started: Y Started: Y
           Scan: Y Enabled: Y Preferred: Y
   Registered instances:
     salespro%11
     salespro%12
Database: "oragdspr" Registered: Y State: Ok ONS: Y. Role: PRIMARY Instances: 2 Region: east
   Service: "sales_reporting_rac_srvc" Globally started: Y Started: N
           Scan: Y Enabled: Y Preferred: Y
   Registered instances:
     salespro%1
     salespro%2
Database: "oragdstr" Registered: Y State: Ok ONS: Y. Role: PH_STNDBY Instances: 2
Region: south
   Service: "sales_reporting_rac_srvc" Globally started: Y Started: Y
           Scan: Y Enabled: Y Preferred: Y
   Registered instances:
     salespro%21
     salespro%22
GDSCTL>
```

Checking the Configuration of the Service

Here are the details:

```
GDSCTL> config service -service sales_reporting_rac_srvc;
Name: sales_reporting_rac_srvc
Network name: sales_reporting_rac_srvc.salespro.oradbcloud
Pool: salespro
Started: Yes
Preferred all: Yes
Locality: ANYWHERE
Region Failover: No
Role: PHYSICAL_STANDBY
Primary Failover: Yes
Lag: ANY
Runtime Balance: SERVICE_TIME
Connection Balance: LONG
Notification: Yes
TAF Policy: NONE
Policy: AUTOMATIC
DTP: No
Failover Method: NONE
Failover Type: NONE
Failover Retries:
Failover Delay:
Edition:
PDB:
Commit Outcome:
Retention Timeout:
Replay Initiation Timeout:
Session State Consistency:
SQL Translation Profile:
Stop option: NONE
Drain timeout:
Table family:
```

```
Databases
-----------------------
Database                 Preferred Status
--------                 --------- ------
oragdsdr                 Yes       Enabled
oragdspr                 Yes       Enabled
oragdstr                 Yes       Enabled

GDSCTL>
```

Checking the Configuration of All the Components

To display the config information of all the components that are part of a given GDS configuration, we can run config at the GDSCTL prompt.

```
GDSCTL> config

Regions
-----------------------
east
north
regionora
south

GSMs
-----------------------
gsmeast
gsmnorth
gsmsouth

GDS pools
-----------------------
dbpoolora
salespro

Databases
-----------------------
oragdsdr
oragdspr
```

```
oragdstr

Services
-----------------------
sales_reporting_rac_srvc

GDSCTL pending requests
-----------------------
Command                          Object                          Status
-------                          ------                          ------

Global properties
-----------------------
Name: oradbcloud
Master GSM: gsmnorth
DDL sequence #: 0

GDSCTL>
```

Checking the Active Services in the Database, oragdspr

Now that the global service has been created and started, we can query the dba_
services and v$active_services views to learn more about the global services. So, let's
connect to the physical standby database where the global service is currently running.

First check the status of the service in the primary database. Connect to the primary
database (oragdspr) and query the dba_services view.

```
[oracle@gdshol-p1 ~]$ . oraenv
ORACLE_SID = [catgdspr1] ? oragdspr1
The Oracle base remains unchanged with value /u01/app/oracle
[oracle@gdshol-p1 ~]$ sqlplus / as sysdba

SQL*Plus: Release 19.0.0.0.0 - Production on Thu Nov 3 15:16:05 2022
Version 19.17.0.0.0

Copyright (c) 1982, 2022, Oracle.  All rights reserved.

Connected to:
Oracle Database 19c Enterprise Edition Release 19.0.0.0.0 - Production
Version 19.17.0.0.0
```

```
SQL> column name format a30
SQL> column network_name format a40
SQL> column name format a30
SQL> column name format a30
SQL> set linesize 120
SQL> select name, network_name, global_service from dba_services;

NAME                           NETWORK_NAME
GLOBAL_SERVICE
------------------------------ ----------------------------------------
--------------
SYS$BACKGROUND                                                          NO
SYS$USERS                                                               NO
oragdspr_CFG                   oragdspr_CFG                             NO
sales_reporting_rac_srvc       sales_reporting_rac_srvc.salespro.oradbc YES
                               loud
oragdsprXDB                    oragdsprXDB                              NO
oragdspr                       oragdspr                                NO

6 rows selected.
SQL>
```

From this output, we can see that for sales_reporting_rac_srvc, the value of the column GLOBAL_SERVICE is YES, denoting that it is a global service.

Now if we query the v$active_services view in the primary database (oragdspr), we can see that the global service sales_reporting_srvc is not listed, indicating that it is not started in the primary database.

```
SQL> select name, network_name, global from v$active_services;

NAME                           NETWORK_NAME                             GLO
------------------------------ ---------------------------------------- ---
oragdspr_CFG                   oragdspr_CFG                             NO
SYS$BACKGROUND                                                          NO
SYS$USERS                                                               NO
oragdsprXDB                    oragdsprXDB                              NO
oragdspr                       oragdspr                                NO

SQL>
```

Checking the Active Services in the Physical Standby Databases, oragdsdr and oragdstr

Log in to the first physical standby database, oragdstr, and check the services.

```
[oracle@gdshol-s1 admin]$ . oraenv
ORACLE_SID = [gsm2] ? oragdstr1
The Oracle base remains unchanged with value /u01/app/oracle

[oracle@gdshol-s1 admin]$ sqlplus / as sysdba

SQL*Plus: Release 19.0.0.0.0 - Production on Thu Nov 3 15:18:51 2022
Version 19.17.0.0.0
Copyright (c) 1982, 2022, Oracle.  All rights reserved.

Connected to:
Oracle Database 19c Enterprise Edition Release 19.0.0.0.0 - Production
Version 19.17.0.0.0

SQL>@/home/oracle/databases_info.sql;
```

DATABASE_HOST	INST_NAME	DB_UNIQUE_NAME	DATABASE_ROLE	OPEN_MODE	STARTUP_TIME
gdshol-s1.localdomain	oragdstr1	oragdstr	PHYSICAL STANDBY	READ ONLY WITH APPLY	03-NOV-22
gdshol-s2.localdomain	oragdstr2	oragdstr	PHYSICAL STANDBY	READ ONLY WITH APPLY	03-NOV-22

NAME	NETWORK_NAME	GLOBAL_SERVICE
SYS$BACKGROUND		NO
SYS$USERS		NO
oragdspr_CFG	oragdspr_CFG	NO
sales_reporting_rac_srvc	sales_reporting_rac_srvc.salespro.oradb cloud	YES ⬅━━━━
oragdsprXDB	oragdsprXDB	NO
oragdspr	oragdspr	NO

```
6 rows selected.

SQL> select name, network_name, global from v$active_services;
```

```
NAME                      NETWORK_NAME                              GLO
------------------------- ----------------------------------------- ---
oragdspr_CFG              oragdspr_CFG                              NO
SYS$BACKGROUND                                                      NO
SYS$USERS                                                           NO
sales_reporting_rac_srvc  sales_reporting_rac_srvc.salespro.oradb  YES  ◄══════════════
                          cloud

SQL>
```

As you can see from the previous output, `sales_reporting_rac_srvc` is started and running in the standby database, `oragdstr`.

Check the same queries in another physical standby database, `oragdsdr`.

```
[oracle@gdshol-s1 admin]$ . oraenv
ORACLE_SID = [gsm1] ? oragdsdr1
The Oracle base remains unchanged with value /u01/app/oracle
[oracle@gdshol-s1 admin]$ sqlplus / as sysdba

SQL*Plus: Release 19.0.0.0.0 - Production on Thu Nov 3 15:18:36 2022
Version 19.17.0.0.0

Copyright (c) 1982, 2022, Oracle.  All rights reserved.

Connected to:
Oracle Database 19c Enterprise Edition Release 19.0.0.0.0 - Production
Version 19.17.0.0.0

SQL>@/home/oracle/databases_info.sql;
```

DATABASE_HOST	INST_NAME	DB_UNIQUE_NAME	DATABASE_ROLE	OPEN_MODE	STARTUP_TIME
gdshol-s1.localdomain	oragdsdr1	oragdsdr	PHYSICAL STANDBY	READ ONLY WITH APPLY	03-NOV-22
gdshol-s2.localdomain	oragdsdr2	oragdsdr	PHYSICAL STANDBY	READ ONLY WITH APPLY	03-NOV-22

```
SQL> select name, network_name, global_service from dba_services;
```

```
NAME                      NETWORK_NAME                     GLOBAL_SERVICE
------------------------- -------------------------------- --------------------
SYS$BACKGROUND                                             NO
SYS$USERS                                                  NO
oragdspr_CFG              oragdspr_CFG                     NO
sales_reporting_rac_srvc  sales_reporting_rac_srvc.salespro  YES  ◄══════════════
                          .oradbcloud
oragdsprXDB               oragdsprXDB                      NO
oragdspr                  oragdspr                         NO

6 rows selected.
```

321

```
SQL> select name, network_name, global from v$active_services;

NAME                        NETWORK_NAME                       GLOBAL
-------------------------   ----------------------------------  ----------
oragdspr_CFG                oragdspr_CFG                       NO
SYS$BACKGROUND                                                 NO
SYS$USERS                                                      NO
sales_reporting_rac_srvc    sales_reporting_rac_srvc.salespro  YES  ⬅
                            .oradbcloud
SQL>
```

So, we can see that the service is running only on the databases that have the role physical_standby.

We can create the TNS entry for this service and test the database connection using this service.

```
sales_reporting_rac_srvc =
  (DESCRIPTION =
    (FAILOVER = ON)
    (ADDRESS_LIST =
      (LOAD_BALANCE = ON)
      (ADDRESS = (PROTOCOL = TCP)(HOST = gdshol-p-scan)(PORT = 1581)))
    (ADDRESS_LIST =
      (LOAD_BALANCE = ON)
      (ADDRESS = (PROTOCOL = TCP)(HOST = gdshol-s-scan)(PORT = 1582)))
    (ADDRESS_LIST =
      (LOAD_BALANCE = ON)
      (ADDRESS = (PROTOCOL = TCP)(HOST = gdshol-s-scan)(PORT = 1583)))
    (CONNECT_DATA =
      (SERVICE_NAME = sales_reporting_rac_srvc.salespro.oradbcloud) (REGION = east)
    )
  )
```

The connect descriptor in tnsnames.ora in a GDS config will be using the GSM listener endpoints and not the RAC SCAN listeners or local listeners. Also, note that 1581 is the GSM listener port on gdshol-p-scan, 1582 is the GSM1 listener port on gdshol-s-scan, and 1583 is the port of the GSM2 listener on gdshol-s-scan.

Testing the Database Connection

We can test the database connection using the TNS alias, as shown here:

```
[oracle@gdshol-p1 admin]$ sqlplus system/welcome@sales_reporting_rac_srvc

SQL*Plus: Release 19.0.0.0.0 - Production on Thu Nov 3 20:37:16 2022
Version 19.17.0.0.0
Copyright (c) 1982, 2022, Oracle.  All rights reserved.

Last Successful login time: Wed Nov 02 2022 23:50:59 -05:00

Connected to:
Oracle Database 19c Enterprise Edition Release 19.0.0.0.0 - Production
Version 19.17.0.0.0

SQL>@/home/oracle/databases_info.sql
```

```
DATABASE_HOST         INST_NAME DB_UNIQUE_NAME DATABASE_ROLE    OPEN_MODE            STARTUP_TIME
--------------------- --------- -------------- ---------------- -------------------- ------------
gdshol-s1.localdomain oragdsdr1 oragdsdr       PHYSICAL STANDBY READ ONLY WITH APPLY 03-NOV-22
gdshol-s2.localdomain oragdsdr2 oragdsdr       PHYSICAL STANDBY READ ONLY WITH APPLY 03-NOV-22

SQL>
```

As you can see, the service is routed to the standby database, oragdsdr.

When we check the services to see where it's currently running, we can see it is running in both the physical standby databases, oragdsdr and oragdstr.

```
GDSCTL> services;
Service "sales_reporting_rac_srvc.sales.oradbcloud" has 4 instance(s).
Affinity: ANYWHERE
   Instance "sales%11", name: "oragdstr1", db: "oragdstr", region: "north",
   status: ready.
   Instance "sales%12", name: "oragdstr2", db: "oragdstr", region: "north",
   status: ready.
   Instance "sales%21", name: "oragdsdr1", db: "oragdsdr", region: "north",
   status: ready.
   Instance "sales%22", name: "oragdsdr2", db: "oragdsdr", region: "north",
   status: ready.
GDSCTL>
```

Shutting Down Both Physical Standby Databases

Shut down both physical standby databases, oragdsdr and oragdstr, since these are the RAC databases, and also, we can use the server control utility (srvctl) to stop the physical standby databases.

First stop the physical standby database, oragdstr.

```
[oracle@gdshol-s1 ~]$ srvctl status database -d oragdstr
Instance oragdstr1 is running on node gdshol-s1
Instance oragdstr2 is running on node gdshol-s2
[oracle@gdshol-s1 ~]$ srvctl stop database -d oragdstr
[oracle@gdshol-s1 ~]$ srvctl status database -d oragdstr
Instance oragdstr1 is not running on node gdshol-s1
Instance oragdstr2 is not running on node gdshol-s2
[oracle@gdshol-s1 ~]$
```

If we check the services from the GDSCTL prompt, we will see that the service is now running only on the other physical standby database.

```
GDSCTL> services;
Service "sales_reporting_rac_srvc.salespro.oradbcloud" has 2 instance(s).
Affinity: ANYWHERE
   Instance "salespro%11", name: "oragdsdr1", db: "oragdsdr", region:
   "north", status: ready.
   Instance "salespro%12", name: "oragdsdr2", db: "oragdsdr", region:
   "north", status: ready.
GDSCTL>
```

Stop the second physical standby database, oragdsdr.

```
[oracle@gdshol-s1 ~]$ srvctl status database -d oragdsdr
Instance oragdsdr1 is running on node gdshol-s1
Instance oragdsdr2 is running on node gdshol-s2

[oracle@gdshol-s1 ~]$ srvctl stop database -d oragdsdr

[oracle@gdshol-s1 ~]$ srvctl status database -d oragdsdr
Instance oragdsdr1 is not running on node gdshol-s1
Instance oragdsdr2 is not running on node gdshol-s2
[oracle@gdshol-s1 ~]$
```

If we check `services` now, we can see that the service had to failover to the primary database.

Check the status of the service `sales_reporting_rac_srvc` when both the physical standby databases are up and running.

```
GDSCTL> services
Service "sales_reporting_rac_srvc.salespro.oradbcloud" has 4 instance(s).
Affinity: ANYWHERE
  Instance "salespro%11", name: "oragdsdr1", db: "oragdsdr", region:
  "north", status: ready.
  Instance "salespro%12", name: "oragdsdr2", db: "oragdsdr", region:
  "north", status: ready.
  Instance "salespro%21", name: "oragdstr1", db: "oragdstr", region:
  "south", status: ready.
  Instance "salespro%22", name: "oragdstr2", db: "oragdstr", region:
  "south", status: ready.
GDSCTL>
```

Check the status of the service `sales_reporting_rac_srvc` when both the physical standby databases are shut down.

```
Service "sales_reporting_rac_srvc.salespro.oradbcloud" has 2 instance(s).
Affinity: ANYWHERE
  Instance "salespro%1", name: "oragdspr1", db: "oragdspr", region:
  "east", status: ready.
  Instance "salespro%2", name: "oragdspr2", db: "oragdspr", region:
  "east", status: ready.
GDSCTL>
```

Testing the Database Connection

Connect to the database using the service name, and it should connect to the primary database.

```
[oracle@gdshol-p1 admin]$ sqlplus system/welcome@sales_reporting_rac_srvc

SQL*Plus: Release 19.0.0.0.0 - Production on Thu Nov 3 20:41:21 2022
Version 19.17.0.0.0
```

Copyright (c) 1982, 2022, Oracle. All rights reserved.

Last Successful login time: Wed Nov 02 2022 23:50:59 -05:00

Connected to:
Oracle Database 19c Enterprise Edition Release 19.0.0.0.0 - Production
Version 19.17.0.0.0

SQL>@/home/oracle/databases_info.sql

```
DATABASE_HOST          INSTANCE_NAME  DB_UNIQUE_NAME  DATABASE_ROLE  OPEN_MODE   STARTUP_TIME
--------------------   -------------  --------------  -------------  ----------  ------------
gdshol-p1.localdomain  oragdspr1      oragdspr        PRIMARY        READ WRITE  03-NOV-22
gdshol-p2.localdomain  oragdspr2      oragdspr        PRIMARY        READ WRITE  03-NOV-22
```

We can see that the service sales_reporting_rac_srvc has automatically failed over to the primary database (oragdspr) when both the physical standby databases are unavailable.

Starting Both Standby Databases

We can start both the physical standby databases and see if the service will connect to the physical standby databases. Using server control, we can start both the physical standby databases.

```
[oracle@gdshol-s1 admin]$ srvctl start database -d oragdsdr

[oracle@gdshol-s1 admin]$ srvctl start database -d oragdstr

[oracle@gdshol-s1 admin]$ srvctl status database -d oragdsdr
Instance oragdsdr1 is running on node gdshol-s1
Instance oragdsdr2 is running on node gdshol-s2

[oracle@gdshol-s1 admin]$ srvctl status database -d oragdstr
Instance oragdstr1 is running on node gdshol-s1
Instance oragdstr2 is running on node gdshol-s2
[oracle@gdshol-s1 admin]$
```

Check the services from the GDSCTL command prompt.
Check the status of the services when both the physical standby databases are down.

```
Service "sales_reporting_rac_srvc.salespro.oradbcloud" has 2 instance(s).
Affinity: ANYWHERE
   Instance "salespro%1", name: "oragdspr1", db: "oragdspr", region:
   "east", status: ready.
   Instance "salespro%2", name: "oragdspr2", db: "oragdspr", region:
   "east", status: ready.
GDSCTL>
```

Check the status of the services when both the physical standby databases are started. We can see that the service has failed over from the primary to the physical standby databases.

```
GDSCTL> services
Service "sales_reporting_rac_srvc.salespro.oradbcloud" has 4 instance(s).
Affinity: ANYWHERE
   Instance "salespro%11", name: "oragdsdr1", db: "oragdsdr", region:
   "north", status: ready.
   Instance "salespro%12", name: "oragdsdr2", db: "oragdsdr", region:
   "north", status: ready.
   Instance "salespro%21", name: "oragdstr1", db: "oragdstr", region:
   "south", status: ready.
   Instance "salespro%22", name: "oragdstr2", db: "oragdstr", region:
   "south", status: ready.
GDSCTL>
```

Connect to the database using the service, and it will connect to one of the available physical standby databases.

```
[oracle@gdshol-p1 admin]$ sqlplus system/welcome@sales_reporting_rac_srvc

SQL*Plus: Release 19.0.0.0.0 - Production on Thu Nov 3 20:45:17 2022
Version 19.17.0.0.0

Copyright (c) 1982, 2022, Oracle.  All rights reserved.

Last Successful login time: Thu Nov 03 2022 20:41:21 -05:00

Connected to:
Oracle Database 19c Enterprise Edition Release 19.0.0.0.0 - Production
Version 19.17.0.0.0
```

```
SQL>@/home/oracle/databases_info.sql;

DATABASE_HOST          DB_NAME   DB_UNIQUE_NAME  DATABASE_ROLE     OPEN_MODE             STARTUP_TIME
---------------------  --------  --------------  ----------------  --------------------  ------------
gdshol-p1.localdomain  oragdstr1 oragdstr        PHYSICAL STANDBY  READ ONLY WITH APPLY  14-AUG-21
gdshol-p2.localdomain  oragdstr2 oragdstr        PHYSICAL STANDBY  READ ONLY WITH APPLY  14-AUG-21
```

As we know, the service failed over to the physical standby databases as soon as the physical standby database became available.

Stopping and Removing the Service

At this point, we can stop and remove the services that we created for this test case.

```
GDSCTL>stop service -service sales_reporting_rac_srvc -gdspool sales
The operation completed successfully

GDSCTL>remove service -gdspool sales -service sales_reporting_rac_srvc
The operation completed successfully
GDSCTL>
```

Summary of This Test Case

This test case illustrated the automatic global service failover capability of Oracle GDS. You learned that as soon as all the physical standby databases are not available, then the global data service fails over to the primary database and then fails back as soon as the physical standby databases are available to connect.

Adding a New Physical Standby Database to the Global Data Service Configuration

As mentioned earlier, if the gdspool databases are part of the Data Guard broker configuration, then instead of adding the primary and physical standby databases individually to the catalog, we should add them to the Data Guard broker configuration directly to the catalog. We already know how to add the broker configuration to the GDS catalog. Now we can add a new physical standby database in the new region and add the new physical standby database to the Data Guard broker configuration using the Oracle Data Guard command-line interface DGMGRL. In this case, does the new physical standby database get automatically added to the global data service configuration? Or do we need to run any additional commands? After we add the new physical standby database to the Data Guard broker configuration, we must run the GDSCTL sync brokerconfig command to synchronize the GDS configuration with the Oracle Data Guard configuration. Let's see this with an example.

For this demonstration, we have created a new region called west, set up a new physical standby database in that region, and added it to the broker configuration. This new physical standby database has been created on the same servers (gdshol-s1 and gdshols-s2) where other two physical standby databases are running. The following is the new broker configuration:

```
[oracle@gdshol-p1 admin]$ dgmgrl
DGMGRL for Linux: Release 19.0.0.0.0 - Production on Tue Nov 8
16:19:54 2022
Version 19.17.0.0.0

Copyright (c) 1982, 2019, Oracle and/or its affiliates.  All rights reserved.

Welcome to DGMGRL, type "help" for information.
DGMGRL> connect sys/welcome;
Connected to "oragdspr"
Connected as SYSDBA.

DGMGRL> show configuration;

Configuration - oragdsprdg

  Protection Mode: MaxPerformance
  Members:
  oragdspr - Primary database
    oragdsdr - Physical standby database
    oragdstr - Physical standby database
    oragdswr - Physical standby database

Fast-Start Failover:  Disabled

Configuration Status:
SUCCESS   (status updated 29 seconds ago)

DGMGRL>
```

Here is the current configuration of the gdspool databases in the GDS configuration:

```
GDSCTL: Version 19.0.0.0.0 - Production on Tue Nov 08 16:20:30 CST 2022

Copyright (c) 2011, 2019, Oracle.  All rights reserved.

Welcome to GDSCTL, type "help" for information.

Current GSM is set to GSMEAST
GDSCTL> databases;
Database: "oragdsdr" Registered: Y State: Ok ONS: Y. Role: PH_STNDBY
Instances: 2 Region: north
   Service: "sales_reporting_rac_srvc" Globally started: Y Started: Y
           Scan: Y Enabled: Y Preferred: Y
   Registered instances:
     salespro%11
     salespro%12
Database: "oragdspr" Registered: Y State: Ok ONS: Y. Role: PRIMARY
Instances: 2 Region: east
   Service: "sales_reporting_rac_srvc" Globally started: Y Started: N
           Scan: Y Enabled: Y Preferred: Y
   Registered instances:
     salespro%1
     salespro%2
Database: "oragdstr" Registered: Y State: Ok ONS: Y. Role: PH_STNDBY
Instances: 2 Region: south
   Service: "sales_reporting_rac_srvc" Globally started: Y Started: Y
           Scan: Y Enabled: Y Preferred: Y
   Registered instances:
     salespro%21
     salespro%22

GDSCTL>
```

So even though a new physical standby database was added to the broker configuration, it is not immediately added to the global data service configuration. We still must run the GDSCTL command sync brokerconfig. This command synchronizes the Oracle Data Guard broker configuration with the configuration in the GDS database pool.

Check the following syntax for the sync brokerconfig command:

```
sync brokerconfig -gdspool poolname
```

Let's run the sync brokerconfig command. When we recheck the databases, we can see that the Oracle Data Guard broker configuration has been synchronized with the GDS catalog and the new physical standby database has been added to the GDS configuration.

```
GDSCTL> sync brokerconfig -gdspool salespro;
The operation completed successfully
Check the database status again.

GDSCTL> databases;
Database: "oragdsdr" Registered: Y State: Ok ONS: Y. Role: PH_STNDBY
Instances: 2 Region: north
   Service: "sales_reporting_rac_srvc" Globally started: Y Started: Y
           Scan: Y Enabled: Y Preferred: Y
   Registered instances:
     salespro%11
     salespro%12
Database: "oragdspr" Registered: Y State: Ok ONS: Y. Role: PRIMARY
Instances: 2 Region: east
   Service: "sales_reporting_rac_srvc" Globally started: Y Started: N
           Scan: Y Enabled: Y Preferred: Y
   Registered instances:
     salespro%1
     salespro%2
Database: "oragdstr" Registered: Y State: Ok ONS: Y. Role: PH_STNDBY
Instances: 2 Region: south
   Service: "sales_reporting_rac_srvc" Globally started: Y Started: Y
           Scan: Y Enabled: Y Preferred: Y
   Registered instances:
     salespro%21
     salespro%22
Database: "oragdswr" Registered: N State: Uninitialized ONS: N. Role: N/A
Instances: 0 Region: N/A
```

```
Service: "sales_reporting_rac_srvc" Globally started: Y Started: N
         Scan: Y Enabled: Y Preferred: Y
GDSCTL>
```

From this output, we can see that the new physical standby database was successfully added to the global data service configuration, and we can also see that a service named sales_reporting_rac_srvc that was running in the other physical standby databases got started automatically on this newly added physical standby database as well. But we can see that the role of the newly added physical standby database shows as N/A and its state still shows as Uninitialized, and also we can see that it's not assigned to any region yet.

Let's first assign the database to a new region. But first, we need to add the new physical standby database net service details to the tnsnames.ora file of the GSM home. Once we do that, we can run the database.

```
GDSCTL> modify database -database oragdswr -region west -gdspool salespro
The operation completed successfully
GDSCTL>
```

Execute the validate catalog command to cross-check the GDS catalog and all its components that includes the GSM, pool databases, and global data services, and it reports any inconsistencies or errors.

```
GDSCTL> validate catalog;
Validation results:

[Warning] VLD2: Region "regionora" does not have buddy region
[Warning] VLD4: Database "oragdswr" has an invalid status: Uninitialized
[Warning] VLD9: Region "regionora" does not contain any databases
[Warning] VLD10: Region "regionora" does not contain any GSMs
[Warning] VLD11: GDS pool "dbpoolora" does not contain any databases
[Warning] VLD12: GDS pool "dbpoolora" does not contain any global services
[Warning] VLD13: Status of database "oragdswr" in GDS catalog is likely to
               be obsolete
[Error] VLD30: Database oragdswr : wrong GDS configuration name detected ""
[Error] VLD31: Database oragdswr : wrong pool name detected ""
[Error] VLD32: Database oragdswr : wrong GDS region name detected ""
```

```
[Error] VLD33: Database oragdswr : wrong database number detected "0"
[Error] VLD34: Database oragdswr : wrong SCAN name detected in GDS catalog
           "gdshol-s-scan"
[Error] VLD35: Database oragdswr : wrong ONS port number detected in GDS
catalog "0"
[Warning] VLD44: Database oragdswr : Configuration mismatch detected.
Parameter name: CPU. Database value: 0. in GDS catalog: 75
[Warning] VLD44: Database oragdswr : Configuration mismatch detected.
Parameter name: Disk Read Latency. Database value: 0. in GDS catalog: 20
[Error] VLD36: Database oragdswr : GDS region "regionora" is not found in
database
[Error] VLD36: Database oragdswr : GDS region "north" is not found in database
[Error] VLD36: Database oragdswr : GDS region "south" is not found in database
[Error] VLD36: Database oragdswr : GDS region "west" is not found in database
[Error] VLD36: Database oragdswr : GDS region "east" is not found in database
[Warning] VLD39: Database oragdswr : gsm "gsmeast" is not found in database
[Warning] VLD39: Database oragdswr : gsm "gsmsouth" is not found in database
[Warning] VLD39: Database oragdswr : gsm "gsmwest" is not found in database
[Warning] VLD39: Database oragdswr : gsm "gsmnorth" is not found in database
[Warning] VLD24: GSM "GSMEAST" is not connected to any GSM from GDS region
"regionora"
[Error] VLD26: Database "oragdswr" is not registered in GSM "GSMEAST"
[Warning] VLD28: Instance "oragdswr2" of Database "oragdswr" is not
registered in GSM "GSMEAST"

Total errors: 12. Total warnings:15
GDSCTL>
```

We noticed from the previous output a few errors and warnings reported from the validate catalog command. We can run the sync database command for the newly added physical standby database to sync its information with the GDS configuration and see if that helps with the previous errors.

The following is the syntax for the sync database command:

```
GDSCTL> sync database -database dbname -gdspool poolname
```

Let's synchronize the database, oragdswr.

```
GDSCTL> sync database -database oragdswr -gdspool salespro;
The operation completed successfully
```

Let's check the database command and see if the database role/instances and the state of the new physical standby database gets updated with the correct info.

```
GDSCTL> databases;
Database: "oragdsdr" Registered: Y State: Ok ONS: Y. Role: PH_STNDBY
Instances: 2 Region: north
   Service: "sales_reporting_rac_srvc" Globally started: Y Started: Y
           Scan: Y Enabled: Y Preferred: Y
   Registered instances:
     salespro%11
     salespro%12
Database: "oragdspr" Registered: Y State: Ok ONS: Y. Role: PRIMARY
Instances: 2 Region: east
   Service: "sales_reporting_rac_srvc" Globally started: Y Started: N
           Scan: Y Enabled: Y Preferred: Y
   Registered instances:
     salespro%1
     salespro%2
Database: "oragdstr" Registered: Y State: Ok ONS: Y. Role: PH_STNDBY
Instances: 2 Region: south
   Service: "sales_reporting_rac_srvc" Globally started: Y Started: Y
           Scan: Y Enabled: Y Preferred: Y
   Registered instances:
     salespro%21
     salespro%22
Database: "oragdswr" Registered: Y State: Ok ONS: Y. Role: PH_STNDBY
Instances: 2 Region: west
   Service: "sales_reporting_rac_srvc" Globally started: Y Started: Y
           Scan: Y Enabled: Y Preferred: Y
```

```
Registered instances:
  salespro%31
  salespro%32
```

GDSCTL>

From the output, the sync database command is involved in fixing the issue. If we run the validate catalog command now, most of the errors will be cleared. Let's check the following output:

```
GDSCTL> validate catalog;
Validation results:

[Warning] VLD2: Region "regionora" does not have buddy region
[Warning] VLD9: Region "regionora" does not contain any databases
[Warning] VLD10: Region "regionora" does not contain any GSMs
[Warning] VLD11: GDS pool "dbpoolora" does not contain any databases
[Warning] VLD12: GDS pool "dbpoolora" does not contain any global services
[Warning] VLD24: GSM "GSMEAST" is not connected to any GSM from GDS region
"regionora"

 Total errors: 0. Total warnings:6
GDSCTL>
```

As you can see from this output, all the errors/warnings related to the newly added physical standby database disappeared.

So, whenever a new physical standby database is added to or removed from the Oracle Data Guard configuration, we should follow these steps to update the GDS configuration:

1. Add the TNS entry of the newly added physical standby database to the tnsnames.ora file of all the GSM homes.

2. If the new physical standby database is created on new servers, we must add those new database servers to the GDS configuration by using the add invitednode command.

3. Run the Sync brokerconfig command from the GDSCTL command line.

4. Run the Sync database command for the new database.

Removing the Physical Standby Database from the Global Data Service Configuration

In the previous section, we deal with the GDS configuration whenever a new physical standby database has been added to the Data Guard broker configuration. In this section, we will see how to synchronize the global data service configuration when a physical standby database is removed from the Data Guard broker configuration.

For this demonstration, we will use the same databases that we used in the previous section.

The following is the current Data Guard configuration:

```
DGMGRL> show configuration ;

Configuration - oragdsprdg

  Protection Mode: MaxPerformance
  Members:
  oragdspr - Primary database
    oragdsdr - Physical standby database
    oragdstr - Physical standby database
    oragdswr - Physical standby database

Fast-Start Failover:  Disabled

Configuration Status:
SUCCESS   (status updated 42 seconds ago)

DGMGRL>
```

The following is the current global data service configuration:

```
GDSCTL> databases;
Database: "oragdsdr" Registered: Y State: Ok ONS: Y. Role: PH_STNDBY
Instances: 2 Region: north
   Service: "sales_reporting_rac_srvc" Globally started: Y Started: Y
           Scan: N Enabled: Y Preferred: Y
   Registered instances:
     salespro%11
     salespro%12
```

```
Database: "oragdspr" Registered: Y State: Ok ONS: Y. Role: PRIMARY
Instances: 2 Region: east
   Service: "sales_reporting_rac_srvc" Globally started: Y Started: N
            Scan: N Enabled: Y Preferred: Y
   Registered instances:
     salespro%1
     salespro%2
Database: "oragdstr" Registered: Y State: Ok ONS: Y. Role: PH_STNDBY
Instances: 2 Region: south
   Service: "sales_reporting_rac_srvc" Globally started: Y Started: Y
            Scan: N Enabled: Y Preferred: Y
   Registered instances:
     salespro%21
     salespro%22
Database: "oragdswr" Registered: Y State: Ok ONS: Y. Role: PH_STNDBY
Instances: 2 Region: west
   Service: "sales_reporting_rac_srvc" Globally started: Y Started: Y
            Scan: N Enabled: Y Preferred: Y
   Registered instances:
     salespro%31
     salespro%32

GDSCTL>
```

In our current setup, we have three physical standby databases in our Data Guard environment and GDS configuration.

Let's try to remove one of the databases from the Data Guard broker configuration and see how we can synchronize the broker configuration in the GDS configuration.

We will remove the physical standby database, oragdswr, from the Data Guard configuration.

```
DGMGRL> disable database oragdswr;
Disabled.

DGMGRL> remove database oragdswr;
Removed database "oragdswr" from the configuration
```

```
DGMGRL> show configuration;

Configuration - oragdsprdg

  Protection Mode: MaxPerformance
  Members:
  oragdspr - Primary database
    oragdsdr - Physical standby database
    oragdstr - Physical standby database

Fast-Start Failover:  Disabled

Configuration Status:
SUCCESS    (status updated 27 seconds ago)
DGMGRL>
```

The following is the configuration in the GDS catalog, after we remove the database from the broker configuration:

```
GDSCTL> databases;
Database: "oragdsdr" Registered: Y State: Ok ONS: Y. Role: PH_STNDBY
Instances: 2 Region: north
   Service: "sales_reporting_rac_srvc" Globally started: Y Started: Y
            Scan: N Enabled: Y Preferred: Y
   Registered instances:
     salespro%11
     salespro%12
Database: "oragdspr" Registered: Y State: Ok ONS: Y. Role: PRIMARY
Instances: 2 Region: east
   Service: "sales_reporting_rac_srvc" Globally started: Y Started: N
            Scan: N Enabled: Y Preferred: Y
   Registered instances:
     salespro%1
     salespro%2
Database: "oragdstr" Registered: Y State: Ok ONS: Y. Role: PH_STNDBY
Instances: 2 Region: south
   Service: "sales_reporting_rac_srvc" Globally started: Y Started: Y
            Scan: N Enabled: Y Preferred: Y
```

```
Registered instances:
  salespro%21
  salespro%22
Database: "oragdswr" Registered: Y State: Ok ONS: Y. Role: PH_STNDBY
Instances: 2 Region: west
  Service: "sales_reporting_rac_srvc" Globally started: Y Started: Y
          Scan: N Enabled: Y Preferred: Y
  Registered instances:
    salespro%31
    salespro%32
GDSCTL>
```

Let's synchronize brokerconfig in the GDS configuration and also validate the catalog.

```
GDSCTL> sync brokerconfig -gdspool salespro;
Catalog connection is established
The operation completed successfully
GDSCTL>
```

Check the status of databases, and we can see that the physical standby database, oragdspr, has been removed from the GDS configuration.

```
GDSCTL> databases;
Database: "oragdsdr" Registered: Y State: Ok ONS: Y. Role: PH_STNDBY
Instances: 2 Region: north
  Service: "sales_reporting_rac_srvc" Globally started: Y Started: Y
          Scan: N Enabled: Y Preferred: Y
  Registered instances:
    salespro%11
    salespro%12
Database: "oragdspr" Registered: Y State: Ok ONS: Y. Role: PRIMARY
Instances: 2 Region: east
  Service: "sales_reporting_rac_srvc" Globally started: Y Started: N
          Scan: N Enabled: Y Preferred: Y
  Registered instances:
    salespro%1
    salespro%2
```

```
Database: "oragdstr" Registered: Y State: Ok ONS: Y. Role: PH_STNDBY
Instances: 2 Region: south
   Service: "sales_reporting_rac_srvc" Globally started: Y Started: Y
            Scan: N Enabled: Y Preferred: Y
   Registered instances:
     salespro%21
     salespro%22
GDSCTL>
```

We can run the validate catalog command to cross-check the GDS information.

```
GDSCTL> validate catalog;
Validation results:

[Warning] VLD2: Region "regionora" does not have buddy region
[Warning] VLD9: Region "regionora" does not contain any databases
[Warning] VLD10: Region "regionora" does not contain any GSMs
[Warning] VLD9: Region "west" does not contain any databases
[Warning] VLD11: GDS pool "dbpoolora" does not contain any databases
[Warning] VLD12: GDS pool "dbpoolora" does not contain any global services
[Warning] VLD24: GSM "GSMEAST" is not connected to any GSM from GDS region
"regionora"
[Error] VLD19: GSM "GSMEAST" - global service "sales_reporting_rac_srvc" is
offered by unknown database "oragdswr"
 Total errors: 1. Total warnings:7
GDSCTL>
```

In this section, you saw how to synchronize the GDS configuration whenever a physical standby database is removed from the Data Guard configuration.

Summary

In this chapter, you learned how to create a global data service and how to utilize the service in a RAC environment with a physical standby database configured. You also learned to add a new physical standby database to the database to the global data service configuration and how to remove a physical standby database from the GDS configuration.

CHAPTER 9

Exploring Raft Replication in Oracle 23c

In Chapter 2, you learned what sharding is, as well as two sharding methods: user-defined sharding and composite sharding. Oracle has introduced a new feature called *Raft Replication* in Oracle 23c. In this chapter, we will cover this new feature, and we will demonstrate a few scenarios using the Raft Replication feature in sharding.

Raft Replication

Replication in Oracle Sharding provides high availability, scalability, and disaster recovery of data. Prior to Oracle 21c, Oracle had two replication technologies, Oracle Data Guard and Oracle GoldenGate, to replicate the data in a sharded database. Another option was to leverage Oracle Real Application Cluster (RAC) for shard-level high availability, complemented by replication, to maintain shard-level data availability in the event of a cluster outage. In Oracle 21c, Oracle depreciated the support of the Oracle GoldenGate replication method for Oracle Sharding. In Oracle 23c, Oracle introduced a new replication topology to replicate the data in sharded databases, that is, Raft Replication.

Raft Replication is a new built-in Oracle sharding feature in Oracle 23c that provides a way to configure the sharding for replication without the need for Oracle Data Guard or Oracle GoldenGate. When compared to other sharding methods, Raft Replication makes the replication simple; it is a built-in feature, and it also removes any configuration overhead from having either Data Guard or Oracle GoldenGate. Raft Replication makes use of the consensus protocol to maintain the consistency between the replicas in the replication units in case of any failures with the network or messages. While the present focus is on supporting Raft Replication exclusively for system-managed sharding, Oracle aims to broaden its capabilities by incorporating support for other methods such as composite and user-defined sharding.

In shard-level replication, data is replicated at the shard database level, whereas the Oracle Sharding Raft Replication method works on the smaller replication units of the shard database. When Raft Replication is enabled, a sharded database is divided into multiple replication units, and each replication unit (RU) contains a set of chunks that have the same replication topology. Each of these chunks contains a single partition from each sharded table. Each replication unit has three replicas that are placed on different shards. Each of the shards contains replicas from multiple replication units. All the replicas of the replication unit form a Raft group where one of the shards is elected as the leader and two shards are elected as the followers. By default, each shard is a leader of two replication units, and the same shard is a follower of the other four replication units. It is the leader shard that processes and executes all the DML and sends the committed log records to the followers. The Raft protocol ensures and guarantees that the log and commit records are received by all the followers in the same order as they were generated by the leader. A transaction running on the leader shard is committed only after at least one of the follower shards sends back the acknowledgment that it has received the commit records. See Figure 9-1 for a visual representation.

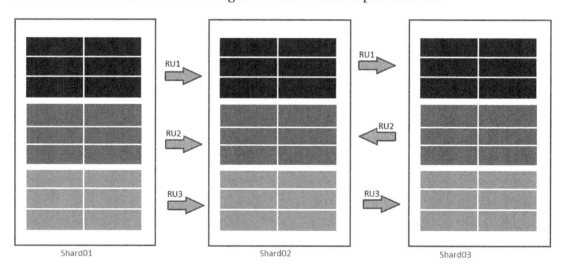

Figure 9-1. *Raft Replication, RUs*

All the DML changes and the committed records are written to logs known as Raft *logs*. These Raft logs are different from the Oracle redo logs, and they are maintained independently. Oracle creates additional OS processes and assigns them to each replication unit. These OS processes maintain the Raft logs, and they also replicate all the changes that are happening in the leader shards to the follower shards. As each replication unit has its own set of OS processes, it makes the replication unit work independently, and since each RU can work independently, it becomes easy to scale up or down the replication units.

Enabling Raft Replication

Raft Replication is enabled during shard catalog creation for a sharded database. When we create the shard catalog using the GDSCTL command shardcatalog, we just need to specify the -repl native option, and this option will enable Raft Replication.

GDSCTL > create shardcatalog -database databasename -repl native

Once the shard catalog is created, we can add the precreated shards to the shard database. It is mandatory that we have at least three shards in the sharded database for the Raft Replication to work.

In the following section, we will work on a few test cases to demonstrate a few features of Raft Replication. We will see how we can move one replication unit from one shard to another shard, how we can scale up the shard Raft Replication, how we can copy one RU from one shard to another shard, and how we can change the leader of the RU.

For this setup, we will need five servers, and the details are given here:

- gsmcat: Shard catalog database (gsmdbp) and shard director

- prsh01: First shard database server

- prsh02: Second shard database server

- stsh01: Third shard database server

- stsh02: Fourth shard database server

All these servers have the Oracle 23c database binaries installed, and additionally, in the catalog server, we have the Oracle 23c GSM software installed. The following shows the location and version of the Oracle software used for this chapter:

```
Database home    :/u01/app/oracle/product/23.0.0.0/dbhome_1
Database version : Oracle Database 23c Enterprise Edition Release
                   23.0.0.0.0 - Beta
```

```
GSM Home           :/u01/app/oracle/product/23.0.0.0/gsmhome_1
GSM version        : GDSCTL: Version 23.0.0.0.0 - Beta
```

All the shard databases and the catalog database are single-instance multitenant databases.

GSM Catalog Database Details

Here are the details:

```
Database host: gsmcat
Container DB: gsmdbp
Catalog PDB: GSMCATDB
```

Shard Database Details

The following are the precreated 4 Oracle 23c multitenant databases that we are going to add as shards to the sharded database.

For the first shard, we will use the following database:

```
Database host: prsh01
Container DB: shdcdb1
Shard1 PDB: shard1
```

For the second shard, we will use the following database:

```
Database host: prsh02
Container DB: shdcdb2
Shard2 PDB: shard2
```

For the third shard, we will use the following database:

```
Database host: stsh01
Container DB: shdcdb3
Shard3 PDB: shard3
```

For the fourth shard, we will use the following database:

```
Database host: stsh02
Container DB: shdcdb
Shard4 PDB: shard4
```

We must make sure the following sharding prerequisites of SQL statements are run in the CDB and PDB accordingly to ensure that they are ready to be added as shards.

The following are the SQL statements that we must run in each of the container databases:

```
alter user gsmrootuser account unlock;
alter user gsmrootuser identified by welcome;
grant SYSDG, SYSBACKUP to gsmrootuser;
alter user gsmuser account unlock;
grant read, write on directory DATA_PUMP_DIR to gsmadmin_internal;
alter user gsmuser identified by welcome container=all;
grant SYSDG, SYSBACKUP to gsmuser;
alter system set db_files=1024 scope=spfile;
alter database force logging;
alter database flashback on;
alter system set db_create_file_dest='/u01/app/oracle/oradata/data';
```

The following are the set of SQL statements needing to be run in each of the shard pluggable databases:

```
alter user gsmuser account unlock;
grant read, write on directory DATA_PUMP_DIR to gsmadmin_internal;
grant SYSDG, SYSBACKUP to gsmuser;
alter system set db_files=1024 scope=spfile;
```

We have a GSM with the name mygsm running in the region1 region.

```
GDSCTL> config gsm
Name      Region    ENDPOINT
----      ------    ------------------------------------
mygsm     region1   (ADDRESS=(HOST=gsmcat.localdomain)
                    (PORT=1522)(PROTOCOL=tcp))
GDSCTL>
```

We will create a shard group named shardgroup_primary for this exercise.

```
GDSCTL> add shardgroup -shardgroup shardgroup_primary -region region1
The operation completed successfully
GDSCTL>
```

We will enable Raft Replication, and as mentioned earlier, we need to use the repl native option when we create the shard catalog.

```
GDSCTL> create shardcatalog -database gsmcat.localdomain:1521/gsmcatdb
-region region1 -user gsm_admin/welcome -agent_port 8080 -agent_password
welcome -chunks 12 -repl native
Catalog is created
GDSCTL>
```

To check whether the Raft Replication is enabled, we can use the command config sdb. This command will also show which sharding method is used in the sharded database and what services are currently configured in the GDS configuration.

```
DSCTL> config sdb

GDS Pool administrators
-----------------------

Replication Type
```

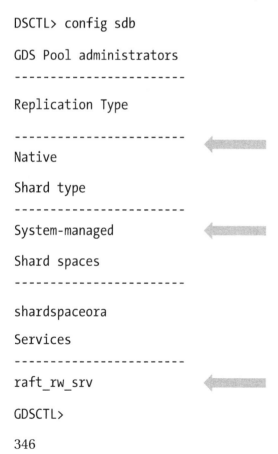

```
-----------------------
Native

Shard type
-----------------------
System-managed

Shard spaces
-----------------------

shardspaceora

Services
-----------------------
raft_rw_srv

GDSCTL>
```

Once the shard catalog is created, we can add the shards to the sharded database. To add the pluggable database (PDB) as a shard, we must first add its CDB to the GDS pool and then add the PDB as a shard.

Add cdbs, shdcdb1, shdcdb2, shdcdb3, and shdcdb to the sharded GDS pool, as shown here:

```
[oracle@gsmcat admin]$ GDSCTL
GDSCTL: Version 23.0.0.0.0 - Beta on Thu May 04 21:11:48 CDT 2023
Copyright (c) 2011, 2022, Oracle.  All rights reserved.
Welcome to GDSCTL, type help for information.

Current GSM is set to MYGSM
GDSCTL> connect gsm_admin/welcome@gsmcatdb
Catalog connection is established

GDSCTL> add cdb -connect prsh01:1521/shdcdb1 -pwd welcome
DB Unique Name: shdcdb1
The operation completed successfully
GDSCTL>

GDSCTL> add cdb -connect prsh02:1521/shdcdb2 -pwd welcome
DB Unique Name: shdcdb2
The operation completed successfully
GDSCTL>

GDSCTL> add cdb -connect stsh01:1521/shdcdb3 -pwd welcome
DB Unique Name: shdcdb3
The operation completed successfully
GDSCTL>
```

We will now add three PDBs (shard1 from the container database shdcdb1, shard2 from the CDB shdcdb2, and shard3 from the CDB shdcdb3) as a shard to the sharded GDS pool.

Add the first shard, shard1.

```
GDSCTL> add shard -cdb shdcdb1 -connect shard1 -shardgroup
shardgroup_primary
"gsmuser" password:
```

INFO: Native shard validation requested.
INFO: Database role is PRIMARY.
INFO: Database name is SHDCDB1.
INFO: Database unique name is shdcdb1.
INFO: Database ID is 421918568.
INFO: Database open mode is READ WRITE.
INFO: Database in archivelog mode.
INFO: Flashback is on.
INFO: Force logging is on.
INFO: Database platform is Linux x86 64-bit.
INFO: Database character set is AL32UTF8. This value must match the
character set of the catalog database.
INFO: 'compatible' initialization parameter validated successfully.
INFO: Database is a multitenant container database.
INFO: Current container is SHARD1.
INFO: Database is using a server parameter file (spfile).
INFO: db_create_file_dest set to: '/u01/app/oracle/oradata/data'
INFO: db_recovery_file_dest set to: '/u01/app/oracle/oradata/fra'
INFO: db_files=200. Must be greater than the number of chunks and/or
tablespaces to be created in the shard.
INFO: remote_login_passwordfile set to EXCLUSIVE.
WARNING: db_file_name_convert is not set.
INFO: GSMUSER account validated successfully.
INFO: DATA_PUMP_DIR is '/u01/app/oracle/admin/shdcdb1/dpdump/
FAE5FC1A103C5CDAE053480278C06941'.
DB Unique Name: shdcdb1_shard1
The operation completed successfully
GDSCTL>

Add a second shard, shard2, to the sharded GDS pool.

GDSCTL> add shard -cdb shdcdb2 -connect shard2 -shardgroup
shardgroup_primary
"gsmuser" password:
INFO: Native shard validation requested.
INFO: Database role is PRIMARY.

INFO: Database name is SHDCDB2.

INFO: Database unique name is shdcdb2.

INFO: Database ID is 29360455.

INFO: Database open mode is READ WRITE.

INFO: Database in archivelog mode.

INFO: Flashback is on.

INFO: Force logging is on.

INFO: Database platform is Linux x86 64-bit.

INFO: Database character set is AL32UTF8. This value must match the character set of the catalog database.

INFO: 'compatible' initialization parameter validated successfully.

INFO: Database is a multitenant container database.

INFO: Current container is SHARD2.

INFO: Database is using a server parameter file (spfile).

INFO: db_create_file_dest set to: '/u01/app/oracle/oradata/data'

INFO: db_recovery_file_dest set to: '/u01/app/oracle/oradata/fra'

INFO: db_files=200. Must be greater than the number of chunks and/or tablespaces to be created in the shard.

INFO: remote_login_passwordfile set to EXCLUSIVE.

WARNING: db_file_name_convert is not set.

INFO: GSMUSER account validated successfully.

INFO: DATA_PUMP_DIR is '/u01/app/oracle/admin/shdcdb2/dpdump/FAE60D2DEB6C54D2E053490278C0FDA9'.

DB Unique Name: shdcdb2_shard2

The operation completed successfully

GDSCTL>

Add the third shard, shard3, to the GDS pool.

GDSCTL> add shard -cdb shdcdb3 -connect shard3 -shardgroup shardgroup_primary

"gsmuser" password:

INFO: Native shard validation requested.

INFO: Database role is PRIMARY.

INFO: Database name is SHDCDB3.

INFO: Database unique name is shdcdb3.

INFO: Database ID is 4285663656.

INFO: Database open mode is READ WRITE.
INFO: Database in archivelog mode.
INFO: Flashback is on.
INFO: Force logging is on.
INFO: Database platform is Linux x86 64-bit.
INFO: Database character set is AL32UTF8. This value must match the character set of the catalog database.
INFO: 'compatible' initialization parameter validated successfully.
INFO: Database is a multitenant container database.
INFO: Current container is SHARD3.
INFO: Database is using a server parameter file (spfile).
INFO: db_create_file_dest set to: '/u01/app/oracle/oradata/data'
INFO: db_recovery_file_dest set to: '/u01/app/oracle/oradata/fra'
INFO: db_files=200. Must be greater than the number of chunks and/or tablespaces to be created in the shard.
INFO: remote_login_passwordfile set to EXCLUSIVE.
WARNING: db_file_name_convert is not set.
INFO: GSMUSER account validated successfully.
INFO: DATA_PUMP_DIR is '/u01/app/oracle/admin/shdcdb3/dpdump/FAE607A8DC4 7D571E0534A0278C0791E'.
DB Unique Name: shdcdb3_shard3
The operation completed successfully
GDSCTL>

We can check the configuration now by running the databases and config shard commands in GDSCTL.

```
GDSCTL> databases
Database: "shdcdb1_shard1" Registered: Y State: Ok ONS: N. Role: PRIMARY
Instances: 1 Region: region1
   Registered instances:
     orasdb%1
Database: "shdcdb2_shard2" Registered: Y State: Ok ONS: N. Role: PRIMARY
Instances: 1 Region: region1
   Registered instances:
     orasdb%11
```

```
Database: "shdcdb3_shard3" Registered: Y State: Ok ONS: N. Role: PRIMARY
Instances: 1 Region: region1
   Registered instances:
     orasdb%21

GDSCTL>

GDSCTL> config shard
Name               Shard Group         Status  State   Region     Availability
----               ------------------  -----   -----   ------     ------------
shdcdb1_shard1     shardgroup_primary  U       none    region1    -
shdcdb2_shard2     shardgroup_primary  U       none    region1    -
shdcdb3_shard3     shardgroup_primary  U       none    region1    -

GDSCTL>
```

We can observe that the name of the shard is registered with the naming convention cdb_pdb in the configuration. Since we have added three shards to the sharded GDS pool, we can now run the deploy command, which will first cross-check all the parameters to ensure that all the required parameters are set, and if it finds any parameters are not set, it will report the error. For example, if the db_create_file_dest parameter is not set, it will report the following error:

```
ERROR: db_create_file_dest is not set
```

Connect to the catalog and run the deploy command.

```
GDSCTL> connect gsm_admin/welcome@gsmcatdb
Catalog connection is established

GDSCTL> deploy
deploy: examining configuration...
deploy: shards configured successfully
The operation completed successfully
GDSCTL>
```

If we now run the config shard command, we can see that all the shards will show the status of ONLINE.

```
GDSCTL> config shard
Name               Shard Group         Status  State   Region    Availability
----               ------------------  -----   -----   ------    ------------
shdcdb1_shard1     shardgroup_primary  U       none    region1   ONLINE
shdcdb2_shard2     shardgroup_primary  U       none    region1   ONLINE
shdcdb3_shard3     shardgroup_primary  U       none    region1   ONLINE
GDSCTL>
```

We will now create a schema and will load some data to test the Raft Replication.

```
SQL> create user app_shard identified by app_shard;
User created.

SQL> grant connect, resource, alter session, select_catalog_role, gsmadmin_
role, dba to app_shard;
Grant succeeded.

SQL> grant all privileges to app_shard;
Grant succeeded.

SQL> grant execute on dbms_crypto to app_shard;
Grant succeeded.

SQL> grant create table, create procedure, create tablespace, create
materialized view to app_shard;
Grant succeeded.

SQL> SQL> grant unlimited tablespace to app_shard;
Grant succeeded.

SQL> create tablespace set TSP_SET_1;
Tablespace created.

SQL>
```

We will now connect to the catalog database as the schema app_shard and create a sharded table with a system-managed sharding method, i.e., using the partition by consistent hash, as shown here:

```
sqlplus app_shard/app_shard@gsmcatdb

SQL> create sharded table Customers
  (
    CustId       varchar2(100) NOT NULL,
    FirstName    varchar2(100),
    LastName     varchar2(100),
    Passwd       raw(60),
    CONSTRAINT pk_customers PRIMARY KEY (CustId)
  ) tablespace SET TSP_SET_1
  partition by CONSISTENT HASH (CustId) partitions AUTO;

Table created.
```

We will also load some dummy data that is useful for our test cases.

```
SQL> insert into Customers values(1,'moody','ragi',utl_raw.cast_to_
raw('hello world'));
SQL> insert into Customers values(2,'randy','Beridze',utl_raw.cast_to_
raw('hello world1'));
SQL> insert into Customers values(3,'ravi','Bettle',utl_raw.cast_to_
raw('hello world2'));
SQL> insert into Customers values(4,'zach','boron',utl_raw.cast_to_
raw('hello world3'));
SQL> insert into Customers values(5,'laura','crain',utl_raw.cast_to_
raw('hello world4'));
SQL> insert into Customers values(6,'shreya','sharma',utl_raw.cast_to_
raw('hello world6'));
SQL> insert into Customers values(7,'trish','jackson',utl_raw.cast_to_
raw('hello world7'));
SQL> insert into Customers values(8,'ilena','samme',utl_raw.cast_to_
raw('hello world8'));
```

```
SQL> insert into Customers values(9,'brad','crusee',utl_raw.cast_to_
raw('hello world9'));
SQL> insert into Customers values(10,'tom','peats',utl_raw.cast_to_
raw('hello world20'));
SQL>commit;
```

We can check the replication status and chunks using the GDSCTL commands config chunks and status ru -show_chunks.

```
DSCTL> config chunks
Chunks
------------------------
```

Database	From	To
--------	----	--
shdcdb1_shard1	1	12
shdcdb2_shard2	1	12
shdcdb3_shard3	1	12

```
GDSCTL> STATUS REPLICATION
Replication units
------------------------
```

Database	RU#	Role	Term	Log Index	Status
--------	---	----	----	---------	------
shdcdb1_shard1	1	Leader	3	8	Ok
shdcdb1_shard1	2	Follower	1	3	Ok
shdcdb1_shard1	3	Follower	2	2	Ok
shdcdb1_shard1	4	Leader	2	5	Ok
shdcdb1_shard1	5	Follower	1	4	Ok
shdcdb1_shard1	6	Follower	2	4	Ok
shdcdb2_shard2	1	Follower	3	8	Ok
shdcdb2_shard2	2	Leader	1	3	Ok
shdcdb2_shard2	3	Follower	2	2	Ok
shdcdb2_shard2	4	Follower	2	5	Ok
shdcdb2_shard2	5	Leader	1	4	Ok
shdcdb2_shard2	6	Follower	2	4	Ok
shdcdb3_shard3	1	Follower	3	8	Ok
shdcdb3_shard3	2	Follower	1	3	Ok

shdcdb3_shard3	3	Leader	2	2	Ok
shdcdb3_shard3	4	Follower	2	5	Ok
shdcdb3_shard3	5	Follower	1	4	Ok
shdcdb3_shard3	6	Leader	2	4	Ok

GDSCTL>

GDSCTL> status ru -show_chunks
Chunks

RU#	From	To
---	----	--
1	1	2
2	3	4
3	5	6
4	7	8
5	9	10
6	11	12

Replication units

Database	RU#	Role	Term	Log Index	Status
--------	---	----	----	---------	------
shdcdb2_shard2	1	Follower	3	8	Ok
shdcdb2_shard2	2	Leader	1	3	Ok
shdcdb2_shard2	3	Follower	2	2	Ok
shdcdb2_shard2	4	Follower	2	5	Ok
shdcdb2_shard2	5	Leader	1	4	Ok
shdcdb2_shard2	6	Follower	2	4	Ok
shdcdb3_shard3	1	Follower	3	8	Ok
shdcdb3_shard3	2	Follower	1	3	Ok
shdcdb3_shard3	3	Leader	2	2	Ok
shdcdb3_shard3	4	Follower	2	5	Ok
shdcdb3_shard3	5	Follower	1	4	Ok
shdcdb3_shard3	6	Leader	2	4	Ok
shdcdb1_shard1	1	Leader	3	8	Ok
shdcdb1_shard1	2	Follower	1	3	Ok

```
shdcdb1_shard1                  3      Follower  2    2         Ok
shdcdb1_shard1                  4      Leader    2    5         Ok
shdcdb1_shard1                  5      Follower  1    4         Ok
shdcdb1_shard1                  6      Follower  2    4         Ok
GDSCTL>
```

Test Cases for Raft Replication

The following are the test cases that explore Raft Replication.

Test Case 1: Moving Chunks from One Replication Unit to Another

For our first test case, we will see how we can move chunks from one RU to another. To move the chunk from one RU to another RU, we will use the command `relocate chunk`.

In our test case, we will try to move chunk 2 from RU# 1 to RU# 4. The following is the status of the chunks:

```
GDSCTL> status ru -show_chunks
Chunks

------------------------

RU#           From       To
---           ----       --          <───────
1             1          2
2             3          4
3             5          6
4             7          8
5             9          10
6             11         12
```

Relocate chunk 2 from RU# 1 to RU# 4.

```
GDSCTL> relocate chunk -chunk 2 -sourceru 1 -targetru 4
The operation completed successfully
GDSCTL>

GDSCTL> status ru -show_chunks
```

```
Chunks
------------------------
RU#             From    To
---             ----    --
1               1       1
2               3       4
3               5       6
4               2       2       <--------
4               7       8
5               9       10
6               11      12

Replication units
------------------------
Database                RU#  Role      Term Log Index Status
--------                ---  ----      ---- --------- ------
shdcdb3_shard3          1    Follower  3    8         Ok
shdcdb3_shard3          2    Follower  1    3         Ok
shdcdb3_shard3          3    Leader    2    2         Ok
shdcdb3_shard3          4    Follower  2    5         Ok
shdcdb3_shard3          5    Follower  1    4         Ok
shdcdb3_shard3          6    Leader    2    4         Ok
shdcdb2_shard2          1    Follower  3    8         Ok
shdcdb2_shard2          2    Leader    1    3         Ok
shdcdb2_shard2          3    Follower  2    2         Ok
shdcdb2_shard2          4    Follower  2    5         Ok
shdcdb2_shard2          5    Leader    1    4         Ok
shdcdb2_shard2          6    Follower  2    4         Ok
shdcdb1_shard1          1    Leader    3    8         Ok
shdcdb1_shard1          2    Follower  1    3         Ok
shdcdb1_shard1          3    Follower  2    2         Ok
shdcdb1_shard1          4    Leader    2    5         Ok
shdcdb1_shard1          5    Follower  1    4         Ok
shdcdb1_shard1          6    Follower  2    4         Ok
GDSCTL>
```

As we can see, we were able to move the chunk from one RU to another.

Test Case 2: Scaling Up the Raft Replication

For the second test case, let's try to scale up the Raft Replication. For this test, we will try to add the fourth pluggable database, shard4, as a new shard to the sharded database. Whenever a shard is added to a sharded database, the redistribution of the chunks occurs, and multiple chunks from the current shards are migrated to the other shards, including to the new shards. For a system-managed replication method, chunk migration occurs automatically to maintain the balanced distribution of chunks across all shards and to maintain the workload across all shards.

We must run all the parameter-related SQL statements (which we ran in the other three databases earlier) in the fourth CDB database, shdcdb, and its PDB, shard4, to ensure that this database is ready to be added to the shard GDS pool. Once the database is ready, we can add the CDB and PDB to the same shard group, shardgroup_primary, as follows:

```
GDSCTL> add cdb -connect stsh02:1521/shdcdb -pwd welcome
DB Unique Name: shdcdb
The operation completed successfully
GDSCTL>

GDSCTL> add shard -cdb shdcdb -connect shard4 -shardgroup
shardgroup_primary
"gsmuser" password:
INFO: Native shard validation requested.
INFO: Database role is PRIMARY.
INFO: Database name is SHDCDB.
INFO: Database unique name is shdcdb.
INFO: Database ID is 3986305272.
INFO: Database open mode is READ WRITE.
INFO: Database in archivelog mode.
INFO: Flashback is on.
INFO: Force logging is on.
INFO: Database platform is Linux x86 64-bit.
INFO: Database character set is AL32UTF8. This value must match the
character set of the catalog database.
INFO: 'compatible' initialization parameter validated successfully.
INFO: Database is a multitenant container database.
```

INFO: Current container is SHARD4.

INFO: Database is using a server parameter file (spfile).

INFO: db_create_file_dest set to: '/u01/app/oracle/oradata/data'

INFO: db_recovery_file_dest set to: '/u01/app/oracle/oradata/fra'

INFO: db_files=1024. Must be greater than the number of chunks and/or tablespaces to be created in the shard.

INFO: remote_login_passwordfile set to EXCLUSIVE.

WARNING: db_file_name_convert is not set.

INFO: GSMUSER account validated successfully.

INFO: DATA_PUMP_DIR is '/u01/app/oracle/admin/shdcdb/dpdump/ FAEB652564455D5EE0534B0278C097CB'.

DB Unique Name: shdcdb_shard4

The operation completed successfully

GDSCTL>

Now, if we run the config shard command, we can see that the fourth shard, shard4, is added, but it is not ONLINE yet.

```
GDSCTL> config shard
Name              Shard Group         Status  State   Region    Availability
----              ------------------  ------  -----   ------    ------------
shdcdb1_shard1    shardgroup_primary  U       none    region1   ONLINE
shdcdb2_shard2    shardgroup_primary  U       none    region1   ONLINE
shdcdb3_shard3    shardgroup_primary  U       none    region1   ONLINE
shdcdb_shard4     shardgroup_primary  U       none    region1   -
GDSCTL>
```

We must run the deploy command, which will cross-check all the parameters in the newly added database, shard4, and will add it to the replication configuration.

```
GDSCTL> deploy
deploy: examining configuration...
deploy: shards configured; background operations in progress
The operation completed successfully
```

```
GDSCTL> config shard
Name                Shard Group         Status  State   Region    Availability
----                -----------------   -----   -----   ------    ------------
shdcdb1_shard1      shardgroup_primary  U       none    region1   ONLINE
shdcdb2_shard2      shardgroup_primary  U       none    region1   ONLINE
shdcdb3_shard3      shardgroup_primary  U       none    region1   ONLINE
shdcdb_shard4       shardgroup_primary  U       none    region1   ONLINE
GDSCTL>
```

We can see that the status of shard4 is now ONLINE, and we can also see that chunk migration occurred and a few chunks migrated to the newly added shard, shdcdb_shard4.

```
GDSCTL> config chunks
Chunks
------------------------
Database                From        To
--------                ----        --
shdcdb1_shard1          1           12
shdcdb2_shard2          1           12
shdcdb3_shard3          1           1
shdcdb3_shard3          3           3
shdcdb3_shard3          5           12
shdcdb_shard4           2           2          <=======
shdcdb_shard4           4           4          <=======
GDSCTL>
GDSCTL> status ru -show_chunks

Chunks
------------------------
RU#                     From        To
---                     ----        --
1                       1           1
2                       3           3
3                       5           5
4                       7           8
```

```
5                         9          10
6                         11         12
7                         2          2
7                         6          6
8                         4          4
```

Replication units

Database	RU#	Role	Term	Log Index	Status
shdcdb3_shard3	1	Follower	3	8	Ok
shdcdb3_shard3	2	Follower	1	3	Ok
shdcdb3_shard3	3	Leader	2	2	Ok
shdcdb3_shard3	4	Follower	2	5	Ok
shdcdb3_shard3	5	Follower	1	4	Ok
shdcdb3_shard3	6	Leader	2	4	Ok
shdcdb_shard4	7	Leader	2	3	Ok
shdcdb_shard4	8	Leader	2	3	Ok
shdcdb_shard4	2	Follower	1	4	Ok
shdcdb_shard4	5	Follower	1	6	Ok
shdcdb_shard4	3	Follower	2	3	Ok
shdcdb_shard4	6	Follower	2	6	Ok
shdcdb2_shard2	1	Follower	3	8	Ok
shdcdb2_shard2	2	Leader	1	3	Ok
shdcdb2_shard2	4	Follower	2	5	Ok
shdcdb2_shard2	5	Leader	1	4	Ok
shdcdb2_shard2	7	Follower	2	3	Ok
shdcdb2_shard2	8	Follower	2	3	Ok
shdcdb1_shard1	1	Leader	3	8	Ok
shdcdb1_shard1	3	Follower	2	2	Ok
shdcdb1_shard1	4	Leader	2	5	Ok
shdcdb1_shard1	6	Follower	2	4	Ok
shdcdb1_shard1	7	Follower	2	3	Ok
shdcdb1_shard1	8	Follower	2	3	Ok

GDSCTL>

We can also run the database command for checking the status of all databases, including the newly added database, shard4.

```
GDSCTL> databases
Database: "shdcdb1_shard1" Registered: Y State: Ok ONS: N. Role: PRIMARY
Instances: 1 Region: region1
    Service: "raft_rw_srv" Globally started: Y Started: Y
            Scan: N Enabled: Y Preferred: Y
    Registered instances:
      orasdb%1
Database: "shdcdb2_shard2" Registered: Y State: Ok ONS: N. Role: PRIMARY
Instances: 1 Region: region1
    Service: "raft_rw_srv" Globally started: Y Started: Y
            Scan: N Enabled: Y Preferred: Y
    Registered instances:
      orasdb%11
Database: "shdcdb3_shard3" Registered: Y State: Ok ONS: N. Role: PRIMARY
Instances: 1 Region: region1
    Service: "raft_rw_srv" Globally started: Y Started: Y
            Scan: N Enabled: Y Preferred: Y
    Registered instances:
      orasdb%21
Database: "shdcdb_shard4" Registered: N State: null ONS: N. Role: N/A
Instances: 0 Region: region1
    Service: "raft_rw_srv" Globally started: Y Started: N
            Scan: N Enabled: Y Preferred: Y
GDSCTL>
```

We were successfully able to add a new shard to the existing sharded database.

Test Case 3: Moving a Replication Unit from One Shard to Another

In this test case, you will see how we can move a replication unit from one shard to another. We can move replication unit replicas from one shard to another by using the move ru command. When moving the replication unit, we must move it to a shard that does *not* have that replication unit replica.

When we check the following output, we can see that shard and shdcdb_shard4 do not have RU# 4. We can try to move RU# 4 from another shard, shdcdb3_shard3, to shdcdb_shard4.

```
GDSCTL> status ru -show_chunks
Chunks
------------------------
```

RU#	From	To
1	1	1
2	3	3
3	5	5
4	7	8
5	9	10
6	11	12
7	2	2
7	6	6
8	4	4

```
Replication units
------------------------
```

Database	RU#	Role	Term	Log Index	Status	
shdcdb3_shard3	1	Follower	3	8	Ok	
shdcdb3_shard3	2	Follower	2	3	Ok	
shdcdb3_shard3	3	Leader	2	2	Ok	⬅
shdcdb3_shard3	4	Follower	2	5	Ok	
shdcdb3_shard3	5	Follower	1	4	Ok	
shdcdb3_shard3	6	Leader	2	4	Ok	
shdcdb_shard4	7	Leader	2	3	Ok	
shdcdb_shard4	8	Leader	2	3	Ok	
shdcdb_shard4	2	Follower	1	4	Ok	
shdcdb_shard4	5	Follower	1	6	Ok	
shdcdb_shard4	3	Follower	2	3	Ok	
shdcdb_shard4	6	Follower	2	6	Ok	
shdcdb2_shard2	1	Follower	3	8	Ok	
shdcdb2_shard2	2	Leader	1	3	Ok	

shdcdb2_shard2	4	Follower	2	5	Ok
shdcdb2_shard2	5	Leader	1	4	Ok
shdcdb2_shard2	7	Follower	2	3	Ok
shdcdb2_shard2	8	Follower	2	3	Ok
shdcdb1_shard1	1	Leader	3	8	Ok
shdcdb1_shard1	3	Follower	2	2	Ok
shdcdb1_shard1	4	Leader	2	5	Ok
shdcdb1_shard1	6	Follower	2	4	Ok
shdcdb1_shard1	7	Follower	2	3	Ok
shdcdb1_shard1	8	Follower	2	3	Ok

```
GDSCTL>
```

Let's move RU# 4 from another shard, shdcdb3_shard3, to shdcdb_shard4.

```
GDSCTL> move ru -ru 4 -source shdcdb3_shard3  -target shdcdb_shard4
Target database metadata retrieval and availability check.
Backup 0 creation.
Backup 0 replication and restoration.
Transition to read-only mode.
Shutdown of apply process group
User metadata export.
Backup 1 creation, replication and restoration.
Chunk import.
Chunk migration is successful. Performing data transition and cleanup.
The operation completed successfully
GDSCTL>
```

Let's check the status of the replication units again; we can see from the following that RU #4 is moved from shdcdb3_shard3 to shdcdb_shard4.

```
GDSCTL> status ru -show_chunks
Chunks
------------------------
RU#                     From     To
---                     ----     --
1                       1        1
2                       3        3
3                       5        5
```

4	7	8
5	9	10
6	11	12
7	2	2
7	6	6
8	4	4

Replication units

Database	RU#	Role	Term	Log Index	Status
shdcdb1_shard1	1	Leader	3	8	Ok
shdcdb1_shard1	3	Follower	2	2	Ok
shdcdb1_shard1	4	Leader	2	5	Ok
shdcdb1_shard1	6	Follower	2	4	Ok
shdcdb1_shard1	7	Follower	2	3	Ok
shdcdb1_shard1	8	Follower	2	3	Ok
shdcdb_shard4	7	Leader	2	3	Ok
shdcdb_shard4	8	Leader	2	3	Ok
shdcdb_shard4	2	Follower	1	4	Ok
shdcdb_shard4	5	Follower	1	6	Ok
shdcdb_shard4	3	Follower	2	3	Ok
shdcdb_shard4	6	Follower	2	6	Ok
shdcdb_shard4	4	Follower	2	9	Ok	⬅
shdcdb3_shard3	1	Follower	3	8	Ok
shdcdb3_shard3	2	Follower	1	3	Ok
shdcdb3_shard3	3	Leader	2	2	Ok
shdcdb3_shard3	5	Follower	1	4	Ok
shdcdb3_shard3	6	Leader	2	4	Ok
shdcdb2_shard2	1	Follower	3	8	Ok
shdcdb2_shard2	2	Leader	1	3	Ok
shdcdb2_shard2	4	Follower	2	5	Ok
shdcdb2_shard2	5	Leader	1	4	Ok
shdcdb2_shard2	7	Follower	2	3	Ok
shdcdb2_shard2	8	Follower	2	3	Ok

GDSCTL>

Test Case 4: Copying a Replication Unit from One Shard to Another

We might have a situation where we must copy a replication unit from one shard to another. We can use the command copy ru to copy the replication units.

We will try to copy RU #1 from shard shdcdb2_shard2 to shard shdcdb_shard4. The following is the status of replication units:

```
GDSCTL> status ru -show_chunks
Chunks
------------------------
```

RU#	From	To
1	1	1
2	3	3
3	5	5
4	7	8
5	9	10
6	11	12
7	2	2
7	6	6
8	4	4

```
Replication units
------------------------
```

Database	RU#	Role	Term	Log Index	Status	
--------	---	----	----	---------	------	
shdcdb_shard4	7	Leader	2	3	Ok	
shdcdb_shard4	8	Leader	2	3	Ok	
shdcdb_shard4	2	Follower	1	4	Ok	
shdcdb_shard4	5	Follower	1	6	Ok	
shdcdb_shard4	3	Follower	2	3	Ok	
shdcdb_shard4	6	Follower	2	6	Ok	
shdcdb_shard4	4	Follower	2	9	Ok	
shdcdb2_shard2	1	Follower	3	8	Ok	⬅
shdcdb2_shard2	2	Leader	2	3	Ok	
shdcdb2_shard2	4	Follower	2	5	Ok	

shdcdb2_shard2	5	Leader	1	4	Ok
shdcdb2_shard2	7	Follower	2	3	Ok
shdcdb2_shard2	8	Follower	2	3	Ok
shdcdb3_shard3	1	Follower	3	8	Ok
shdcdb3_shard3	2	Follower	1	3	Ok
shdcdb3_shard3	3	Leader	2	2	Ok
shdcdb3_shard3	5	Follower	1	4	Ok
shdcdb3_shard3	6	Leader	2	4	Ok
shdcdb1_shard1	1	Leader	3	8	Ok
shdcdb1_shard1	3	Follower	2	2	Ok
shdcdb1_shard1	4	Leader	2	5	Ok
shdcdb1_shard1	6	Follower	2	4	Ok
shdcdb1_shard1	7	Follower	2	3	Ok
shdcdb1_shard1	8	Follower	2	3	Ok

```
GDSCTL>
```

Let's try to copy RU# 1 from shard shdcdb2_shard2 to shard shdcdb_shard4 using the GDSCTL copy ru command.

```
GDSCTL> copy ru -ru 1 -source shdcdb2_shard2 -target shdcdb_shard4
GSM-45029: SQL error
ORA-03982: invalid number of replicas
ORA-06512: at "GSMADMIN_INTERNAL.DBMS_GSM_POOLADMIN", line 15863
ORA-06512: at "SYS.DBMS_SYS_ERROR", line 79
ORA-06512: at "GSMADMIN_INTERNAL.DBMS_GSM_POOLADMIN", line 15787
ORA-06512: at "GSMADMIN_INTERNAL.DBMS_GSM_POOLADMIN", line 15437
ORA-06512: at line 1
GDSCTL>
```

It errored out, as we can see; it complained about the invalid number of replicas, as we already have the three replicas of RU# 1, and it fails, as the replication unit should be following the replication factor (3). To fix the issue, we must use the replace option in the copy command.

```
GDSCTL> copy ru -ru 1 -source shdcdb2_shard2 -target shdcdb_shard4 -replace
shdcdb3_shard3
The operation completed successfully
GDSCTL>
```

We can see that the RU was copied from shard2 to shard4, and it deleted the RU in shard3, as it must maintain the replication factor of 3.

```
GDSCTL> status ru -show_chunks
Chunks
-------------------------
RU#                      From      To
---                      ----      --
1                        1         1
2                        3         3
3                        5         5
4                        7         8
5                        9         10
6                        11        12
7                        2         2        <----
7                        6         6
8                        4         4

Replication units
-------------------------
Database           RU#   Role        Term  Log Index  Status
--------           ---   ----        ----  ---------  ------
shdcdb_shard4      7     Leader      2     3          Ok
shdcdb_shard4      8     Leader      2     3          Ok
shdcdb_shard4      2     Follower    1     4          Ok
shdcdb_shard4      5     Follower    1     6          Ok
shdcdb_shard4      3     Follower    2     3          Ok
shdcdb_shard4      6     Follower    2     6          Ok
shdcdb_shard4      4     Follower    2     9          Ok
shdcdb_shard4      1     Follower    3     12         Ok        <----

shdcdb2_shard2     1     Follower    3     8          Ok        <----
shdcdb2_shard2     2     Leader      1     3          Ok
shdcdb2_shard2     4     Follower    2     5          Ok
shdcdb2_shard2     5     Leader      1     4          Ok
shdcdb2_shard2     7     Follower    2     3          Ok
```

```
shdcdb2_shard2      8    Follower  2   3         Ok
shdcdb1_shard1      1    Leader    3   8         Ok          ⬅
shdcdb1_shard1      3    Follower  2   2         Ok
shdcdb1_shard1      4    Leader    2   5         Ok
shdcdb1_shard1      6    Follower  2   4         Ok
shdcdb1_shard1      7    Follower  2   3         Ok
shdcdb1_shard1      8    Follower  2   3         Ok
shdcdb3_shard3      2    Follower  1   3         Ok
shdcdb3_shard3      3    Leader    2   2         Ok
shdcdb3_shard3      5    Follower  1   4         Ok
shdcdb3_shard3      6    Leader    2   4         Ok
GDSCTL>
```

Test Case 5: Changing the Leader of the Replication Unit

There might be a scenario where we have a need to change the replication unit leader from one shard to another; we can achieve this by using the GDSCTL command, switchover ru.

We can check the current leader by running the following command:

```
GDSCTL>  status ru -leaders
Replication units
-----------------------
Database          RU#  Role      Term Log Index Status
--------          ---  ----      ---- --------- -----
shdcdb3_shard3    3    Leader    2   2         Ok
shdcdb3_shard3    6    Leader    2   4         Ok          ⬅
shdcdb_shard4     7    Leader    2   3         Ok
shdcdb_shard4     8    Leader    2   3         Ok
shdcdb2_shard2    2    Leader    1   3         Ok
shdcdb2_shard2    5    Leader    1   4         Ok
shdcdb1_shard1    1    Leader    3   8         Ok
shdcdb1_shard1    4    Leader    2   5         Ok
GDSCTL>
```

As of now, shdcdb3_shard3 is the leader of RU# 6. Let's change the leader of RU# 6 to shdcdb1_shard1 using the GDSCTL command switchover ru.

```
GDSCTL>  switchover ru -ru 6 -database shdcdb1_shard1
Switchover process has been started
Switchover process completed
The operation completed successfully
GDSCTL>

GDSCTL>  status ru -leaders
Replication units
------------------------
Database          RU#   Role      Term   Log Index   Status
--------          ---   ----      ----   ---------   ------
shdcdb1_shard1    1     Leader    3      8           Ok
shdcdb1_shard1    4     Leader    2      5           Ok
shdcdb1_shard1    6     Leader    3      6           Ok        <---
shdcdb3_shard3    3     Leader    2      2           Ok
shdcdb2_shard2    2     Leader    1      3           Ok
shdcdb2_shard2    5     Leader    1      4           Ok
shdcdb_shard4     7     Leader    2      3           Ok
shdcdb_shard4     8     Leader    2      3           Ok
GDSCTL>
```

We can see from the previous that the leader of RU# 6 has been changed from shdcdb3_shard3 to shdcdb1_shard1.

Test Case 6: Scaling Down in Raft Replication

We might have a need to scale down the shards. In this exercise, we will scale down the Raft Replication by removing the shard shdcdb3_shard3 from the configuration. As of now, we have four shards in the configuration.

```
GDSCTL> config shard
Name               Shard Group          Status  State   Region    Availability
----               ------------------   ------  -----   ------    ------------
shdcdb1_shard1     shardgroup_primary   U       none    region1   ONLINE
shdcdb2_shard2     shardgroup_primary   U       none    region1   ONLINE
shdcdb3_shard3     shardgroup_primary   U       none    region1   ONLINE
shdcdb_shard4      shardgroup_primary   U       none    region1   ONLINE
GDSCTL>
```

Please note that when removing one of the shards, we must first empty the shard by moving all of the replication units present in it to other available shards, and only then will we be able to remove the shard. If we try to remove the shard that has replication units, it will error out. Please see the following when we try to remove a nonempty shard, shdcdb3_shard3:

```
GDSCTL> remove shard -shard shdcdb3_shard3;
GSM-45029: SQL error
ORA-02659: cannot remove a shard which contains chunks or replication units
ORA-06512: at "GSMADMIN_INTERNAL.DBMS_GSM_POOLADMIN", line 19147
ORA-06512: at "SYS.DBMS_SYS_ERROR", line 79
ORA-06512: at "GSMADMIN_INTERNAL.DBMS_GSM_POOLADMIN", line 18837
ORA-06512: at "GSMADMIN_INTERNAL.DBMS_GSM_POOLADMIN", line 18541
ORA-06512: at line 1
GDSCTL>
```

As you can see from the previous error, we cannot remove any shard containing the replication units or chunks. Let's see how many chunks the shard shdcdb3_shard3 does have.

```
GDSCTL> status ru -show_chunks
Chunks
------------------------
RU#                      From    To
---                      ----    --
1                        1       1
2                        3       3
3                        5       5
4                        7       8
```

5	9	10
6	11	12
7	2	2
7	6	6
8	4	4

Replication units

Database	RU#	Role	Term	Log Index	Status
shdcdb3_shard3	6	Leader	4	7	Ok
shdcdb3_shard3	2	Follower	1	6	Ok
shdcdb3_shard3	5	Leader	2	6	Ok
shdcdb3_shard3	3	Leader	5	6	Ok
shdcdb2_shard2	1	Follower	6	16	Ok
shdcdb2_shard2	2	Leader	1	3	Ok
shdcdb2_shard2	4	Follower	7	14	Ok
shdcdb2_shard2	5	Follower	2	6	Ok
shdcdb2_shard2	7	Follower	9	12	Ok
shdcdb2_shard2	8	Follower	4	5	Ok
shdcdb1_shard1	1	Follower	6	16	Ok
shdcdb1_shard1	3	Follower	5	6	Ok
shdcdb1_shard1	4	Leader	7	14	Ok
shdcdb1_shard1	6	Follower	4	7	Ok
shdcdb1_shard1	7	Leader	9	12	Ok
shdcdb1_shard1	8	Follower	4	5	Ok
shdcdb_shard4	7	Follower	9	12	Ok
shdcdb_shard4	8	Leader	4	5	Ok
shdcdb_shard4	2	Follower	1	4	Ok
shdcdb_shard4	5	Follower	2	6	Ok
shdcdb_shard4	3	Follower	5	6	Ok
shdcdb_shard4	6	Follower	4	7	Ok
shdcdb_shard4	4	Follower	7	14	Ok
shdcdb_shard4	1	Leader	6	16	Ok

GDSCTL>

Therefore, we have three Rus (6, 2, and 5) in shard shdcdb3_shard3. We must move these replication units to other shards, and then we should be able to drop the shard, shdcdb3_shard3. We should be able to move RUs #2 and #5 without any issues, but the thing is that shdcdb3_shard3 is the leader for RU# 6, so we first need to change its leader and then move it to the other shard.

Let's move RU# 2 and RU# 5 from shdcdb3_shard3 -target shdcdb2_shard2.

```
GDSCTL> move ru -ru 2 -source shdcdb3_shard3 -target shdcdb1_shard1
Target database metadata retrieval and availability check.
Backup 0 creation.
Backup 0 replication and restoration.
move ru -ru 2 -source shdcdb3_shard3 -target shdcdb2_shard2
Transition to read-only mode.
Shutdown of apply process group
User metadata export.
Backup 1 creation, replication and restoration.
Chunk import.
Chunk migration is successful. Performing data transition and cleanup.
status ru -show_chunks
The operation completed successfully
GDSCTL>

GDSCTL> move ru -ru 5 -source shdcdb3_shard3 -target shdcdb1_shard1
Target database metadata retrieval and availability check.
Backup 0 creation.
Backup 0 replication and restoration.
move ru -ru 2 -source shdcdb3_shard3 -target shdcdb2_shard2
Transition to read-only mode.
Shutdown of apply process group
User metadata export.
Backup 1 creation, replication and restoration.
Chunk import.
Chunk migration is successful. Performing data transition and cleanup.
status ru -show_chunks
The operation completed successfully
GDSCTL>
```

Let's try moving RU# 6 and see what it says.

```
GDSCTL>  move ru -ru 6 -source shdcdb3_shard3 -target shdcdb2_shard2
GSM-45029: SQL error
ORA-03980: shard shdcdb3_shard3 is the leader for replication unit 6
ORA-06512: at "GSMADMIN_INTERNAL.DBMS_GSM_POOLADMIN", line 16142
ORA-06512: at "SYS.DBMS_SYS_ERROR", line 121
ORA-06512: at "GSMADMIN_INTERNAL.DBMS_GSM_POOLADMIN", line 16028
ORA-06512: at "GSMADMIN_INTERNAL.DBMS_GSM_POOLADMIN", line 15874
ORA-06512: at line 1
GDSCTL>
```

As mentioned, shdcdb3_shard3 is the leader for replication unit 6. So, let's change the leader of RU# 6 to shdcdb_shard4.

```
GDSCTL> switchover ru -ru 6 -database shdcdb_shard4
Switchover process has been started
Switchover process completed
The operation completed successfully
GDSCTL>
```

Now, if the move operation for RU #6 is retried, it will work.

```
GDSCTL> move ru -ru 6 -source shdcdb3_shard3 -target shdcdb2_shard2
Target database metadata retrieval and availability check.
Backup 0 creation.
Backup 0 replication and restoration.
Transition to read-only mode.
Shutdown of apply process group
User metadata export.
Backup 1 creation, replication and restoration.
Chunk import.
Chunk migration is successful. Performing data transition and cleanup.
The operation completed successfully
GDSCTL>
```

If we check the status of the replication units, we will not see anything for shdcdb3_shard3.

```
GDSCTL>status ru -show_chunks

GDSCTL> Chunks
------------------------
RU#                      From      To
---                      ----      --
1                        1         1
2                        3         3
3                        5         5
4                        7         8
5                        9         10
6                        11        12
7                        2         2
7                        6         6
8                        4         4

Replication units
------------------------
Database                 RU#  Role      Term Log Index Status
--------                 ---  ----      ---- --------- ------
shdcdb_shard4            7    Follower  9    12        Ok
shdcdb_shard4            8    Leader    4    5         Ok
shdcdb_shard4            2    Follower  1    4         Ok
shdcdb_shard4            5    Follower  3    7         Ok
shdcdb_shard4            3    Leader    6    7         Ok
shdcdb_shard4            6    Leader    5    8         Ok
shdcdb_shard4            4    Follower  7    14        Ok
shdcdb_shard4            1    Leader    6    16        Ok
shdcdb1_shard1           1    Follower  6    16        Ok
shdcdb1_shard1           3    Follower  6    7         Ok
shdcdb1_shard1           4    Leader    7    14        Ok
shdcdb1_shard1           6    Follower  5    8         Ok
shdcdb1_shard1           7    Leader    9    12        Ok
shdcdb1_shard1           8    Follower  4    5         Ok
```

shdcdb1_shard1	5	Follower	3	8	Ok
shdcdb1_shard1	2	Follower	1	6	Ok
shdcdb2_shard2	1	Follower	6	16	Ok
shdcdb2_shard2	2	Leader	1	3	Ok
shdcdb2_shard2	4	Follower	7	14	Ok
shdcdb2_shard2	5	Leader	3	7	Ok
shdcdb2_shard2	7	Follower	9	12	Ok
shdcdb2_shard2	8	Follower	4	5	Ok
shdcdb2_shard2	6	Follower	5	9	Ok
shdcdb2_shard2	3	Follower	6	8	Ok

```
GDSCTL> GSM-45018: Command not found
Chunks
GDSCTL>
```

We can now remove the shard shdcdb3_shard3.

```
GDSCTL>remove shard -shard shdcdb3_shard3;
The operation completed successfully
GDSCTL>
GDSCTL> config shard
Name                Shard Group         Status  State   Region      Availability
----                ------------------  ------  -----   ------      ------------
shdcdb1_shard1      shardgroup_primary  U       none    region1     ONLINE
shdcdb2_shard2      shardgroup_primary  U       none    region1     ONLINE
shdcdb_shard4       shardgroup_primary  U       none    region1     ONLINE
GDSCTL>

GDSCTL>
```

As we saw, if we want to remove a shard from the existing configuration, we must first empty the shard by moving all the replication units present in that shard to other shards, and then we will be able to remove the shard from the configuration.

Test Case 7: Testing the High Availability of Shards

What happens when one of the available shard databases goes down or is taken down for maintenance? Will the other shards continue to provide access to the replicated data? Well, let's determine the answer.

For this test case, we will shut down one of the shards. The following are the available shards now:

```
GDSCTL> config shard
Name              Shard Group          Status  State   Region    Availability
----              ------------------   -----   -----   ------    ------------
shdcdb1_shard1    shardgroup_primary   U       none    region1   ONLINE
shdcdb2_shard2    shardgroup_primary   U       none    region1   ONLINE
shdcdb_shard4     shardgroup_primary   U       none    region1   ONLINE
GDSCTL>
```

As we can see, the availability for all three shards is shown as ONLINE, and we are able to access the data when we run the following SELECT statement on the precreated table called customers in the catalog database.

```
[oracle@stsh01 ~]$ sqlplus app_shard/app_shard@gsmcatdb

SQL*Plus: Release 23.0.0.0.0 - Beta on Mon May 8 11:27:28 2023
Version 23.1.0.0.0

Copyright (c) 1982, 2022, Oracle.  All rights reserved.

Last Successful login time: Mon May 08 2023 09:58:13 -05:00

Connected to:
Oracle Database 23c Enterprise Edition Release 23.0.0.0.0 - Beta
Version 23.1.0.0.0

SQL> select * from customers order by 1;

CUSTID        FIRSTNAME   LASTNAME    PASSWD
-----------   ---------   ---------   ----------------------------------
1             moody       ragi        68656C6C6F20776F726C64
10            tom         peats       68656C6C6F20776F726C643230
2             randy       Beridze     68656C6C6F20776F726C6431
```

3	ravi	Bettle	68656C6C6F20776F726C6432
4	zach	boron	68656C6C6F20776F726C6433
5	laura	crain	68656C6C6F20776F726C6434
6	shreya	sharma	68656C6C6F20776F726C6436
7	trish	jackson	68656C6C6F20776F726C6437
8	ilena	samme	68656C6C6F20776F726C6438
9	brad	crusee	68656C6C6F20776F726C6439

10 rows selected.

SQL>

Now let's shut down the shard shdcdb_shard4, which is the database shdcdb. We can shut down either its CDB, shdcdb, or just the pdb, shard4. In this case, we will shut down the CDB itself.

```
[oracle@stsh02 ~]$ sqlplus/as sysdba

SQL*Plus: Release 23.0.0.0.0 - Beta on Mon May 8 11:24:52 2023
Version 23.1.0.0.0

Copyright (c) 1982, 2022, Oracle.  All rights reserved.

Connected to:
Oracle Database 23c Enterprise Edition Release 23.0.0.0.0 - Beta
Version 23.1.0.0.0

SQL> show pdbs

    CON_ID CON_NAME                         OPEN MODE  RESTRICTED
---------- ------------------------------ ---------- ----------
         2 PDB$SEED                         READ ONLY  NO
         3 SHARD4                           READ WRITE NO
SQL> shut immediate;
Database closed.
Database dismounted.
ORACLE instance shut down.
SQL>
```

If we check the `config shard` command, we will see that the availability of shard shdcdb_shard4 is not ONLINE.

```
GDSCTL> config shard
Name              Shard Group          Status  State   Region    Availability
----              ------------------   ------  -----   ------    ------------
shdcdb1_shard1    shardgroup_primary   U       none    region1   ONLINE
shdcdb2_shard2    shardgroup_primary   U       none    region1   ONLINE
shdcdb_shard4     shardgroup_primary   U       none    region1   -
GDSCTL>
```

If we run the same SELECT statement by connecting either to the catalog or to one of the available shards, it will return the same set of data.

```
[oracle@stsh01 ~]$ sqlplus app_shard/app_shard@gsmcatdb

SQL*Plus: Release 23.0.0.0.0 - Beta on Mon May 8 11:53:42 2023
Version 23.1.0.0.0
Copyright (c) 1982, 2022, Oracle.  All rights reserved.          .
Last Successful login time: Mon May 08 2023 11:52:01 -05:00

Connected to:
Oracle Database 23c Enterprise Edition Release 23.0.0.0.0 - Beta
Version 23.1.0.0.0

SQL> select * from customers;

CUSTID        FIRSTNAME  LASTNAME    PASSWD
-----------   ---------- ----------- ------------------------------------
7             trish      jackson     68656C6C6F20776F726C6437
10            tom        peats       68656C6C6F20776F726C643230
3             ravi       Bettle      68656C6C6F20776F726C6432
5             laura      crain       68656C6C6F20776F726C6434
9             brad       crusee      68656C6C6F20776F726C6439
6             shreya     sharma      68656C6C6F20776F726C6436
4             zach       boron       68656C6C6F20776F726C6433
1             moody      ragi        68656C6C6F20776F726C64
```

| 2 | randy | Beridze | 68656C6C6F20776F726C6431 |
| 8 | ilena | samme | 68656C6C6F20776F726C6438 |

10 rows selected.

SQL>

Since the replication is enabled, we can fetch the data without any issues. This shows that when one or more shards are not available, the high availability of data is provided by the remaining shards as long as at least one of the shards is available.

The following are a few useful commands that we can use to check the chunks.

We can use the GDSCTL command config chunks -cross_shard to check which shards are running in READ ONLY mode and which ones are running in READ WRITE mode.

```
GDSCTL> config chunks -cross_shard
Read-Only cross shard targets
------------------------
Database                       From To
--------                       ---- --
shdcdb2_shard2                 1    2
shdcdb2_shard2                 4    4
shdcdb2_shard2                 6    7
shdcdb3_shard3                 9    9
shdcdb3_shard3                 11   11
shdcdb_shard4                  3    3
shdcdb_shard4                  5    5
shdcdb_shard4                  8    8
shdcdb_shard4                  10   10
shdcdb_shard4                  12   12

Chunks not offered for cross-shard
```

```
-----------------------
Shard space     From To
-----------     ---- --

Read-Write cross-shard targets
-----------------------
Database                    From To
--------                    ---- --
shdcdb1_shard1              1    1
shdcdb1_shard1              5    5
shdcdb1_shard1              7    8
shdcdb1_shard1              11   12
shdcdb2_shard2              3    3
shdcdb2_shard2              9    10
shdcdb_shard4              2    2
shdcdb_shard4              4    4
shdcdb_shard4              6    6

Chunks not offered for Read-Write cross-shard activity
-----------------------
Data N/A
GDSCTL>
```

We can run the following SQL command in the GDS catalog database to check the number of chunks per shard:

```
SQL > col SHARD_NAME for a20
select i.name SHARD_NAME,count(j.chunk_number) NUM_OF_CHUNKS from gsmadmin_
internal.database i, gsmadmin_internal.chunk_loc j where i.database_num=j.
database_num group by i.name;

SHARD_NAME              NUM_OF_CHUNKS
------------------     -------------
shdcdb1_shard1                    9
shdcdb2_shard2                    9
shdcdb3_shard3                    6
shdcdb_shard4                    12
SQL>
```

We can run the following command to check the leaders of the replication units:

```
GDSCTL> ru -leaders
Replication units
------------------------
```

Database	RU#	Role	Term	Log Index	Status
--------	---	----	----	---------	------
shdcdb1_shard1	12	Leader	2	5	Ok
shdcdb1_shard1	1	Leader	27	37	Ok
shdcdb1_shard1	2	Leader	20	25	Ok
shdcdb1_shard1	7	Leader	33	38	Ok
shdcdb1_shard1	5	Leader	27	33	Ok
shdcdb1_shard1	6	Leader	21	26	Ok
shdcdb1_shard1	8	Leader	22	26	Ok
shdcdb1_shard1	11	Leader	17	21	Ok
shdcdb1_shard1	13	Leader	1	1	Ok
shdcdb3_shard3	4	Leader	31	42	Ok
shdcdb3_shard3	10	Leader	16	22	Ok
shdcdb3_shard3	3	Leader	25	29	Ok

```
GDSCTL>
```

What Happens When a New Shard Is Added to the Sharded Database

Whenever a new shard is added to the sharded database, a redistribution of data occurs, ensuring that the data is evenly distributed in all the available shards. We can see how the distribution is happening internally using the command config task.

```
GDSCTL> config task
```

task ID	status	GDS command
-------	------	--
423	started	move ru -ru 10 -source shdcdb2_shard2 -target shdcdb1_shard1
424	scheduled	switchover ru -ru 3 -database shdcdb_shard4
425	scheduled	move ru -ru 3 -source shdcdb3_shard3 -target shdcdb1_shard1

426	scheduled	switchover ru -ru 5 -database shdcdb_shard4
427	scheduled	move ru -ru 5 -source shdcdb3_shard3 -target shdcdb1_shard1
428	scheduled	switchover ru -ru 6 -database shdcdb_shard4
429	scheduled	move ru -ru 6 -source shdcdb3_shard3 -target shdcdb1_shard1
430	scheduled	switchover ru -ru 8 -database shdcdb_shard4
431	scheduled	move ru -ru 8 -source shdcdb3_shard3 -target shdcdb1_shard1
432	scheduled	switchover ru -ru 11 -database shdcdb_shard4
433	scheduled	move ru -ru 11 -source shdcdb3_shard3 -target shdcdb1_shard1
434	scheduled	switchover ru -ru 12 -database shdcdb1_shard1
435	scheduled	switchover ru -ru 12 -database shdcdb1_shard1
436	scheduled	relocate chunk -chunk 8 -sourceru 12 -targetru 13
437	scheduled	switchover ru -ru 13 -database shdcdb1_shard1

As a part of the redistribution process, we can see that replication units move to the new shard, and the leaders of the few replication units change to the new shard. From the previous output, we can see that task ID 423 is currently running, and all other tasks are added to the queue waiting for their turn. All the tasks will run in order. This might take time depending upon the size of the data.

Known Issues

The following are a few known issues along with the solutions.

Problem 1

The relocate command fails with the ORA-03985 error.

```
GDSCTL> relocate chunk -chunk 2 -sourceru 1 -targetru 2
GSM-45029: SQL error
ORA-03985: replication units 1 and 2 are not collocated
ORA-06512: at "GSMADMIN_INTERNAL.DBMS_GSM_POOLADMIN", line 16933
ORA-06512: at "SYS.DBMS_SYS_ERROR", line 130
ORA-06512: at "GSMADMIN_INTERNAL.DBMS_GSM_POOLADMIN", line 16863
```

```
ORA-06512: at "GSMADMIN_INTERNAL.DBMS_GSM_POOLADMIN", line 16593
ORA-06512: at line 1
```

The previous failed as the source and target RUs are not collated.

```
oerr ora 03985
03985, 00000, "replication units %s and %s are not collocated"
//*Cause: The specified replication units were not located on the same set
//          of shards or did not have the same leader.
//*Action: Validate parameter values and replication topology then retry
command.
```

Solution

Here is the solution:

```
GDSCTL> relocate chunk -chunk 2 -sourceru 1 -targetru 4
The operation was completed successfully
GDSCTL>
```

Problem 2

The status of a replication unit is showing as Error.

```
GDSCTL> status ru -show_chunks
Chunks
------------------------
Catalog connection is established
```

RU#	From	To
1	1	1
2	3	3
3	5	5
4	7	8
5	9	10
6	11	12
7	2	2
7	6	6
8	4	4

```
Replication units
-----------------------
Database            RU#  Role      Term  Log Index  Status
--------            ---  ----      ----  ---------  ------
shdcdb3_shard3      6    Follower  3     7          Ok
shdcdb3_shard3      2    Follower  1     6          Ok
shdcdb3_shard3      5    Follower  1     6          Ok
shdcdb3_shard3      3    Leader    5     6          Ok
shdcdb_shard4       7    Follower  9     12         Ok
shdcdb_shard4       8    Leader    4     5          Ok
shdcdb_shard4       2    Follower  1     4          Ok
shdcdb_shard4       5    Follower  1     6          Ok
shdcdb_shard4       3    Follower  5     6          Ok
shdcdb_shard4       6    Follower  3     6          Ok
shdcdb_shard4       4    Follower  7     14         Ok
shdcdb_shard4       1    Leader    6     16         Ok
shdcdb1_shard1      1    Follower  6     16         Ok
shdcdb1_shard1      3    Follower  5     6          Ok
shdcdb1_shard1      4    Leader    7     14         Ok
shdcdb1_shard1      6    Leader    3     6          Errors   ⬅
shdcdb1_shard1      7    Leader    9     12         Ok
shdcdb1_shard1      8    Follower  4     5          Ok
shdcdb2_shard2      1    Follower  6     16         Ok
shdcdb2_shard2      2    Leader    1     3          Ok
shdcdb2_shard2      4    Follower  7     14         Ok
shdcdb2_shard2      5    Leader    1     4          Errors   ⬅
shdcdb2_shard2      7    Follower  9     12         Ok
shdcdb2_shard2      8    Follower  4     5          Ok
GDSCTL>
```

Solution

We can switch over the leader of those specific RUs; in this case, we can switch over the leader of RU #6 and RU #5. We must select another shard database that has this RU and make it the leader.

```
GDSCTL> switchover ru -ru 5 -database shdcdb3_shard3
Switchover process has been started
Switchover process completed
The operation completed successfully
GDSCTL>

GDSCTL> switchover ru -ru 6 -database shdcdb3_shard3
Switchover process has been started
Switchover process completed
The operation completed successfully
GDSCTL>
```

Now if we recheck the status, the status should be clean.

```
GDSCTL> status ru -show_chunks
Chunks
------------------------
RU#                      From      To
---                      ----      --
1                        1         1
2                        3         3
3                        5         5
4                        7         8
5                        9         10
6                        11        12
7                        2         2
7                        6         6
8                        4         4
```

```
Replication units
------------------------
Database                    RU#  Role      Term Log Index Status
--------                    ---  ----      ---- --------- ------
shdcdb3_shard3              6    Leader    4    7         Ok
shdcdb3_shard3              2    Follower  1    6         Ok
shdcdb3_shard3              5    Leader    2    6         Ok
shdcdb3_shard3              3    Leader    5    6         Ok
shdcdb2_shard2              1    Follower  6    16        Ok
shdcdb2_shard2              2    Leader    1    3         Ok
shdcdb2_shard2              4    Follower  7    14        Ok
shdcdb2_shard2              5    Follower  2    6         Ok
shdcdb2_shard2              7    Follower  9    12        Ok
shdcdb2_shard2              8    Follower  4    5         Ok
shdcdb1_shard1              1    Follower  6    16        Ok
shdcdb1_shard1              3    Follower  5    6         Ok
shdcdb1_shard1              4    Leader    7    14        Ok
shdcdb1_shard1              6    Follower  4    7         Ok
shdcdb1_shard1              7    Leader    9    12        Ok
shdcdb1_shard1              8    Follower  4    5         Ok
shdcdb_shard4              7    Follower  9    12        Ok
shdcdb_shard4              8    Leader    4    5         Ok
shdcdb_shard4              2    Follower  1    4         Ok
shdcdb_shard4              5    Follower  2    6         Ok
shdcdb_shard4              3    Follower  5    6         Ok
shdcdb_shard4              6    Follower  4    7         Ok
shdcdb_shard4              4    Follower  7    14        Ok
shdcdb_shard4              1    Leader    6    16        Ok
GDSCTL>
```

Problem 3

We got the error ORA-03984 when trying to change the replication unit leader.

```
GDSCTL> switchover ru -ru 6 -database shdcdb2_shard2
GSM-45029: SQL error
ORA-03984: shard shdcdb2_shard2 does not contain replication unit 6
ORA-06512: at "GSMADMIN_INTERNAL.DBMS_GSM_POOLADMIN", line 16583
ORA-06512: at "SYS.DBMS_SYS_ERROR", line 121
ORA-06512: at "GSMADMIN_INTERNAL.DBMS_GSM_POOLADMIN", line 16546
ORA-06512: at "GSMADMIN_INTERNAL.DBMS_GSM_POOLADMIN", line 16409
ORA-06512: at line 1
GDSCTL>
```

Solution

This error means that the mentioned RU (in this case #6) is not present in the shard database shdcdb2_shard2. We must select one of the other shard databases that has RU #6 and select it as the leader.

```
GDSCTL> switchover ru -ru 6 -database shdcdb_shard4
Switchover process has been started
Switchover process completed
The operation completed successfully
GDSCTL>
```

Problem 4

We received error ORA-03980 when trying to move the replication unit.

```
GDSCTL>  move ru -ru 6 -source shdcdb3_shard3 -target shdcdb2_shard2
GSM-45029: SQL error
ORA-03980: shard shdcdb3_shard3 is the leader for replication unit 6
ORA-06512: at "GSMADMIN_INTERNAL.DBMS_GSM_POOLADMIN", line 16142
ORA-06512: at "SYS.DBMS_SYS_ERROR", line 121
ORA-06512: at "GSMADMIN_INTERNAL.DBMS_GSM_POOLADMIN", line 16028
ORA-06512: at "GSMADMIN_INTERNAL.DBMS_GSM_POOLADMIN", line 15874
ORA-06512: at line 1
GDSCTL>
```

Solution

Change the leader of the RU to another shard and retry the move ru command.

```
GDSCTL> switchover ru -ru 6 -database shdcdb_shard4
Switchover process has been started
Switchover process completed
The operation completed successfully
GDSCTL>

GDSCTL> move ru -ru 6 -source shdcdb3_shard3 -target shdcdb2_shard2  ⬅
Target database metadata retrieval and availability check.
Backup 0 creation.
Backup 0 replication and restoration.
Transition to read-only mode.
Shutdown of apply process group
User metadata export.
Backup 1 creation, replication and restoration.
Chunk import.
Chunk migration is successful. Performing data transition and cleanup.
The operation completed successfully
GDSCTL>
```

Problem 5

When a user runs a SELECT statement on the shard table, it errors out with an ORA-02519 error.

```
select * from Customers order by custid
*
ERROR at line 1:
ORA-02519: cannot perform cross-shard operation. Chunk "5" is unavailable
ORA-06512: at "GSMADMIN_INTERNAL.DBMS_GSM_POOLADMIN", line 31556
ORA-06512: at "SYS.DBMS_SYS_ERROR", line 86
ORA-06512: at "GSMADMIN_INTERNAL.DBMS_GSM_POOLADMIN", line 31521
ORA-06512: at "GSMADMIN_INTERNAL.DBMS_GSM_POOLADMIN", line 31573
ORA-06512: at line 1
SQL>
```

Solution

Check if all the shards in the configuration are up and available. In this case, one of the shards, shdcdb_shard4, is not available.

```
GDSCTL> config shard
Name             Shard Group        Status  State      Region   Availability
-------------    ----------------   ------  -----      ------   ------------
shdcdb1_shard1   shardgroup_primary Ok      Deployed   region1  ONLINE
shdcdb2_shard2   shardgroup_primary Ok      Deployed   region1  ONLINE
shdcdb_shard4    shardgroup_primary Ok      Deployed   region1  -
GDSCTL>
```

In the previous example, the database that was added as shard shdcdb_shard4 was down. Once this database is started, the issue will be fixed.

Problem 6

The role of the replication unit is disabled in the ru -sort command output.

```
Replication units
-----------------------
Database            RU#  Role       Term Log Index Status
--------            ---  ----       ---- --------- ------
shdcdb1_shard1      1    Follower   26   36        Ok
shdcdb3_shard3      1    Leader     26   35        Ok
shdcdb_shard4       1    Follower   26   35        Ok
shdcdb1_shard1      2    Follower   19   25        Ok
shdcdb3_shard3      2    Leader     19   24        Ok
shdcdb_shard4       2    Follower   19   24        Ok
shdcdb1_shard1      3    Follower   24   29        Ok
shdcdb2_shard2      3    Disabled   10   11        Ok
```

Solution

We were not able to identify the root cause for this issue. For now, as a workaround, we can add a new shard and move the RU from the issue shard to the new shard, and that will help with the issue.

Problem 7

When trying to move the replication unit, the move command errors out with ORA-03992.

```
GDSCTL> move ru -ru 3 -source shdcdb3_shard3 -target shdcdb2_shard2
GSM-45029: SQL error
ORA-03992: background tasks are pending
ORA-06512: at "GSMADMIN_INTERNAL.DBMS_GSM_POOLADMIN", line 16142
ORA-06512: at "SYS.DBMS_SYS_ERROR", line 79
ORA-06512: at "GSMADMIN_INTERNAL.DBMS_GSM_POOLADMIN", line 15916
ORA-06512: at "GSMADMIN_INTERNAL.DBMS_GSM_POOLADMIN", line 15874
ORA-06512: at line 1
```

Solution

We can find what background tasks are running by using the config task command.

```
GDSCTL> config task
task ID    status    GDS command
-------    ------    -------------------------------------------
405        failed    copy ru -ru 3 -source shdcdb_shard4 -target
                     shdcdb2_shard2 -replace shdcdb3_shard3 -force
```

We can see that one of the tasks is in a failed state, which prevents the move command from working. We can cancel the failed task by using the alter task command. Once the task is cleared, the move ru command will work without any issue.

```
GDSCTL> alter task -task 405 -cancel
The operation completed successfully
GDSCTL> config task
task ID    status                       GDS command
-------    ------                       -----------
GDSCTL>
```

Summary

In this chapter, you learned about Oracle 23c's new feature, the Raft Replication method, and observed how it can be used to provide high data availability without the need for Oracle Active Data Guard or Oracle GoldenGate. We also observed how to configure Raft Replication and tested a few scenarios using GDSCTL commands to manage the Raft Replication. We also observed how easy it is to scale up and scale down the shards in the Raft Replication method.

CHAPTER 10

High Availability of the Global Service Manager

This chapter examines how high availability of the global service manager (GSM) is achieved and how it works in a real-time environment. Specifically, this chapter will address the following topics:

- How high availability of the GSM can be achieved

- How the global service will work when one of the regions becomes unavailable

- How the GDS components and services work when the GDS catalog database becomes unavailable.

Setting Up the Environment

The setup includes a single-instance primary database and two single-instance physical standby databases. We have installed and configured Oracle 19c (19.3.0) on both the primary and physical standby database servers and applied the October 2022 patch set update (PSU) to the environment.

For this demonstration, we will use the same databases that we used in Chapter 6. Also, we will use the same two scripts that were used in Chapter 6 to check the info of the primary database and the lag in the physical standby database.

© Y V Ravi Kumar, Mariami Kupatadze, Sambaiah Sammeta 2023
Y V Ravi Kumar et al., *Oracle Global Data Services for Mission-critical Systems*,
https://doi.org/10.1007/978-1-4842-9553-3_10

Primary Database Version and the Patch Set

Here are the details:

```
Primary DB server      : prim01.localdomain
OS version             : Oracle Enterprise Linux 7.1 64 bit
Oracle Home            : /u01/app/oracle/product/19.3.0.0/dbhome_1
Database Version        : 19.3.0.0 with October 2022 Database Bundle Patch

[oracle@ prim01 ~]$ export ORACLE_HOME=/u01/app/oracle/product/19.3.0.0/
dbhome_1
[oracle@ prim01 ~]$ export PATH=$ORACLE_HOME/bin:$PATH

[oracle@prim01 ~]$ $ORACLE_HOME/OPatch/opatch lspatches
34419443;Database Release Update : 19.17.0.0.221018 (34419443)
29585399;OCW RELEASE UPDATE 19.3.0.0.0 (29585399)
OPatch succeeded
```

The primary database name is orcldb and is located in the east region. The following are the instance details:

```
SQL> @/home/oracle/database_info.sql
DATABASE_HOST        DB_NAME  DB_UNIQUE_NAME   DATABASE_ROLE  OPEN_MODE    STARTUP_TIME
-------------------  -------  ---------------  -------------  -----------  ----------------
prim01.localdomain   orcldb   orcldb           PRIMARY        READ WRITE   28-OCT-22
```

First Physical Standby Database Server

We have two physical standby databases for this exercise.

The following are the details of the first physical standby database:

```
First Standby server   : stbyh01.localdomain
OS version             : Oracle Enterprise Linux 7.1 64 bit
Oracle Home            : /u01/app/oracle/product/19.3.0.0/dbhome_1
Database Version        : 19.3.0.0 with October 2022 Database Bundle Patch

[oracle@stbyh01 ]$ export ORACLE_HOME=/u01/app/oracle/product/19.3.0.0/
dbhome_1
[oracle@stbyh01 ]$ export PATH=$ORACLE_HOME/bin:$PATH

[oracle@stbyh01 ~]$ $ORACLE_HOME/OPatch/opatch lspatches
```

```
34419443;Database Release Update : 19.17.0.0.221018 (34419443)
29585399;OCW RELEASE UPDATE 19.3.0.0.0 (29585399)
OPatch succeeded.
[oracle@stbyh01 ~]
```

The first physical standby database is orcldbp, and the region is south.

```
SQL> @/home/oracle/database_info.sql
DATABASE_HOST        DB_NAME DB_UNIQUE_NAME DATABASE_ROLE    OPEN_MODE            STARTUP_TIME
-------------------- ------- -------------- ---------------- -------------------- ------------
stbyh01.localdomain  orcldb  orcldbp        PHYSICAL STANDBY READ ONLY WITH APPLY 26-OCT-22
```

Second Physical Standby Database Server

The following are the details of the second physical standby database used in this chapter:

```
Second Standby server : cstbyh01.localdomain
OS version            : Oracle Enterprise Linux 7.1 64 bit
Oracle Home           : /u01/app/oracle/product/19.3.0.0/dbhome_1
Database Version      : 19.3.0.0 with October 2022 Database Bundle Patch

[oracle@cstbyh01 ]$ export ORACLE_HOME=/u01/app/oracle/product/19.3.0.0/
dbhome_1
[oracle@cstbyh01 ]$ export PATH=$ORACLE_HOME/bin:$PATH

[oracle@stbyh01 ~]$ $ORACLE_HOME/OPatch/opatch lspatches
34419443;Database Release Update : 19.17.0.0.221018 (34419443)
29585399;OCW RELEASE UPDATE 19.3.0.0.0 (29585399)
OPatch succeeded.
[oracle@cstbyh01 ~]
```

The name of the second physical standby database is orcldbs, and the region is north.

```
SQL> @/home/oracle/database_info.sql
DATABASE_HOST        DB_NAME DB_UNIQUE_NAME DATABASE_ROLE    OPEN_MODE            STARTUP_TIME
-------------------- ------- -------------- ---------------- -------------------- ------------
cstbyh01.localdomain orcldb  orcldbs        PHYSICAL STANDBY READ ONLY WITH APPLY 26-OCT-22
```

Catalog Database Used in This Chapter

The catalog database named catgds is on the same server, prim01, where we have our primary database running. The following is the catalog database information:

```
SQL> @/home/oracle/database_info.sql
DATABASE_HOST        DB_NAME  DB_UNIQUE_NAME   DATABASE_ROLE  OPEN_MODE     STARTUP_TIME
-------------------  -------  ---------------  -------------  ------------  -------------
prim01.localdomain   catgds   catgds           PRIMARY        READ WRITE    28-OCT-22
```

To provide high availability for the catalog database, a physical standby database named catgdsdr has been set up. The following are its details:

```
SQL> @/home/oracle/database_info.sql
DATABASE_HOST        DB_NAME DB_UNIQUE_NAME   DATABASE_ROLE    OPEN_MODE             STARTUP_TIME
-------------------  ------- ---------------  ---------------  --------------------  -----------
stbyh01.localdomain catgds   catgdsdr         PHYSICAL STANDBY READ ONLY WITH APPLY 28-OCT-22
```

Test Case: High Availability of the GSM

The GSM is one of the main components in the GDS framework. The GSM is very smart as it monitors all the databases in the configuration to gather the required information of the availability and load on the database, and based on these real-time statistics, it will route the incoming connection request. Now what will happen if the GSM running in one region becomes unavailable due to some issue? Will the database running in that region still be accessible? Let's check it out.

In this scenario, we will shut down the GSM in one region and see if the database running in the same region can and will accept any new connections.

Before starting this test case, we need to make sure that all the databases, GSMs, and catalog database are up and running without any issues.

High-Level Steps of This Test Case

Here are the steps:

1. Start all the GSMs, databases, and the catalog database.

2. Check the current configured services.

3. Check the current buddy regions for each of the regions.

4. Modify each region in the GDS configuration to add a
    buddy region.

5. Create a new service named `srvc_ref_region` with a role of
    `primary` so that this service will run only on the primary database.

6. Create a TNS entry for the service named `srvc_ref_region` and
    test the database connection using the service.

7. Stop the GSM `gsmeast` running on the primary database server.

8. Test the database connection using the service `srvc_ref_region`
    and see if the service still connects to the primary database.

9. Stop the buddy region `gsmnorth`, which is running on the
    physical standby database server `stbyh01`, and retry the database
    connection using the same service to see if the service is still able
    to connect to the primary database.

10. Stop the last GSM, `gsmsouth`, which is running on a physical
    standby database server, `cstbyh01`, and see if the service is still
    able to connect to the database or if it errors out.

11. Start all the GSMs.

12. Stop the service `srvc_ref_region` and remove it.

Prerequisites

Before starting this test case, we need to make sure that all the databases, GSMs, and
catalog database are up and running without any issues.

Starting and Checking the Status of the GSM gsmeastl

Here are the details:

```
[oracle@prim01 ~]$ oraenv
ORACLE_SID = [gsm] ?
The Oracle base remains unchanged with value /u01/app/oracle
[oracle@prim01 ~]$ gdsctl
GDSCTL: Version 19.0.0.0.0 - Production on Sun Oct 30 06:58:42 CDT 2022
```

Copyright (c) 2011, 2019, Oracle. All rights reserved.
Welcome to GDSCTL, type "help" for information.

Current GSM is set to GSMEAST
GDSCTL> status
Alias   GSMEAST
Version   19.0.0.0.0
Start Date   29-OCT-2022 08:24:29
Trace Level   off
Listener Log File   /u01/app/oracle/diag/gsm/prim01/gsmeast/
                             alert/log.xml
Listener Trace File   /u01/app/oracle/diag/gsm/prim01/gsmeast/trace/
                             ora_5851_140000528739392.trc
Endpoint summary   (ADDRESS=(HOST=prim01.localdomain)(PORT=1581)
                             (PROTOCOL=tcp))
GSMOCI Version   3.0.180702
Mastership   N
Connected to GDS catalog   Y
Process Id   5854
Number of reconnections   0
Pending tasks.   Total   0
Tasks in process. Total   0
Regional Mastership   TRUE
Total messages published   1620
Time Zone   -05:00
Orphaned Buddy Regions:
    None
GDS region   east
Network metrics:
   Region: south Network factor:0
   Region: north Network factor:0
GDSCTL>

Starting and Checking the Status of the GSM gsmnorth

Here are the details:

```
[oracle@stbyh01 ~]$ . oraenv
ORACLE_SID = [gsm] ?
The Oracle base remains unchanged with value /u01/app/oracle
[oracle@stbyh01 ~]$ gdsctl
GDSCTL: Version 19.0.0.0.0 - Production on Sun Oct 30 06:59:45 CDT 2022
Copyright (c) 2011, 2019, Oracle.  All rights reserved.
Welcome to GDSCTL, type "help" for information.

Current GSM is set to GSMNORTH
GDSCTL> status
Alias                    GSMNORTH
Version                  19.0.0.0.0
Start Date               29-OCT-2022 08:24:14
Trace Level              off
Listener Log File        /u01/app/oracle/diag/gsm/stbyh01/gsmnorth/
                         alert/log.xml
Listener Trace File      /u01/app/oracle/diag/gsm/stbyh01/gsmnorth/trace/
                         ora_5187_139757816208448.trc
Endpoint summary         (ADDRESS=(HOST=stbyh01.localdomain)(PORT=1582)
                         (PROTOCOL=tcp))
GSMOCI Version           3.0.180702
Mastership               N
Connected to GDS catalog Y
Process Id               5190
Number of reconnections  0
Pending tasks.     Total 0
Tasks in  process. Total 0
Regional Mastership      TRUE
Total messages published 1620
Time Zone                -05:00
Orphaned Buddy Regions:
    None
GDS region               north
```

```
Network metrics:
   Region: south Network factor:0
   Region: east Network factor:0
GDSCTL>
```

Starting and Checking the Status of the GSM gsmsouth

Here are the details:

```
[oracle@cstbyh01 ~]$ . oraenv
ORACLE_SID = [gsm] ?
The Oracle base remains unchanged with value /u01/app/oracle
[oracle@cstbyh01 ~]$ gdsctl
GDSCTL: Version 19.0.0.0.0 - Production on Sun Oct 30 07:00:16 CDT 2022

Copyright (c) 2011, 2019, Oracle.  All rights reserved.


Welcome to GDSCTL, type "help" for information.

Current GSM is set to GSMSOUTH
GDSCTL> status
Alias                    GSMSOUTH
Version                  19.0.0.0.0
Start Date               29-OCT-2022 08:23:54
Trace Level              off
Listener Log File        /u01/app/oracle/diag/gsm/cstbyh01/gsmsouth/
                         alert/log.xml
Listener Trace File      /u01/app/oracle/diag/gsm/cstbyh01/gsmsouth/trace/
                         ora_5059_140348924025920.trc
Endpoint summary         (ADDRESS=(HOST=cstbyh01.localdomain)(PORT=1583)
                         (PROTOCOL=tcp))
GSMOCI Version           3.0.180702
Mastership               Y
Connected to GDS catalog Y
Process Id               5062
Number of reconnections  0
Pending tasks.    Total  0
```

```
Tasks in  process. Total  0
Regional Mastership       TRUE
Total messages published  1620
Time Zone                 -05:00
Orphaned Buddy Regions:
    None
GDS region                south
Network metrics:
   Region: north Network factor:0
   Region: east Network factor:0

GDSCTL>
```

Check the status of the databases.

```
GDSCTL> databases;
Database: "orcldb" Registered: Y State: Ok ONS: N. Role: PRIMARY Instances:
1 Region: east
   Registered instances:
     sales%1
Database: "orcldbp" Registered: Y State: Ok ONS: N. Role: PH_STNDBY
Instances: 1 Region: north
   Registered instances:
     sales%11
Database: "orcldbs" Registered: Y State: Ok ONS: N. Role: PH_STNDBY
Instances: 1 Region: south
   Registered instances:
     sales%21
GDSCTL>
```

Check the current configured services.

```
GDSCTL> services;
```

Check the current gdspools in the GSM configuration.

```
GDSCTL> config gdspool
Catalog connection is established
Name                          Broker                      Sharded
----                          ------                      -------
dbpoolora                     No                          No
hr                            No                          No
sales                         Yes                         No

GDSCTL>
```

Check the configuration of the regions.

```
GDSCTL> config region;
Name                          Buddy
----                          -----
east
north
south

GDSCTL>
```

You can see from the previous output that we don't have any buddy regions configured yet for any of the regions. What is a buddy region, and what is its purpose?

A buddy region is a region that will also have GSMs running, and this GSM can provide continuous access to the GDSs if the GSM running on the local region is unable to provide any services as it becomes unavailable.

For each region that we create in the GDS configuration, we should assign a buddy region so that when the local GSM stops unexpectedly or becomes unavailable due to various reasons, the GSM running on the buddy region will take over the responsibility and will provide continuous access to the GDSs running in the local regions.

None of the regions has a buddy region, so let's add them now. We can modify each of the regions to update the buddy as follows:

```
GDSCTL> modify region -region east -buddy north;
The operation completed successfully

GDSCTL> modify region -region north -buddy south;
The operation completed successfully
```

```
GDSCTL> modify region -region south -buddy east;
The operation completed successfully

GDSCTL> config region;
Name                        Buddy
----                        -----
east                        north
north                       south
south                       east

GDSCTL>
```

Check the updated configuration of each region.

```
GDSCTL> config region;
Name                        Buddy
----                        -----
east                        north
north                       south
south                       east

GDSCTL>
GDSCTL>

GDSCTL> config gsm
Name       Region   ENDPOINT
----       ------   --------
gsmeast    east     (ADDRESS=(HOST=prim01.localdomain)(PORT=1581)
                    (PROTOCOL=tcp))
gsmnorth   north    (ADDRESS=(HOST=stbyh01.localdomain)(PORT=1582)
                    (PROTOCOL=tcp))
gsmsouth   south    (ADDRESS=(HOST=cstbyh01.localdomain)(PORT=1583)
                    (PROTOCOL=tcp))

GDSCTL>
```

Check the current services configured.

```
GDSCTL>services

GDSCTL> databases;
Database: "orcldb" Registered: Y State: Ok ONS: N. Role: PRIMARY Instances:
1 Region: east
   Registered instances:
      sales%1
Database: "orcldbp" Registered: Y State: Ok ONS: N. Role: PH_STNDBY
Instances: 1 Region: north
   Registered instances:
      sales%11
Database: "orcldbs" Registered: Y State: Ok ONS: N. Role: PH_STNDBY
Instances: 1 Region: south
   Registered instances:
      sales%21

GDSCTL>
```

Let's create a new role-based global service with the name srvc_ref_region, as shown here:

```
GDSCTL> connect gsmcatuser/welcome@prim01:1521/CATGDS;
Catalog connection is established

GDSCTL> add service -service srvc_ref_region -gdspool sales -preferred_all
-role PRIMARY
The operation completed successfully
```

Since we created the service with -role set to primary, this service will run only on the primary database.

Starting the Service

Here's how:

```
GDSCTL>start service -service srvc_ref_region -gdspool sales
The operation completed successfully
```

Checking the Status of the Service and the Databases

Here are the details:

```
GDSCTL> services;
Service "srvc_ref_region .sales.oradbcloud" has 1 instance(s). Affinity:
ANYWHERE
    Instance "sales%1", name: "orcldb", db: "orcldb", region: "east",
status: ready.

GDSCTL> databases;
Database: "orcldb" Registered: Y State: Ok ONS: N. Role: PRIMARY Instances:
1 Region: east
    Service: "srvc_ref_region " Globally started: Y Started: Y
            Scan: Y Enabled: Y Preferred: Y
    Registered instances:
      sales%1
Database: "orcldbp" Registered: Y State: Ok ONS: N. Role: PH_STNDBY
Instances: 1 Region: north
    Service: "srvc_ref_region " Globally started: Y Started: N
            Scan: Y Enabled: Y Preferred: Y
    Registered instances:
      sales%11
Database: "orcldbs" Registered: Y State: Ok ONS: N. Role: PH_STNDBY
Instances: 1 Region: south
    Service: "srvc_ref_region " Globally started: Y Started: N
            Scan: Y Enabled: Y Preferred: Y
    Registered instances:
      sales%21

GDSCTL>
```

Testing the Database Connection

We can use the following TNS entry for the global service srvc_ref_region:

```
srvc_ref_region =
  (DESCRIPTION =
    (FAILOVER = ON)
    (ADDRESS_LIST =
      (LOAD_BALANCE = ON)
      (ADDRESS = (PROTOCOL = TCP)(HOST = prim01)(PORT = 1581)))
    (ADDRESS_LIST =
      (LOAD_BALANCE = ON)
      (ADDRESS = (PROTOCOL = TCP)(HOST = stbyh01)(PORT = 1582)))
    (ADDRESS_LIST =
      (LOAD_BALANCE = ON)
      (ADDRESS = (PROTOCOL = TCP)(HOST = cstbyh01)(PORT = 1583)))
    (CONNECT_DATA =
      (SERVICE_NAME = srvc_ref_region .sales.oradbcloud)
    )
  )
```

Let's connect to the database using this global service srvc_ref_region.

```
[oracle@cstbyh01 admin]$ sqlplus system/welcome@srvc_ref_region

SQL*Plus: Release 19.0.0.0.0 - Production on Sun Oct 30 07:11:43 2022
Version 19.17.0.0.0

Copyright (c) 1982, 2022, Oracle.  All rights reserved.

Last Successful login time: Sat Oct 29 2022 22:41:30 -05:00

Connected to:
Oracle Database 19c Enterprise Edition Release 19.0.0.0.0 - Production
Version 19.17.0.0.0
```

```
SQL> @/home/oracle/atabase_info.sql

DATABASE_HOST        DB_NAME  DB_UNIQUE_NAME  DATABASE_ROLE  OPEN_MODE    STARTUP_TIME
-------------------  -------  --------------  -------------  -----------  ---------------
prim01.localdomain   orcldb   orcldb          PRIMARY        READ WRITE   29-OCT-22

SQL>
```

As we can see, we are able to connect the database, and it's connecting to the primary database, orcldb.

Check the status of the GSM gsmeast, which is running in the primary database server.

```
GDSCTL> status
Alias                      GSMEAST
Version                    19.0.0.0.0
Start Date                 29-OCT-2022 08:24:29
Trace Level                off
Listener Log File          /u01/app/oracle/diag/gsm/prim01/gsmeast/
                           alert/log.xml
Listener Trace File        /u01/app/oracle/diag/gsm/prim01/gsmeast/trace/
                           ora_5851_140000528739392.trc
Endpoint summary           (ADDRESS=(HOST=prim01.localdomain)(PORT=1581)
                           (PROTOCOL=tcp))
GSMOCI Version             3.0.180702
Mastership                 N
Connected to GDS catalog   Y
Process Id                 5854
Number of reconnections    0
Pending tasks.     Total   0
Tasks in  process. Total   0
Regional Mastership        TRUE
Total messages published   1631
Time Zone                  -05:00
Orphaned Buddy Regions:
    None
GDS region                 east
```

```
Network metrics:
   Region: south Network factor:0
   Region: north Network factor:0

GDSCTL>
```

Stopping the GSM gsmeast

Stop the GSM gsmeast that is running in the primary database server.

```
GDSCTL> stop gsm -gsm GSMEAST;
GSM is stopped successfully

GDSCTL> status
GSM-45075: No response from GSM
GDSCTL>
```

Testing the Database Connection

So, the GSM gsmeast that is running on the primary database server is now down and unavailable. Now let's try to connect to the service srvc_ref_region that is running on the primary database with the GSM down running on the same servers.

```
[oracle@cstbyh01 admin]$ sqlplus system/welcome@srvc_ref_region

SQL*Plus: Release 19.0.0.0.0 - Production on Sun Oct 30 07:15:25 2022
Version 19.17.0.0.0
Copyright (c) 1982, 2022, Oracle.  All rights reserved.
Last Successful login time: Sun Oct 30 2022 07:11:43 -05:00

Connected to:
Oracle Database 19c Enterprise Edition Release 19.0.0.0.0 - Production
Version 19.17.0.0.0

SQL> @/home/oracle/rac_database_info.sql;
```

DATABASE_HOST	DB_NAME	DB_UNIQUE_NAME	DATABASE_ROLE	OPEN_MODE	STARTUP_TIME
prim01.localdomain	orcldb	orcldb	PRIMARY	READ WRITE	29-OCT-22

```
SQL>
```

As you can see, even though the GSM gsmeast is running on the primary database server that is down, the connection did not fail. This is all happening because of the buddy region. Let's check the region configuration again once.

```
GDSCTL> config region;
Name                          Buddy
----                          -----
east                          north
north                         south
south                         east

GDSCTL>
```

As you can see, the buddy region for the east region is north. When the GSM running on the east region went down, the GSM running on the north region took over the responsibility of managing the database connections and started accepting all the connections that were going to the GSM running in the east region.

What happens if the GSM running in the north region goes down? Let's see it ourselves.

Stopping the Second GSM gsmnorth

Stop the GSM gsmnorth that is running on node 1 of the physical standby database server, connect to GDSCTL, and stop the GSM, as shown here:

```
[oracle@stbyh01 ~]$ gdsctl
GDSCTL: Version 19.0.0.0.0 - Production on Sun Oct 30 07:20:07 CDT 2022

Copyright (c) 2011, 2019, Oracle.  All rights reserved.

Welcome to GDSCTL, type "help" for information.

Current GSM is set to GSMNORTH
GDSCTL>stop gsm -gsm GSMNORTH;
GSM is stopped successfully
GDSCTL> status
GSM-45075: No response from GSM
GDSCTL>
```

Testing the Database Connection

If we try to connect the database using the service again, it will connect to the database that is up and running in the other region, which in this case is orcldb running in the region gsmeast.

```
[oracle@cstbyh01 admin]$ sqlplus system/welcome@srvc_ref_region

SQL*Plus: Release 19.0.0.0.0 - Production on Sun Oct 30 07:20:48 2022
Version 19.17.0.0.0

Copyright (c) 1982, 2022, Oracle.  All rights reserved.

Last Successful login time: Sun Oct 30 2022 07:15:25 -05:00

Connected to:
Oracle Database 19c Enterprise Edition Release 19.0.0.0.0 - Production
Version 19.17.0.0.0

SQL>@/home/oracle/database_info.sql;
```

DATABASE_HOST	DB_NAME	DB_UNIQUE_NAME	DATABASE_ROLE	OPEN_MODE	STARTUP_TIME
prim01.localdomain	orcldb	orcldb	PRIMARY	READ WRITE	29-OCT-22

```
SQL>
```

As you can see, even though both GSMs running in the region east and on its buddy region north are down, we are still able to connect to the database using the service. This is because, for the region north, we have the region south as its buddy region, and this time, the GSM running on south took over responsibility and provided continuous support for GDS. Isn't it that amazing? So, it is always recommended that you define and keep a buddy region for each of the regions present in the GDS configuration.

Note that if all the GSMs are down, we cannot connect to GDS as it will complain, saying that there are no more GSM listeners to accept any new connections. Let's test this! Stop the last GSM, gsmsouth, that is running on the physical standby database server cstbyh01.

```
GDSCTL: Version 19.0.0.0.0 - Production on Sun Oct 30 07:24:17 CDT 2022

Copyright (c) 2011, 2019, Oracle.  All rights reserved.

Welcome to GDSCTL, type "help" for information.
```

```
Current GSM is set to GSMSOUTH
GDSCTL> stop gsm -gsm GSMSOUTH;
GSM is stopped successfully
GDSCTL>
```

Testing the Database Connection

With all the GSMs being down, now if we try to connect to the database using the same service, it will give the No listener error.

```
[oracle@cstbyh01 admin]$ sqlplus system/welcome@srvc_ref_region
```

```
SQL*Plus: Release 19.0.0.0.0 - Production on Sun Oct 30 07:24:48 2022
Version 19.17.0.0.0
```

```
Copyright (c) 1982, 2022, Oracle.  All rights reserved.
```

```
ERROR:
ORA-12541: TNS:no listener
```

```
Enter user-name:
```

This proves that we should have at least one GSM up and running, and that the GSM that is up must be a buddy region for the other region that is down; only then will GDS be able to provide a successful connection for the global service to the database.

Starting All the GSMs

We can start all the GSMs and stop and remove the services created for demonstrating this test case.

```
GDSCTL> start gsm -gsm GSMEAST;
GSM is started successfully
```

```
GDSCTL> start gsm -gsm GSMNORTH;
GSM is started successfully
```

```
GDSCTL> start gsm -gsm GSMSOUTH;
GSM is started successfully
```

Stopping and Removing the Service

We can now stop the service that was created to demonstrate this test case. Please note that while stopping the service, we can also give the database name on which the service is currently running.

```
GDSCTL> stop service -service srvc_ref_region -gdspool sales
The operation completed successfully

GDSCTL> remove service -service srvc_ref_region -gdspool sales;
The operation completed successfully
GDSCTL>
```

Summary of This Test Case

Buddy regions play an important role in providing high availability for the GSMs and for GDS, and thus we should always define a buddy region for each of the regions in the GDS configuration.

Test Case: Crash of the GDS Catalog Database

The GDS catalog is the repository in the GDS configuration that stores all the metadata and configuration information for all the GDS components in the catalog. This repository is created in a separate Oracle database that we call the GDS catalog database. Since the catalog database is the only place that GDS uses to store all the configuration information, Oracle strongly recommends considering highly available solutions such as Real Application Cluster (RAC) and Data Guard for the catalog database. In our case, even though our catalog database is a single-instance database, we do have a physical standby database configured to it.

Here is the catalog primary database information:

```
SQL> @/home/oracle/database_info.sql;
```

DATABASE_HOST	DB_NAME	DB_UNIQUE_NAME	DATABASE_ROLE	OPEN_MODE	STARTUP_TIME
prim01.localdomain	catgds	catgds	PRIMARY	READ WRITE	29-OCT-22

Here is the catalog physical standby database information:

```
SQL> @/home/oracle/database_info.sql;

DATABASE_HOST        DB_NAME DB_UNIQUE_NAME DATABASE_ROLE    OPEN_MODE            STARTUP_TIME
------------------- ------- -------------- ---------------- -------------------- ---------------
stbyh01.localdomain catgds  catgdsdr       PHYSICAL STANDBY READ ONLY WITH APPLY 29-OCT-22
```

Now what happens when the catalog database crashes abruptly? Will it have an immediate impact or any impact on the GDS services? Let's check it out.

In this test case, we will see whether when the GDS catalog database suddenly goes down and is not available if it will have an impact on the existing GSMs and services.

High-Level Steps of This Test Case

Here are the steps:

1. Start all the GSMs, databases, and catalog database.

2. Check the current configured services in the GSM.

3. Create a new service named `sales_catlog_srvc` with the role set to `primary` so that this service will run only on the primary database.

4. Create a TNS entry for the service named `sales_catlog_srvc` and test the database connection using the service.

5. Shut down the catalog database, `catgds`.

6. Test the database connection using the service `srvc_ref_region` and see if the service still connects to the primary database.

7. Try to create a new service and see what happens.

8. Try to stop the GSM and restart it to see what happens.

9. Start the catalog database.

Prerequisites

Before starting this test case, we need to make sure that all the databases, GSMs, and catalog database are up and running without any issues.

Starting All the GSMs and Checking Their Status

Start and check the status of the GSM gsmeast.

```
GDSCTL> status
Alias                      GSMEAST
Version                    19.0.0.0.0
Start Date                 30-OCT-2022 07:25:57
Trace Level                off
Listener Log File          /u01/app/oracle/diag/gsm/prim01/gsmeast/
                           alert/log.xml
Listener Trace File        /u01/app/oracle/diag/gsm/prim01/gsmeast/trace/
                           ora_26403_139900265258048.trc
Endpoint summary           (ADDRESS=(HOST=prim01.localdomain)(PORT=1581)
                           (PROTOCOL=tcp))
GSMOCI Version             3.0.180702
Mastership                 Y
Connected to GDS catalog   Y
Process Id                 26406
Number of reconnections    0
Pending tasks.     Total   0
Tasks in  process. Total   0
Regional Mastership        TRUE
Total messages published   11
Time Zone                  -05:00
Orphaned Buddy Regions:
     None
GDS region                 east
Network metrics:
   Region: south Network factor:0
   Region: north Network factor:0

GDSCTL>
```

Start and check the status of the GSM gsmnorth.

```
GDSCTL> status
Alias                     GSMNORTH
Version                   19.0.0.0.0
Start Date                30-OCT-2022 07:26:08
Trace Level               off
Listener Log File         /u01/app/oracle/diag/gsm/stbyh01/gsmnorth/
                          alert/log.xml
Listener Trace File       /u01/app/oracle/diag/gsm/stbyh01/gsmnorth/trace/
                          ora_24116_140305203260480.trc
Endpoint summary          (ADDRESS=(HOST=stbyh01.localdomain)(PORT=1582)
                          (PROTOCOL=tcp))
GSMOCI Version            3.0.180702
Mastership                N
Connected to GDS catalog  Y
Process Id                24119
Number of reconnections   0
Pending tasks.     Total  0
Tasks in  process. Total  0
Regional Mastership       TRUE
Total messages published  3
Time Zone                 -05:00
Orphaned Buddy Regions:
    None
GDS region                north
Network metrics:
   Region: south Network factor:0
   Region: east Network factor:0

GDSCTL>
```

Start and check the status of the GSM gsmsouth.

```
GDSCTL> status
Alias                     GSMSOUTH
Version                   19.0.0.0.0
Start Date                30-OCT-2022 07:26:16
```

```
Trace Level              off
Listener Log File        /u01/app/oracle/diag/gsm/cstbyh01/gsmsouth/
                         alert/log.xml
Listener Trace File      /u01/app/oracle/diag/gsm/cstbyh01/gsmsouth/trace/
                         ora_24568_140502229982272.trc
Endpoint summary         (ADDRESS=(HOST=cstbyh01.localdomain)(PORT=1583)
                         (PROTOCOL=tcp))
GSMOCI Version           3.0.180702
Mastership               N
Connected to GDS catalog Y
Process Id               24571
Number of reconnections  0
Pending tasks.    Total  0
Tasks in  process. Total 0
Regional Mastership      TRUE
Total messages published 3
Time Zone                -05:00
Orphaned Buddy Regions:
     None
GDS region               south
Network metrics:
   Region: north Network factor:0
   Region: east Network factor:0

GDSCTL>
```

Checking the Status of the Databases

Here's how:

```
GDSCTL> databases;
Database: "orcldb" Registered: Y State: Ok ONS: N. Role: PRIMARY Instances:
1 Region: east
   Registered instances:
     sales%1
Database: "orcldbp" Registered: Y State: Ok ONS: N. Role: PH_STNDBY
Instances: 1 Region: north
```

```
    Registered instances:
        sales%11
Database: "orcldbs" Registered: Y State: Ok ONS: N. Role: PH_STNDBY
Instances: 1 Region: south
    Registered instances:
        sales%21

GDSCTL>
```

Checking the Current Configured Services

Here's how:

```
GDSCTL> services;
GDSCTL>
```

Checking the Current gdspools in the GSM Configuration

Here's how:

```
GDSCTL> config gdspool
Name                            Broker              Sharded
----                            ------              -------
dbpoolora                       No                  No
hr                              No                  No
sales                           Yes                 No

GDSCTL>
GDSCTL> config gsm
Name       Region      ENDPOINT
----       ------      --------
gsmeast    east        (ADDRESS=(HOST=prim01.localdomain)(PORT=1581)
                       (PROTOCOL=tcp))
gsmnorth   north       (ADDRESS=(HOST=stbyh01.localdomain)(PORT=1582)
                       (PROTOCOL=tcp))
gsmsouth   south       (ADDRESS=(HOST=cstbyh01.localdomain)(PORT=1583)
                       (PROTOCOL=tcp))

GDSCTL>
```

Creating a Role-Based Global Service Named sales_catlog_srvc

Create a new service named sales_catlog_srvc as shown in this section. Since we are creating this service with -role as PRIMARY, the service will run only on the primary database.

```
GDSCTL>add service -service sales_catlog_srvc -gdspool sales -preferred_all
-role PRIMARY
Catalog connection is established
The operation completed successfully
```

Please note that, as mentioned earlier, if the databases are RAC databases, we will have to add the instances of all the RAC primary databases and physical standby databases to this service using the modify service command.

Since we added all the instances, we can now start the service sales_catlog_srvc.

```
GDSCTL> start service -service sales_catlog_srvc -gdspool sales;
The operation completed successfully
GDSCTL>
```

Checking the Status of Services and the Databases

Here's how:

```
GDSCTL> services
Service "sales_catlog_srvc.sales.oradbcloud" has 1 instance(s). Affinity:
ANYWHERE
   Instance "sales%1", name: "orcldb", db: "orcldb", region: "east",
   status: ready.

GDSCTL> databases;
Database: "orcldb" Registered: Y State: Ok ONS: N. Role: PRIMARY Instances:
1 Region: east
   Service: "sales_catlog_srvc" Globally started: Y Started: Y
           Scan: Y Enabled: Y Preferred: Y
   Registered instances:
     sales%1
```

```
Database: "orcldbp" Registered: Y State: Ok ONS: N. Role: PH_STNDBY
Instances: 1 Region: north
   Service: "sales_catlog_srvc" Globally started: Y Started: N
            Scan: Y Enabled: Y Preferred: Y
   Registered instances:
     sales%11
Database: "orcldbs" Registered: Y State: Ok ONS: N. Role: PH_STNDBY
Instances: 1 Region: south
   Service: "sales_catlog_srvc" Globally started: Y Started: N
            Scan: Y Enabled: Y Preferred: Y
   Registered instances:
     sales%21
GDSCTL>
```

We can use the TNS entry to test this service.

```
sales_catlog_srvc =
  (DESCRIPTION =
    (FAILOVER = ON)
    (ADDRESS_LIST =
      (LOAD_BALANCE = ON)
      (ADDRESS = (PROTOCOL = TCP)(HOST = prim01)(PORT = 1581)))
    (ADDRESS_LIST =
      (LOAD_BALANCE = ON)
      (ADDRESS = (PROTOCOL = TCP)(HOST = stbyh01)(PORT = 1582)))
    (ADDRESS_LIST =
      (LOAD_BALANCE = ON)
      (ADDRESS = (PROTOCOL = TCP)(HOST = cstbyh01)(PORT = 1583)))
    (CONNECT_DATA =
      (SERVICE_NAME = sales_catlog_srvc.sales.oradbcloud)
    )
  )
```

Testing the Database Connection

From the server node of the primary database server, try to connect to the database using this global service.

```
SQL*Plus: Release 19.0.0.0.0 - Production on Sun Oct 30 07:43:51 2022
Version 19.17.0.0.0

Copyright (c) 1982, 2022, Oracle.  All rights reserved.

Last Successful login time: Sun Oct 30 2022 07:20:48 -05:00

Connected to:
Oracle Database 19c Enterprise Edition Release 19.0.0.0.0 - Production
Version 19.17.0.0.0

SQL> @/home/oracle/database_info.sql;

DATABASE_HOST        DB_NAME   DB_UNIQUE_NAME  DATABASE_ROLE  OPEN_MODE    STARTUP_TIME
-------------------  -------   --------------- -------------  -----------  ---------------
prim01.localdomain   orcldb    orcldb          PRIMARY        READ WRITE   29-OCT-22
SQL>
```

As you can see, we are able to connect to the database, and it's connecting to the primary database, orcldb. As of now, all the GSMs/databases and the catalog database are up and running.

Shutting Down the GDS Catalog Database

Let's shut down the catalog database, catgds.

```
[oracle@prim01 ~]$ . oraenv
ORACLE_SID = [catgds] ?
The Oracle base remains unchanged with value /u01/app/oracle
[oracle@prim01 ~]$ sqlplus / as sysdba

SQL*Plus: Release 19.0.0.0.0 - Production on Sun Oct 30 07:47:28 2022
Version 19.17.0.0.0

Copyright (c) 1982, 2022, Oracle.  All rights reserved.
```

```
Connected to:
Oracle Database 19c Enterprise Edition Release 19.0.0.0.0 - Production
Version 19.17.0.0.0

SQL> shutdown immediate;
Database closed.
Database dismounted.
ORACLE instance shut down.
```

The catalog database is now down. Let's perform a few different tests to see which operations we need to get the catalog database up and running.

Performing a Switchover Operation When the Catalog Database Is Down

Let's see if we need the catalog database to be up and running while we perform the switchover operation using the Data Guard broker utility DGMGRL and then try to connect the database using the service.

From node 1 of the database server, log in to DGMGRL and check the current configuration.

```
[oracle@prim01 admin]$ dgmgrl
DGMGRL for Linux: Release 19.0.0.0.0 - Production on Sun Oct 30
07:49:02 2022
Version 19.17.0.0.0

Copyright (c) 1982, 2019, Oracle and/or its affiliates.  All rights
reserved.

Welcome to DGMGRL, type "help" for information.
DGMGRL> connect sys/welcome;
Connected to "orcldb"
Connected as SYSDBA.
DGMGRL> show configuration;

Configuration - orcldbcfg
```

```
  Protection Mode: MaxPerformance
  Members:
  orcldb  - Primary database
    orcldbp - Physical standby database
    orcldbs - Physical standby database

Fast-Start Failover:  Disabled

Configuration Status:
SUCCESS (status updated 35 seconds ago)

DGMGRL>
```

As you can see, at this moment, orcldb is the primary database. Perform the switchover to make orcldbp the primary database.

```
DGMGRL> switchover to orcldbp;
Performing switchover NOW, please wait...
Operation requires a connection to database "orcldbp"
Connecting ...
Connected to "orcldbp"
Connected as SYSDBA.
New primary database "orcldbp" is opening...
Operation requires start up of instance "orcldb" on database "orcldb"
Starting instance "orcldb"...
Connected to an idle instance.
ORACLE instance started.
Connected to "orcldb"
Database mounted.
Database opened.
Switchover succeeded, new primary is "orcldbp"

DGMGRL> show configuration;

Configuration - orcldbcfg

  Protection Mode: MaxPerformance
  Members:
  orcldbp - Primary database
```

```
   orcldb  - Physical standby database
      Error: ORA-1034: ORACLE not available

   orcldbs - Physical standby database

Fast-Start Failover:  Disabled

Configuration Status:
ERROR (status updated 80 seconds ago)

DGMGRL>
```

As we can see from the previous output, the database orcldbp is the primary database now. If we check the services again, we can see that the service is a failover to the new primary database, orcldbp, as we created the service with the -role option.

```
GDSCTL> services
Service "sales_catlog_srvc.sales.oradbcloud" has 1 instance(s). Affinity:
ANYWHERE
   Instance "sales%11", name: "orcldbp", db: "orcldbp", region: "north",
status: ready.
GDSCTL>
GDSCTL> databases
Alert: catalog database is not registered on GSM listener.  ◄▬▬▬▬
Database: "orcldb" Registered: Y State: Ok ONS: N. Role: PH_STNDBY Instances: 1 Region: east
   Service: "sales_catlog_srvc" Globally started: Y Started: N
            Scan: N Enabled: Y Preferred: Y
   Registered instances:
     sales%1
Database: "orcldbp" Registered: Y State: Ok ONS: N. Role: PRIMARY
Instances: 1 Region: north
   Service: "sales_catlog_srvc" Globally started: Y Started: Y
            Scan: N Enabled: Y Preferred: Y
   Registered instances:
     sales%11
Database: "orcldbs" Registered: Y State: Ok ONS: N. Role: PH_STNDBY
Instances: 1 Region: south
```

```
Service: "sales_catlog_srvc" Globally started: Y Started: N
          Scan: N Enabled: Y Preferred: Y
Registered instances:
  sales%21

GDSCTL>
```

From the previous output, we can see that the service sales_catlog_srvc has successfully failed over to the new primary database as it should. Since the catalog database is down, we can see an alert regarding the catalog database not being registered to the GSM listener in the previous output.

Let's see what happens if we try connecting to the database using the service name, with the catalog database being down. Will the connection go through or error out? Let's see.

```
[oracle@cstbyh01 admin]$ sqlplus system/welcome@sales_catlog_srvc;

SQL*Plus: Release 19.0.0.0.0 - Production on Sun Oct 30 07:58:36 2022
Version 19.17.0.0.0

Copyright (c) 1982, 2022, Oracle.  All rights reserved.

Last Successful login time: Sun Oct 30 2022 07:43:51 -05:00

Connected to:
Oracle Database 19c Enterprise Edition Release 19.0.0.0.0 - Production
Version 19.17.0.0.0

SQL> @/home/oracle/database_info.sql;
```

DATABASE_HOST	DB_NAME	DB_UNIQUE_NAME	DATABASE_ROLE	OPEN_MODE	STARTUP_TIME
prim01.localdomain	orcldbp	orcldbp	PRIMARY	READ WRITE	30-OCT-22

As we can see, when the GDS catalog database is down, there is no immediate impact on the existing and running GSMs and the GDS services. All the GDS services will work as long as they don't have a need to interact with the catalog database. We can see impact only when the commands that need to interact with the catalog database are executed. For example, a few commands like add service/modify service, add database/modify database, and start gsm/modify gsm will fail as they need to connect to the catalog to update the metadata. The following are a few such commands that fail when the catalog database is down.

Adding a New Service When the Catalog Database Is Down

If we are already connected to GDSCTL and the catalog database becomes unavailable, we will see the following errors if we run any commands that need a catalog database connection:

```
GDSCTL> add service -service test -gdspool sales -preferred_all -role
PRIMARY;
GSM-45036: Error while getting GDS catalog lock
GSM-45036: Error while getting GDS catalog lock
No more data to read from socket

GDSCTL> GSM-45018: Command not found
GSM-45036: Error while getting GDS catalog lock
GDSCTL>
```

If we make a new connection to GDSCTL after the catalog database becomes unavailable and if we run any commands that need a catalog connection, you will get the following errors:

```
[oracle@prim01 ~]$ gdsctl
GDSCTL: Version 19.0.0.0.0 - Production on Sun Oct 30 08:03:35 CDT 2022

Copyright (c) 2011, 2019, Oracle.  All rights reserved.

Welcome to GDSCTL, type "help" for information.

Current GSM is set to GSMEAST
GDSCTL> add service -service test -gdspool sales -preferred_all -role PRIMARY;
GSM-45034: Connection to GDS catalog is not established.
GDSCTL>
```

Stopping and Starting the GSM When the Catalog Database Is Down

If we try to stop and start the GSMs while the GDS catalog database is down, we will see the same errors.

```
[oracle@prim01 ~]$ gdsctl
GDSCTL: Version 19.0.0.0.0 - Production on Sun Oct 30 08:04:10 CDT 2022

Copyright (c) 2011, 2019, Oracle.  All rights reserved.

Welcome to GDSCTL, type "help" for information.

Current GSM is set to GSMEAST
GDSCTL> stop gsm -gsm GSMEAST;
GSM is stopped successfully

GDSCTL> start gsm -gsm GSMEAST;
GSM-45054: GSM error
GSM-40070: GSM is not able to establish connection to GDS catalog
GDSCTL>
```

Summary of This Test Case

In this test case, you saw that when the catalog database is down, there is no effect on the existing GDS operations. However, all the commands such as add/modify/start that run in GDSCTL will fail as they need the catalog database to be up.

Summary

In conclusion, you saw how the high availability of GSM regions is achieved using buddy regions. You also saw what the impact on the GDS services is when the GDS catalog database is not available.

Index

© Y V Ravi Kumar, Mariami Kupatadze, Sambaiah Sammeta 2023
Y V Ravi Kumar et al., *Oracle Global Data Services for Mission-critical Systems*,
https://doi.org/10.1007/978-1-4842-9553-3

H, I, J, K

L

Printed in the United States
by Baker & Taylor Publisher Services